Dedication

This book is dedicated to all those who, since the beginning of manned flight, have taken off into the wild blue yonder and never returned.

First published in 2015 by Zenith Press, an imprint of Quarto Publishing Group USA Inc., 400 First Avenue North, Suite 400, Minneapolis, MN 55401 USA

Zenith Press titles are also available at discounts in bulk quantity for industrial or sales-promotional use. For details write to Special Sales Manager at Quarto Publishing Group USA Inc., 400 First Avenue North, Suite 400, Minneapolis, MN 55401 USA.

To find out more about our books, visit us online at www.zenithpress.com.

ISBN: 978-0-7603-4792-8

Library of Congress Cataloging-in-Publication Data

Ruffin, Steven A.
  Flights of no return : aviation history's most infamous one-way tickets to immortality / Steven A. Ruffin.
    pages cm
  Includes bibliographical references.
  ISBN 978-0-7603-4792-8 (hc w/jacket)
  1. Aircraft accidents--History. I. Title.
  TL553.5.R84 2015
  363.12'409--dc23
                                    2014049416

Acquisitions Editor: Elizabeth Demers
Project Manager: Madeleine Vasaly
Art Director: James Kegley
Cover Designer: Faceout Studios
Page Designer: Carol Holtz
Layout Designer: Simon Larkin

On the front cover: Amelia Earhart posing in front of her Lockheed 10E Electra. It was one of the most advanced civilian airplanes of its day. *NASA*

On the table of contents page: *Ensuper/ Shutterstock*

Printed in China

10 9 8 7 6 5 4 3 2 1

FLIGHTS OF NO RETURN

Aviation History's Most Infamous One-Way Tickets to Immortality

STEVEN A. RUFFIN

ZENITH
PRESS

CONTENTS

SECTION III CRIMINAL AND OTHER POLITICALLY INCORRECT BEHAVIOR

SECTION IV INTO THE TWILIGHT ZONE

PREFACE

I must have been a pioneer aviator in a previous life. This would explain my fascination with aviation history—and why I wrote this book about the most legendary "flights of no return." In a lifetime studying the history of flight, I have found that some of the most captivating true flying tales were those where one or more of the participants never returned. These "last flight" accounts pique my interest, not because of their grim endings, but because they so often form the basis of a more complex story.

I had two goals in writing this collection: I wanted the stories to be unique and interesting enough to appeal to readers of all types and all ages, and I wanted them to be as accurate as possible. A major challenge in achieving the first goal was deciding *which* flights to chronicle. In more than two centuries of manned flight, the overwhelming majority of lost flights are easy to explain and involve little or no mystery: a pilot flew into bad weather and crashed into the side of a mountain, or he lost control of his aircraft and spun into the ground. All are tragic, but not necessarily compelling. However, a few of history's ill-fated flights—or the events associated with them—are fascinating in some particular way. They are mysterious, bizarre, or controversial, and they often involve someone famous. These flights provide all the adventure and drama necessary for good literature, and are therefore the ones I chose to describe.

My second goal—making this book about real historic events as accurate as possible—was equally challenging. Determining what happened before, during, and after each of these historic failed flights required a great deal of research and crosschecking. I spared no effort in describing each flight and each incident as faithfully as possible. I employed in my research as many primary sources as I could, including original documents and photos, official accident reports, maps, and first-person accounts. In the absence of these, I relied on information presented in books, articles, and other sources that were, to the best of my judgment, accurate. Only by meticulously evaluating each of these sources and comparing one to another could I feel confident of describing an event as closely as possible to the way it actually occurred.

Most of these legendary flights have been the subjects of books, articles, documentaries, websites, and movies. However, such an abundance of material is a double-edged sword, for within almost any mass of information exists an unknown quantity of *mis*information. False "facts" are ubiquitous. They can arise, even in official documents, from typos or transcribing errors. Elsewhere, they result from unverified assertions, legends, rumors, and—too often— purposefully made fallacious claims. Although it was sometimes difficult to distinguish fact from fiction, I tried to weed out as many errors as possible. In so doing, I also eliminated some long-held misconceptions. Any untruths that may have survived are unintentional and my responsibility alone.

ACKNOWLEDGMENTS

It is impossible to complete a work as comprehensive as this without a great deal of help from others, and I would like to acknowledge those who assisted me in making it possible. First, I am indebted to my editors at Zenith Press for helping to make this work the best it could possibly be. Their many perceptive comments and suggestions were invaluable. Colonel Walter Boyne—friend, colleague, and mentor—is the "ace of aces" in matters having to do with aviation history. I very much appreciated his encouragement and advice. Terry Irwin, certified flight instructor and friend for more years than seems possible, is also one of the most knowledgeable aviation authorities anywhere. His review of the manuscript and astute observations were exceedingly helpful. Lieutenant Dan Ruffin is a US Navy F/A-18 Super Hornet weapons systems officer—and the smartest young fellow I was ever blessed to have as a son. His technical perspective on this work was vital. Paula Ronald, whom I was lucky enough to have as a sister and personal librarian, has also been a lifetime coach, critic, fan, and friend. She painstakingly reviewed every word of the manuscript and expertly dissected some of my dangling participles, split infinitives, and run-on sentences. My good friend and comrade-in-arms, Col. Steve Robison, showed unparalleled fortitude by laboriously wading through the manuscript. I thank him for his insightful suggestions and much-needed encouragement.

Others who kindly provided assistance included Heather Bourk of the US House of Representatives Collection, the Cessna Aircraft Company, Stephen Miller, Bob Garrard, Minerva Bloom of the NAS Fort Lauderdale Museum, Peter Kilduff, Jon Proctor, Bernhard Ebner, and Otto Gross. Finally, I wish to acknowledge my wife, Janet, and daughter, Katie, both of whom supported and encouraged me in various ways throughout this long process. Many thanks to you, one and all.

Steve Ruffin
Virginia Beach, Virginia
January 2015

INTRODUCTION

A celebrated millionaire—who was also the world's foremost aviator—lifted off in a small plane one clear morning in 2007 and disappeared. Was his loss an accident, or something more sinister?

The glamorous son of a beloved president took off on a hazy summer night in 1999 and plunged himself and two others into the Atlantic Ocean. Was an infamous "curse" to blame? Or did he simply make a bad decision?

In 1943, Nazi fighters deliberately shot down a civilian airliner carrying the famous movie star best known for his role in the epic movie *Gone with the Wind*. Was he the target? Or was this atrocity the result of mistaken identity?

A US Navy blimp landed one Sunday morning in 1942 in the middle of a street in Daly City, California, with no one aboard. What happened to the crew? Were they victims of enemy action, espionage—or, perhaps, even of their own government?

What is the real story behind the perplexing disappearance of Amelia Earhart? Did the Japanese execute her as a spy? Did she die of starvation and exposure on a remote Pacific island? Or did she live to a ripe old age as a housewife in New Jersey?

Some of these tragic flights terminated by accident. Others ended intentionally. A few ended for reasons that to this day remain unknown. What all the flights described in this book have in common, however, is that they are unique and compelling in their own ways, and ended unhappily for the occupants under unusual, mysterious, controversial—or, in some cases, downright spooky—circumstances.

Stories about failed flights precede manned flight itself. Perhaps the earliest ever recorded dates back to ancient Greek mythology. Daedalus and his son Icarus escaped from a fortress on the island of Crete, where they had been imprisoned, by flying from a tower using wings that Daedalus had fabricated from feathers held together by string and wax. Young Icarus ignored his father's warning not to fly too high and, in his youthful exuberance, ascended so close to the sun that it melted the wax holding his wings together. He crashed into the sea and perished.

While the story of Icarus' flight is mythical, man would eventually slip Earth's "surly bonds" and ascend into the heavens. And although the overwhelming majority of flights in aviation's magnificent history have been successful, too many have fallen victim to the unyielding demands of gravity.

The events described in this book cover the entire 230-year span of manned flight. They occurred during both war and peace, over land and sea, and in aircraft of all types: from balloons, blimps, and dirigibles to propeller-driven biplanes, triplanes, and monoplanes to jets and rocket planes. Readers will experience what the doomed occupants of these aircraft—some of them rich, famous, and/or powerful—experienced as they battled, unsuccessfully, a wide variety of deadly aerial adversaries. These include bad weather, bad judgment, enemy combatants, criminal activity, mysterious unknown forces, and a lethal dose of every aviator's nemesis: bad luck.

In the pages to come, you're about to discover true accounts of great aviation mysteries; ghosts and derelicts; aircraft—and the people in them— that seemingly vanished into thin air; political intrigue and conspiracy; an occasional sprinkling of the supernatural; and criminals who committed heinous acts in the air. All these factual events unfold here exactly as they occurred. They are aviation history and human drama at their best— fascinating, informative, poignant, and provocative.

FIRST TO FALL

"SACRIFICES MUST BE MADE."

First to Fly and First to Die

On June 15, 1785, two pioneering French balloonists set out to make history. Early that morning, Jean-François Pilâtre de Rozier and Pierre Romain took off from the French coastal town of Boulogne-sur-Mer in a Rozière balloon—named after its inventor, Monsieur Jean-François Pilâtre de Rozier himself. To achieve buoyancy, this unique craft employed a highly incompatible hybrid of two separate gas chambers: one containing air heated in flight by an open flame suspended beneath it; and the other filled with combustible hydrogen gas. In this floating bomb, the two intrepid aeronauts hoped to be the first ever to fly across the English Channel from France to England.

De Rozier was already an aeronaut of great accomplishment. A year and a half earlier, on the afternoon of November 21, 1783, the young physicist, chemist, and inventor accompanied the Marquis François Laurent d'Arlandes to become the first humans ever to make an untethered balloon flight. On that day, they ascended to three thousand feet above the outskirts of Paris in a Montgolfier hot-air "fire balloon" built by brothers Étienne and Joseph Montgolfier. De Rozier and d'Arlandes remained aloft for twenty-five minutes and drifted a distance of more than five miles. It was only by stubborn persistence that the two men had been able to make this historic first flight. King Louis XVI considered it too dangerous for his loyal subjects, so he initially decreed that only convicted criminals could

Mort de Pilâtre de Rozier et de Romain, an artistic rendering of Jean-François Pilâtre de Rozier and Pierre Romain after their balloon crashed on June 15, 1785, near Wimereux, France. They were the first humans ever to die in an aviation accident.
Library of Congress

make the flight, in exchange for a pardon—if they survived. Only at the last minute did he acquiesce to de Rozier's and d'Arlandes's passionate pleas to allow them—men of status—the honor of being the first to fly.

After this achievement, de Rozier continued to fly and, in so doing, helped establish several other early firsts in aeronautics. With his rapidly expanding résumé of accomplishments came international fame. If he could successfully complete the proposed thirty-mile flight across the forbidding English Channel, his celebrity and fortune would only increase. Two other aeronauts, Frenchman Jean-Pierre Blanchard and American expatriate Dr. John Jeffries, had managed to balloon their way eastward across the Channel, from England to France, earlier that year; however, no one had yet made the more difficult east-to-west flight against the prevailing winds.

↑ The "Flying Man," Otto Lilienthal, in free flight after launching his glider from a German hillside. He died after his glider stalled and plunged to the ground on August 9, 1896. *Library of Congress*

← German engineer and aviation pioneer, Otto Lilienthal. His groundbreaking work in aerodynamics greatly influenced others—most notably, the Wright brothers.

De Rozier's fellow flier, Romain, had an even more compelling reason to make the historic journey. Awaiting his arrival in Britain was a beautiful and wealthy young Englishwoman he intended to marry.

The two aeronauts had to wait for a favorable easterly wind to propel them across the Channel. When the conditions were finally right, they climbed into the basket suspended below the balloon and took off. They made, according to one contemporary newspaper account, "a fine appearance in the ascent, bidding fair for a prosperous voyage to England." Within minutes, the balloon had reached an altitude of several thousand feet and begun to drift westward, out over the Channel.

Soon after, however, the wind shifted and started pushing the two men and their balloon back toward the east. Before long, they were once again floating above the French landscape. Suddenly, onlookers below saw the balloon envelope collapse, and the two pioneers plunged with their deflated balloon to the earth. They fell near the town of Wimereux, three miles north of their launching point. Both died upon impact.

No one knew exactly what had gone wrong; however, the deadly proximity of the open flame and highly combustible hydrogen may have been a factor. This combination was, as fellow ballooning pioneer Jacques Charles had warned de Rozier, akin to "putting fire beside gunpowder."

De Rozier had once again made history—but not in the manner he intended. Instead, the man who made his mark as the first to fly became also the first to die. The world will always remember him and Romain as the first humans ever to die in an aviation accident, marking history's first flight of no return.

Winged Sacrifice

Manned flight progressed significantly during the century following de Rozier and Romain's historic doomed flight. Lighter-than-air flight became almost commonplace—not only balloons, but also a wide variety of steerable, motorized dirigibles. Still, a few aviation pioneers began experimenting with an entirely different form of human flight, one that did not require buoyant gases for lift. One of these early visionaries was a German engineer born in 1848 named Karl Wilhelm Otto Lilienthal.

Otto Lilienthal's fascination with the concept of manned flight began at an early age. He carefully studied the flight of birds, and, while still a teenager, he began experimenting with winged gliders. From his observations, he developed his own designs, theories, and techniques. During the 1890s, his gliding feats earned him international fame—and the title Flying Man—due in part to the many photographs taken of him soaring through the air, suspended from his glider, that regularly appeared in publications throughout the world. Lilienthal's groundbreaking work with wing shapes and other principles of aerodynamics enabled him to make more than two thousand glider flights, during which he set many early flying records.

The scientifically minded engineer further bolstered his legacy by writing and publishing one of history's first aeronautical textbooks, *Der Vogelflug als Grundlage der Fliegekunst*—later translated into English as *Birdflight as the Basis of Aviation*. Even today, well over a century later, the most recent edition of this classic is available. Given Lilienthal's flying achievements and scientific observations in the realm of winged flight, it is no surprise that many still consider him the world's first true aviator.

Otto Lilienthal achieved his many flying accomplishments in gliders of his own design, most of which were similar to today's hang gliders. He routinely made sustained and controlled flights for distances of up to several hundred feet. To get airborne, he launched from a hillside—often using an artificial slope that he constructed near his home in Lichterfelde, Germany. This knoll remains today a memorial to this important aviation pioneer.

Lilienthal's flying accomplishments were of great influence to other prospective aviators of his era, particularly two American bicycle-building brothers from Dayton, Ohio, who were also interested in manned flight. Wilbur and Orville Wright considered Lilienthal the most important aeronautical authority of the day. They carefully studied his writings, designs, and flight techniques as they worked on their own glider, which would be the precursor to the world's first true airplane, the Wright *Flyer*.

On August 9, 1896, Lilienthal flew his glider in the nearby Rhinower Hills. On his fourth flight of the day, he was soaring from a hilltop at a height of about fifty feet when a gust of wind caused his glider to stall. He tried to recover by shifting his weight, but was unable to do so in time. Crashing heavily to the ground, he sustained a fractured spine. Colleagues quickly transported him to Berlin for treatment, but he died the following day.

One of Otto Lilienthal's most quoted statements is "*Opfer müssen gebracht werden*"—sacrifices must be made. His sacrifice made him humanity's first victim of winged flight.

The Airplane Joins the Club

Based on the work of Lilienthal and others, it was only a matter of time before someone figured out how to attach an engine to a winged glider and fly it off the ground. The result would be the world's first airplane.

The first controlled and sustained manned flight of a powered, heavier-than-air machine occurred on December 17, 1903. On this day, Orville

Wright made a twelve-second hop from the windswept sand dunes of Kitty Hawk, North Carolina. It was not overly impressive, but it was a first. Before day's end, he and his brother, Wilbur, would make three additional and progressively longer flights in their *Flyer*, which they designed and built after years of painstaking experimentation.

Still, to many people, these first flights did not seem significant. Balloonists over the past 120 years had already accomplished much greater feats in the realm of human flight. Nevertheless, what the two bicycle makers had managed to do at Kitty Hawk was something special; though they did not invent flight itself, they did invent a *different kind* of flight. The powered airplane would prove to be the way of the future. It would fly faster and higher and carry bigger payloads than any other type of flying machine; however, such exceptional performance would come at a cost.

The events of September 17, 1908, graphically illustrate this point. Orville Wright was at Fort Myer, Virginia, demonstrating his and Wilbur's newest flying machine, the Wright Model A, to the US Army. It had been nearly five years since their first flight, and they had yet to sell the US government on the concept of the airplane. However, Wilbur had begun

The Wright Model A at the US Army flight trials, Fort Myer, Virginia. During the first two weeks of September 1908, this machine—piloted by Orville Wright—would break most of the existing airplane flight records. Despite such success, the trials would end in disaster. *NASA*

Orville Wright flying his Wright Model A over the parade ground at Fort Myer, September 1908. *US Air Force*

demonstrating their flying machine in Europe at the famous automobile racetrack outside of Le Mans, France, and after only one flight had instantly converted the Europeans' widespread skepticism to wild enthusiasm. Now Orville had to make the case in his own country.

On September 3, flying from the parade field at Fort Myer, Orville began putting his Model A through its paces. If successful, he would earn a $25,000 US Army contract for one of their airplanes. Enthusiastic crowds and skeptical US Army evaluators watched intently. They were not disappointed. Over the next two weeks, Orville broke—and broke yet again—several world records. On one flight, he managed to stay airborne for an incredible seventy-five minutes.

The army had several requirements for its first airplane. First, it had to be capable of carrying a passenger. On September 9, Orville took up Lt. Frank P. Lahm for a short hop, and three days later he did the same for Major George O. Squier. At shortly after 5:00 on the afternoon of September 17, it was Lt. Thomas E. Selfridge's turn.

The twenty-six-year-old Selfridge was a 1903 West Point graduate and already a rising star in the US Army. He was also anything but a neophyte when it came to aviation. After being assigned to the army's newly formed Aeronautical Division of the Signal Corps, he had learned to fly dirigibles, making him one of only three with this qualification in the US Army. In addition, the army had assigned him to work with a civilian aeronautical research group known as the Aerial Experiment Association, or AEA. Alexander Graham Bell, best known as the inventor of the first practical telephone, was the driving force behind this nonprofit scientific organization dedicated to building a "practical aeroplane" capable of carrying passengers. Over the most recent few months, Selfridge had completed several flights in aircraft that he and fellow AEA members had designed and built—making him the first member of the US military ever to solo an airplane. In view of Selfridge's unique expertise in the realm of aeronautics, it is not surprising that he was among the assigned army observers at the Wright airplane trials.

The suspicious and highly secretive Wright brothers viewed Bell and his AEA as a competitor—and, therefore, the enemy. Consequently, they had no great love for Lieutenant Selfridge either. Orville believed the young officer's real intent during the Fort Myer flight demonstration was to steal their secrets and use them for his and the AEA's own purposes. This led Orville to write to Wilbur during the Fort Myer trials, "I will be glad to have Selfridge out of the way. I don't trust him an inch." He would soon have reason to regret making that statement.

The September 17, 1908, crash that killed Lt. Thomas E. Selfridge. Orville Wright was piloting the Wright Model A over Fort Myer, when a propeller tip broke and sent the airplane out of control. *National Museum of the US Air Force*

The broken propeller tip that led to the death of Lt. Thomas E. Selfridge. It is displayed at the National Museum of the US Air Force. *Steven A. Ruffin*

Orville's takeoff that afternoon was uneventful, as Selfridge, seated next to him, waved to friends in the crowd of two thousand spectators. The Wright Model A climbed to about 150 feet and began flying circuits over the field. After a few minutes, however, something went terribly wrong; it was later determined that a propeller tip broke. It was the catalyst for a catastrophic series of events that led to the complete uncontrollability of the airplane, which suddenly pitched downward and crashed headlong to the earth. Selfridge, according to Orville, only had time to utter a nearly inaudible "uh-oh."

The stunned group of onlookers made a wild dash across the parade field toward the crash, while mounted cavalry did their best to hold back the mob. A cloud of dust hovered over the wreckage as rescuers extricated the two men from it. Orville, face bloodied, was conscious but badly hurt with a fractured femur, broken ribs, and other injuries. Selfridge was even less fortunate. Those in attendance carried him from the field, unconscious and suffering from a fractured skull. He died three hours later. The crash occurred mere feet outside the western perimeter of Arlington National Cemetery, where Selfridge's body would soon lie.

September 17, 1908, was a day of tragedy and a day of firsts. On that afternoon, Lt. Thomas E. Selfridge had the unfortunate distinction of becoming the first person ever to die in an airplane accident—with none other than the world's first pilot at the controls.

✈★✈

The fateful last flights of de Rozier and Romain, Lilienthal, and Selfridge were only the first of many. Aeronautical science continued to advance in leaps and bounds—all the way to the moon and back—but always at a heavy cost. Albert Einstein once said, "Failure is success in progress." If so, then aviation's many sacrifices have greatly contributed to the advancement of aeronautics. This did not make them any less tragic for those fliers destined never to return.

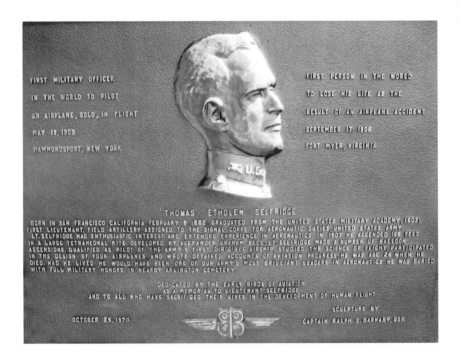

Plaque dedicated to Lt. Thomas E. Selfridge. It is located on the parade ground at Fort Myer, Virginia, near where he died on September 17, 1908. He was the first military officer ever to pilot an airplane solo, and the first person ever to die in an airplane crash. *Steven A. Ruffin*

SECTION I
WHEN LUCK RUNS OUT

CHAPTER ONE

A DEADLY SUNDAY DRIVE

"A MIND-BLOWING THING"

O n the morning of September 3, 2007, a sixty-three-year-old pilot took off on a routine local flight from a desert airstrip in western Nevada. The terrain over which he flew was familiar and the weather was perfect. His plane was a single-engine Bellanca Super Decathlon—a safe and extremely rugged little two-seater—and it was in good operating condition. After lifting off and heading south, man and machine gradually faded into the distance, never to return.

The pilot of the small plane was not, however, just any pilot. He was James Stephen Fossett—millionaire, sailor, and all-around adventurer. As the holder of nearly one hundred aviation world records, he was also one of the most famous and accomplished aviators of all time.

Record Setter Supreme

His biography reads like an adventure novel. After graduating from Stanford and earning an MBA from Washington University, Fossett became wealthy selling commodities futures. Although a phenomenally successful business tycoon and self-made millionaire—more than enough to satisfy most high achievers—he had many other interests. Not surprisingly, he applied the same tenacity to his hobbies. During his life he managed to establish an incredible 115 world records in five different sports. Remarkably, he established most of these records *after* he had reached the age of fifty.

Fossett's range of interests and accomplishments was extraordinary. He was a world-renowned sailor, having set an astounding twenty-three world records, many of which are still standing as of 2015. Perhaps his best-known feats were his transatlantic speed record in 2001 and around-the-world record in 2004. For his many sailing contributions, he won a number of prestigious awards, including recognition by the World Sailing Speed Record Council as "the world's most accomplished speed sailor."

He was also a competitive cross-country skier, Le Mans racecar driver, marathon runner, and Ironman triathlete. As a mountain climber, he had conquered both the Matterhorn and Mount Kilimanjaro. In addition, he competed in—and completed—the ultragrueling 1,165-mile Iditarod Trail Sled Dog Race; and on his fourth attempt, Fossett became the 270th person in history to swim the icy-cold English Channel.

For all of Fossett's accomplishments, his most significant occurred in aviation, placing him in a lofty class all its own. A thorough examination of the data published by the international keeper of aviation records, the *Fédération Aéronautique Internationale* (FAI), reveals the magnitude of Fossett's achievements. During his relatively short active career, he set nearly a hundred world records for altitude, distance, duration, and speed in an unparalleled four different classes of aircraft: balloons, gliders, airships, and airplanes. This made him the first person in history to set world flight records in more than a single category. The most significant of these were major feats of endurance and skill that will be difficult to eclipse.

Fossett's aviation milestones are so numerous that it would be impossible to do them justice in one short chapter; however, a passing mention of the most important ones highlights the fateful irony that characterized the improbable end of his remarkable life.

Balloon — During the sixteen-day period from June 19 to July 4, 2002, Fossett became the first person in history to fly a hot-air balloon solo around the world. This flight, made in the Rozière-type craft named *Bud Light Spirit of Freedom*, was a testament to his amazing perseverance, having failed on five previous attempts—in one case plunging into the shark-infested Coral Sea after his balloon ruptured during a thunderstorm. During his precedent-setting flight, he also set a balloon speed record, covering 3,186.8 miles during June 30 and July 1 for an average speed of 133 miles per hour. At one point, he rode the high-altitude winds to a top speed of 200 miles per hour, the fastest any human had ever flown in a balloon.

Airship — On October 27, 2004, along with copilot Hans-Paul Stroehle, Fossett set an FAI "absolute" airship speed record of 115 kilometers per hour (71.5 miles per hour). They accomplished this in a Zeppelin NT semirigid airship—appropriately enough, at Friedrichshafen, Germany, where history's first Zeppelin airship took flight on July 2, 1900.

Glider — From December 2002 to December 2004, Fossett and copilot Terry Delore dominated international glider competition, setting ten out of a possible twenty-one world speed and distance records. On August 30, 2006, Fossett was at it again, this time with copilot Einar Enevoldson, when they rode Argentinean Andes mountain waves to an unprecedented altitude for unpowered gliders of 50,699 feet—nearly ten miles above sea level. It was a world record Fossett had been pursuing for the previous five years on three different continents—another testament to his tenacity.

Fixed-Wing — Undoubtedly the greatest of all Fossett's many record-shattering achievements occurred while flying the jet-powered Virgin Atlantic GlobalFlyer. Between February 2005 and March 2006, he flew this unique Burt Rutan–designed craft nonstop and unrefueled solo around the world—not once, but on three different occasions.

Steve Fossett landing the Virgin Atlantic GlobalFlyer at NASA's Kennedy Space Center on January 12, 2006. On February 8, Fossett took off from here to make history's longest nonstop flight. *NASA*

The first flight began on February 28, 2005, when Fossett took off from Salina, Kansas. A little more than sixty-seven hours later, he touched down once again at Salina, having circumnavigated the earth for a total of 22,936 miles. Not only was he the first person ever to fly nonstop around the world solo, his average speed of 342.2 miles per hour during this world-record flight qualified it as history's fastest nonstop round-the-world flight.

Fossett's second solo circumnavigation in the GlobalFlyer took place a year later, from February 8 to 11, 2006, beginning at Kennedy Space Center, Florida. This time, however, after completing the first circuit of the earth, he continued east to Bournemouth, England. Here, he landed after flying nonstop and unrefueled for an unprecedented seventy-six hours, forty-two minutes, and fifty-five seconds, having covered a distance of 25,767 miles. This was—and still is—history's longest nonstop aircraft flight.

Finally, a month later, on March 14-17, Fossett completed the GlobalFlyer's record-setting trilogy. Again, he started and ended on the 12,300-foot runway at Salina, Kansas. This time, he flew a total of 25,294 miles, claiming the world record in the FAI category of "absolute distance over a closed circuit."

Fossett's three GlobalFlyer flights set three of the possible seven "absolute" records kept by the FAI: distance without landing, distance over a closed circuit, and speed around the world nonstop and nonrefueled.

These achievements and more marked him as one of history's greatest aviators. He received nearly all of the most prestigious awards available, including the Harmon trophy, the Gold Medal of the *Fédération Aéronautique Internationale*, and induction into both the Balloon and Airship and the National Aviation Halls of Fame. He had more than earned his way into the ultraexclusive club reserved for such icons as Lindbergh, Doolittle, Yeager, and Armstrong.

So how could a pilot of such incredible skill go out for a joyride on a clear day and never return? It was akin to a NASCAR driver dying in a traffic accident on the way to the grocery store.

The Search

Fossett departed at around 8:30 a.m. on September 3, 2007, from a private airstrip on a western Nevada desert plain, adjacent to the Flying M Ranch. This hunting club for sportsmen, located about seventy-five miles southeast of Reno, was a sort of private resort for celebrities and high-profile aviators. The wealthy aviation enthusiast William Barron Hilton—of the Hilton hotel chain—owned and operated both ranch and airport. The world's most famous pilots often gathered there to enjoy good food, good company, and—best of all—the unique collection of aircraft that

EXP

Steve Fossett seated
in the Virgin Atlantic GlobalFlyer
at Kennedy Space Center's Shuttle Landing Facility,
February 8, 2006. He is about to take off on his second solo, nonstop
circumnavigation of the world without refueling. He will fly for more
than three days straight and a distance of 25,767 miles to make history's
longest nonstop aircraft flight. *NASA*

Steve Fossett before his historic round-the-world flight. *NASA*

A Super Decathlon sport aircraft similar to the one Steve Fossett was flying when he disappeared on September 3, 2007. *Adrian Pingstone*

Hilton maintained. It was a pilot's paradise for those few with the "right stuff" to merit an invitation.

By noon, there had been no word from Fossett, and the chief pilot of the Flying M was concerned; he had expected him back by midmorning. Eventually, it became obvious that the Decathlon must be out of fuel and no longer flying. Fossett probably landed somewhere and needed a ride home. That he could have crashed seemed inconceivable.

A search began immediately, with every expectation of quickly finding Fossett unharmed. It soon expanded into the largest rescue effort ever conducted for a single person in the United States, involving Civil Air Patrol search planes from at least a half dozen states, US military aircraft, and numerous private aircraft from all over western Nevada and eastern California. In addition, several of Fossett's well-known pilot friends responded to the call to form what the press dubbed the "Flying M Air Force." There were also several ground search and rescue teams in all-terrain vehicles combing a rugged search area twice the size of Massachusetts. Divers even probed the murky depths of nearby Walker Lake.

The search incorporated others besides those actually hunting for the missing pilot. Experts analyzed radar tracking images from the morning of Fossett's flight for clues, and thousands of Internet users from around the world—who had been following the constant stream of news updates—used satellite imagery to look for some trace of Fossett's downed airplane.

Someone even thought to consult a psychic. In short, the search was unparalleled in scope; it could only be a matter of time before the missing millionaire superpilot would turn up—hopefully alive and well.

Days turned into weeks, however, and still there was nothing. Searchers were baffled at their inability to find even a trace of Fossett's airplane, a situation reminiscent of the search for Amelia Earhart seventy years earlier. The hunt was so thorough that it turned up several other lost aircraft from the past, but nothing of Fossett. Where could he be? And why was his Emergency Locator Transmitter (ELT) not emitting a signal that would lead searchers to him? Even if he had been unable to turn it on, the force of any impact should have automatically activated it. It seemed as though the earth had snatched him from the sky and rendered him and the Decathlon invisible. It was, as Fossett's friend and autobiography co-author, Will Hasley, described it, "a mind-blowing thing."

In February 2008, five months after he disappeared, a judge declared Fossett legally dead. It provided the official and legal closure the family needed, but emotional closure was still months away. The baffling disappearance of the famed aviator, who could not be recovered in spite of one of the most extensive searches in history, gave rise to the inevitable theories and rumors that began to dominate the blogs and tabloids. Perhaps Fossett was just another victim of the so-called "Nevada Triangle," a wild area that has claimed uncounted gold prospectors, hikers, and airmen without leaving a trace. As evidence of this area's remote and rugged nature, the body of a World War II flier had only recently turned up there after being missing for sixty years.

Or was there a more sinister explanation? Various sources alleged that Fossett had faked his own death to escape personal or financial problems; escaped to Argentina to reunite with an illegitimate son; and faked a crash to provide cover for the US government to search for a lost nuclear warhead. The fact that Fossett was not only a man of unlimited resources, but also a recognized survival expert, further fueled this wild speculation. For him, anything was possible. However, there was not a shred of hard evidence on which to base any of these theories. Still, the question remained: why had the massive search failed to turn up a single trace of the lost airman?

Mystery Solved . . . But More Questions

Finally, on September 29, 2008—almost thirteen months after Fossett's disappearance—a man hiking near Mammoth Lakes, in a remote part of the Sierra Nevada Mountains of east-central California, came upon a pilot's license and other personal effects, and a tattered bundle of hundred-dollar

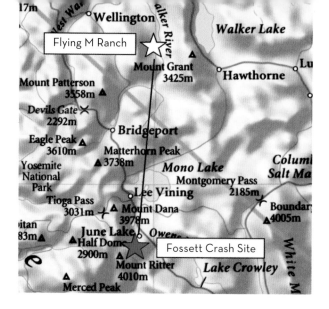

Fossett's presumed flight path of September 3, 2007. After taking off from the Flying M Ranch airstrip, he crashed some sixty-five miles to the south, high in the Sierra Nevada Mountains, near Mammoth Lakes, California.

bills. The license bore the name of James Stephen Fossett. A new search operation quickly ensued, and the wreckage of Fossett's plane was located a half mile from where the documents were found. Bits and pieces of the Decathlon were strewn all over the mountainside at an altitude of ten thousand feet, some sixty-five miles south of the Flying M Ranch. Later DNA tests on the few available bits of human tissue that were found—inexplicably, a half mile from the crash site—confirmed that they were Fossett's. His family and friends finally were able to lay the famed pilot's remains to rest, and with them went the lurid rumors that had circulated. Appropriately, an October 3, 2008, headline in the *Times* of London announced: FACTS RUIN OTHERWISE-GOOD STEVE FOSSETT CONSPIRACY THEORIES.

The badly fragmented and burned wreckage quickly revealed why the ELT had not functioned: it was scattered in pieces all across the debris field. As for the airplane itself, one witness stated, "there wasn't a piece big enough to cover a coffee table." In addition to its unlikely location, it was atomized into a million pieces, rendering it nearly invisible from the air. This explained why search planes had flown over it a reported nineteen times during the operation without spotting it.

The National Transportation Safety Board (NTSB), which investigates the causes of accidents, detected no obvious problem with either the pilot or the airplane. Its report on the accident, finally published nearly two years after Fossett went missing, suggested that the probable cause was "the pilot's inadvertent encounter with downdrafts that exceeded the climb capability of the airplane." In other words, a vicious wind gust may have slammed his airplane down onto the side of the mountain. However, this explanation was only the NTSB's best guess as to why Fossett's airplane crashed into the side of the mountain with such force.

The official report left certain questions unspoken and unanswered. For example, why was Fossett flying at such a high altitude, in mountains more than sixty miles from home? His small plane was hardly suited for mountain flying. The crash location was especially puzzling, as Fossett had indicated before takeoff that he intended to investigate dry lakebeds for a possible future land-speed record attempt.

Also, why, as the NTSB reported, was Fossett's seat belt unbuckled? Severe crashes may rip or burn the webbing, but they seldom unbuckle metal latches; and it is extremely doubtful that this experienced pilot was flying without it securely buckled.

Another question left open for speculation was why the meager remains of Fossett's body were found scattered a half mile away from the crash site. Did wild animals drag them there? Or did he somehow survive the impact and crawl to that spot before dying and being partially devoured by animals?

Finally, was the conjectured powerful downdraft the only factor contributing to the crash? It seems that a pilot of Fossett's experience would have known better than to tempt the notoriously vicious Sierra Nevada air currents in a small aircraft. Was there a problem with either the pilot or plane? Or could it have even been intentional? The latter seems unlikely, given that he was carrying a roll of $100 bills, but no one will ever know.

—★—

Steve Fossett was a highly gifted pilot. It is the ultimate irony that a man who had flown balloons, airships, gliders, airplanes, and jets to their very limits, and who had flown solo nonstop around the world—not just once but three times—would be destined to die on a pleasure flight his wife characterized as "a Sunday drive."

The type of airplane he was flying that fateful day is one of the safest in existence—so safe that, as the saying goes, "it can just barely kill you." However, flight, by its nature, involves a degree of danger—regardless of the pilot's skills or the airplane's safety record. Steve Fossett accepted that risk and had repeatedly cheated death. However, on that September day in 2007, he came up short—perhaps for no better reason than that his luck finally ran out.

CHAPTER TWO

DISAPPEARANCE OF THE MIDNIGHT GHOSTS

"THE EVEREST OF AVIATION MYSTERIES"

At 5:18 on the Sunday morning of May 8, 1927, two famed and highly skilled French aviators took off from Le Bourget Field, near Paris, France. Their destination was New York City. If successful, they would be the first ever to fly nonstop between these two cities. The airplane they were flying was an all-white open-cockpit biplane, appropriately named *l'Oiseau Blanc*—the white bird.

The two fliers, Charles Nungesser and François Coli, lifted off to the cheers of thousands of spectators. They proceeded northwest to the coast of Normandy and then out over the English Channel. After traversing southern England and Ireland, they disappeared into the haze over the Atlantic Ocean and were never seen again.

This internationally publicized world record attempt by two of the most glamorous and widely known aviators of the day remains one of history's most memorable flights of no return. Their still-unexplained disappearance is often compared to that of famed climbers George Leigh Mallory and Andrew Irvine, who vanished on Mount Everest in 1924—it is for this reason that some call the inexplicable loss of the two aviators "the Everest of aviation mysteries." Where they ended up has never been determined (unlike Mallory, whose body turned up in 1999), but evidence exists to suggest that Nungesser and Coli may have been the first ever to fly nonstop from Paris to North America.

Charles Nungesser, the much-decorated World War I French flying ace. He was one of the lucky few high-scoring aces to survive the war.

Nungesser and Coli

Charles Nungesser, born March 15, 1892, first earned international fame as a World War I fighter pilot. With forty-five confirmed kills to his credit, he was France's third-ranking ace and among the top twenty aces from all nations. He was also a much publicized, hard-partying ladies' man, rumored to have consorted with the infamous Dutch exotic dancer and presumptive German spy Mata Hari.

Above all, the flamboyant Nungesser was admired for his grit and resilience. His numerous war wounds were so extensive that his case history could have provided an entire textbook on the treatment of traumatic injuries. Long before the war ended, the indomitable Nungesser was a certified physical wreck. Yet, for all the crippling pain and physical limitations these injuries imposed upon him, he continued to fly—often having to be lifted into and out of the cockpit—and wreak havoc upon the enemy.

His injuries were matched only by his numerous medals and awards, which he wore even when flying. They jangled together as he limped heavily around the airfield, making him sound, as *French Warbirds* author

Charles Nungesser's macabre personal insignia, as it appeared on one of his wartime fighter planes. This logo also adorned *l'Oiseau Blanc*, the airplane in which he and François Coli attempted, unsuccessfully, to fly nonstop from Paris to New York. *US Air Force*

Claude W. Sykes describes it, "rather like a walking ironmongers shop." It is no wonder the public idolized him and that his much-photographed, battle-scarred face was known worldwide.

German pilots also recognized Nungesser from afar by the taunting macabre personal insignia he boldly exhibited on all his fighter aircraft, consisting of a skull and crossbones, candles, and a coffin, all enclosed in a big black heart. It was the brash Frenchman's challenge to enemy pilots: "Here I am—whenever you are ready to die!"

After the war, Nungesser ran a flying school, flew in exhibitions, and eventually ended up in Hollywood. There he flew as a stunt pilot and even made a cameo appearance in the 1925 silent movie *Sky Raider*. However, this was insufficient to satisfy the lust for fame, glory—and danger—that fed the oversized ego of a man like Nungesser. His opportunity to leap back into the limelight came when he was approached by an unlikely looking fellow countryman with a rotund physique, a black patch over his right eye, and a big idea.

François Coli, eleven years older than Nungesser, never achieved the same level of fame as the young ace, although he too had been a successful wartime fighter pilot. Like Nungesser, he had sustained grievous injuries, including the loss of one of his eyes in a crash. In addition to being a pilot, Coli was an accomplished navigator, having been a seafaring man before the war. After the armistice, he maintained his flying and navigational skills by participating in a series of record-setting flights. In 1919, he and fellow pilot Henri Roget set an overseas distance record by making the first double crossing of the Mediterranean Sea. Other record-setting distance flights in the Mediterranean region followed, including a 1,400-mile flight from Paris to Morocco.

A Reward Worth the Risk

In 1923, Coli began planning his biggest venture yet—a nonstop transatlantic flight from Paris to New York. The flight between these two cities had become for aviators on both sides of the Atlantic the ultimate goal. This was partly because of the challenge involved with making this difficult 3,600-mile flight, and partly because of the symbolic significance of linking the two important cities by air. It was also attractive because the first to succeed would collect the $25,000 Orteig Prize. New York hotelier Raymond Orteig had made this offer—equivalent to about $330,000 in present-day dollars—for the first nonstop flight between the two cities. Prize money aside, the fame and glory resulting from this accomplishment would pay a lifetime of dividends.

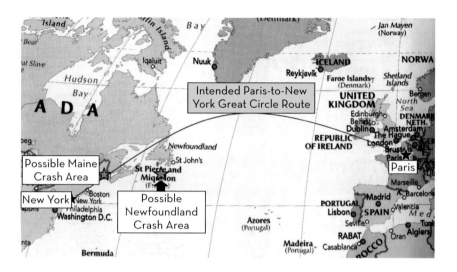

The route Nungesser and Coli planned to take from Paris to New York. Their last confirmed sighting was over the Irish coast. No one knows where their flight ended, but unconfirmed witness reports indicate they may have crashed somewhere south of Newfoundland or in the wilderness of southeastern Maine.

Orteig did not specify in which direction the flight had to be made. Most pilots favored riding the prevailing westerly winds from New York to Paris, but Coli preferred to buck the headwind and fly westward. This way, he calculated, more of the final third of the flight—the most critical part— would be over land. The additional safety outweighed the disadvantage of the headwind. He would follow the great circle route, which extends in a northerly arc between Ireland and Newfoundland. This would also keep the most possible dry land beneath him—although it would also take him well north of the major sea-lanes, where any chance for rescue would be unlikely.

Coli's first choice for a pilot to accompany him was Paul Tarascon. But when Tarascon was injured in a crash in late 1926, Charles Nungesser moved to the top of the list. The dynamic ace flier and darling of the press was the obvious choice, and the adventurous Frenchman was happy to accept the challenge.

For their attempt they chose the Levasseur PL.8, a highly modified version of the French naval long-range PL.4 reconnaissance plane. A 450-horsepower Lorraine-Dietrich twelve-cylinder engine powered this open-cockpit biplane. However, its most remarkable feature was its ability to jettison its heavily reinforced, drag-inducing landing gear soon after

Nungesser and Coli in the flying attire they wore on their last flight.

Nungesser and Coli pictured above their Levasseur PL.8, appropriately named *l'Oiseau Blanc*—the white bird. This widely distributed postcard carried a caption translating to "Nungesser and Coli – The heroes of the flight from Paris to New York." Though truly heroes, they never arrived in New York.

takeoff. This would significantly increase the speed and fuel efficiency throughout the flight, after which the airplane would land on its belly in the water and—at least theoretically—stay afloat until the two French fliers could escape and climb onto a rescuing boat. They decided against taking any radio equipment. In 1927, radios were notoriously heavy and unreliable—and besides, over the North Atlantic there would be virtually no one with whom to communicate.

The intrepid fliers planned to make the biggest splash ever when they triumphantly swooped down into New York Harbor, escorted by a formation of US Army Air Corps fighters. The Frenchmen would land their beautiful white biplane—adorned with Nungesser's signature black-hearted wartime logo—in the water at the foot of the Statue of Liberty. It was a magnificent plan. All they had to do was execute it and collect the cash.

Capturing the Orteig Prize was, however, a much more difficult proposition than simply flying across the big pond. By 1927, several fliers had already conquered the Atlantic, but the Paris–New York flight was *twice* that distance. This meant that twice as much fuel—as well as twice as much engine and crew endurance—was required. Equally important, the additional distance doubled the possibilities for weather, navigational, and mechanical problems. These considerations aside, the ever-treacherous North Atlantic remained by far the most challenging aspect of the flight. With its storms, fog, icing conditions, unpredictable winds, and cold waters, it was a fearsome adversary.

It was dangerous enough simply being airborne in the underpowered and fuel-laden airplanes of the era. On September 21, 1926, two crew members flying with former French ace René Fonck died when their Sikorsky S-35 crashed on takeoff during a New York-to-Paris attempt. And only days before Nungesser's and Coli's attempt, US Navy pilots Noel Davis and Stanton Wooster were killed taking off in the Keystone Pathfinder they were planning to fly from New York to Paris the following week. The 3,600-mile nonstop flight between the two cities would require all that aeronautical technology had to offer in 1927. It would also require more courage—and luck—than most rational people ever have.

It was a long shot, but the potential rewards were worth the risk, so Nungesser and Coli quickly readied themselves and their airplane. Time was of the essence, since several other efforts to capture the enticing Orteig prize were in the making. Three teams were already converging on Long Island, New York, awaiting optimal weather conditions for a flight to Paris. Clarence Chamberlin led one of these and Richard Byrd, recently returned from his record-breaking flight to the North Pole, another. The third American pilot intending to attempt the New York-to-Paris flight had not yet arrived in New York. He was hardly worthy of consideration anyway, since he was by far the least likely to succeed. He was a young, unknown US Air Mail pilot crazy enough to believe he could make the near-impossible trip to Paris flying solo. His name was Charles Lindbergh, and his airplane was a small, single-engine Ryan monoplane he called *Spirit of St. Louis*.

Missing!

Nungesser and Coli lifted off on the morning of May 8, 1927, a week earlier than they had previously planned; the other teams breathing down their necks had forced the Frenchmen to expedite preparations. With only eighty days to build and test *l'Oiseau Blanc*, work progressed at breakneck speed. The rushed arrangements paid off, however, and the two Frenchmen now had the edge.

Nungesser carefully coaxed their grossly overloaded biplane into the air from Le Bourget, using a half mile of runway. The fully laden airplane weighed in at five and a half tons and carried one thousand gallons of fuel—enough for forty hours of flight. Once airborne, the pilots evaluated the airplane's performance, and when all systems checked out, released the heavy landing gear. The aircraft—now a flying boat—was instantly 270 pounds lighter and several miles per hour faster. The two intrepid airmen then proceeded, accompanied by an escort of military and photographic airplanes, to the French coast. From there they headed out over the English Channel, toward their rendezvous with immortality.

Little else is known about the infamous last flight of *l'Oiseau Blanc*, though not for lack of interest. It was the biggest event of the day, with profuse coverage in every newspaper on both sides of the Atlantic. Fans worldwide cheered on the two larger-than-life war heroes in their magnificent white biplane. Thousands of spectators had already started to converge around New York harbor in hopes of seeing history in the making. When the French newspaper *La Presse* prematurely proclaimed Nungesser and Coli's successful arrival in New York, there was dancing in the streets all across France—that is, until the paper had to retract the story. The dancing quickly turned into riots, directed against the newspaper's sloppy journalism.

Exhaustive searches ensued on both sides of the Atlantic, and untold numbers of unsubstantiated reports from nearly every location along their route told of sightings, crashes, mysterious signals, messages in bottles, and the discovery of bodies and wreckage. But in the end, no traces of the big Levasseur or its renowned pilots emerged. The big white biplane never arrived.

It seems certain that *l'Oiseau Blanc* made it safely across the English Channel and over the western Irish coast to the two-thousand-mile expanse of the Atlantic Ocean. What happened next is mostly conjecture. Did they encounter bad weather and crash into the sea? Or did they, as some have speculated, turn back and end up in the English Channel? Convincing evidence points to a third possibility.

The North American Theory

Of the multiple theories proposed to explain the disappearance of Nungesser and Coli, one stands out as the most credible, based on evidence that emerged soon after the flight—but largely ignored and eventually forgotten. Recently, investigators have begun to put these scraps of information together, concluding that the two fliers actually reached North America.

Newfoundland Reports — There is no ironclad evidence to verify this claim, but plenty of documentation points to the possibility that Nungesser and Coli did reach North America. Well over a dozen credible witnesses near the eastern and southern coast of Newfoundland—an area known as the Avalon Peninsula—came forward soon after the flight to report hearing, and in a few cases actually seeing, an airplane overhead on the morning of May 9. Among these sources was the crew of a seagoing vessel, who reported seeing a white airplane matching the description of *l'Oiseau Blanc* south of Newfoundland. A fisherman also reported hearing an airplane crash into the ocean in a dense fog near this location. For *any* airplane to fly over such a remote area in 1927 would have been a rare and memorable event; therefore, if the witnesses truly did see one, it was in all likelihood *l'Oiseau Blanc*.

Recently, a French researcher named Bernard Decré discovered additional evidence in the US National Archives to support the Newfoundland crash theory. A pair of US Coast Guard dispatches revealed that on May 19, 1927, the Coast Guard picked up an airplane aileron in Long Island Sound's Napeague Bay. Three months later, they retrieved part of a white airplane wing floating off the coast of Norfolk, Virginia. One or both could have been from *l'Oiseau Blanc*. If so, these documents support the notion that Nungesser and Coli landed or crashed into the sea somewhere south of Newfoundland, where their airplane broke up and the two men drowned. The detached wings then drifted southward several hundred miles with the Labrador Current until finally spotted.

Why no one ever apparently made this information public is a mystery within a mystery, as is the question of what the Coast Guard did with the wreckage. Some have suggested that the US government withheld the findings to prevent casting a shadow on the American pilot who successfully completed the historic flight less than two weeks after Nungesser and Coli's attempt.

There were other allegations of conspiratorial tactics directed against the two unlucky French fliers. Soon after they disappeared, US meteorologists came under fire for allegedly giving them inaccurate weather information. Others have suggested that *l'Oiseau Blanc* was shot down—either by the US Coast Guard or by Prohibition-era bootleggers. No one has ever proved any of these assertions.

Witnesses in Maine — Another possibility is that *l'Oiseau Blanc* ended its flight in the United States. Late on the overcast afternoon of May 9, 1927, a man in a remote part of eastern Maine's Washington County claimed to have heard a sputtering airplane engine approaching from the northeast. According to him, the engine quit, followed by the sound of a crash. Unfortunately, he did not actually see the airplane in the low-hanging clouds, and he never felt sufficiently inclined to venture into the wilderness to investigate. This area was, however, very close to the two French fliers' original course, and the late-afternoon timeframe was compatible with the earlier sightings of the airplane over Newfoundland. Moreover, the sputtering engine corresponds almost exactly with when *l'Oiseau Blanc* would have been burning its last drops of fuel.

Others in this area also reported hearing an airplane engine that day. Even more incredible, there was a report of what may have been the definitive evidence of the French fliers' arrival in North America: an old, corroded aircraft engine buried beneath the underbrush. Could it have been the big Lorraine-Dietrich from *l'Oiseau Blanc*? Sadly, the engine was never found. Subsequent searches by various aviation archeological teams have likewise failed to find any definitive traces of engine, airplane, or bodies. This apparent dead end is where the search for *l'Oiseau Blanc* ended in Maine.

✈★✈

On May 21, 1927, only twelve days after *l'Oiseau Blanc* went missing, Charles Lindbergh beat all the odds and succeeded where Nungesser and Coli had failed. He became the first person ever to fly nonstop between New York and Paris—and he did it solo. He landed at Le Bourget, the same field from which the two Frenchmen had taken off, thirty-three and a half hours after taking off from New York. Not only did "Lucky Lindy" collect the coveted Orteig Prize, he also instantly became the most celebrated man of his era and an aviation icon of a magnitude never surpassed. If only some of Lindy's legendary luck had gone to Nungesser and Coli, these honors could have been theirs. Instead, as Lindbergh himself noted in his classic autobiography, *The Spirit of St. Louis*, the two Frenchmen simply "vanished like midnight ghosts."

Perhaps these ghosts will reappear someday. Researchers have focused the search south of Newfoundland, near the islands of Saint-Pierre and Miquelon. Their prospects of finding anything tangible after nearly nine decades are slim, but if successful, they will have found what some consider the holy grail of missing airplanes. Until that happens, the only verified surviving piece of *l'Oiseau Blanc* in existence is the landing gear that Nungesser and Coli dropped to the ground after takeoff. It made its way back to Le Bourget and resides there at France's Air and Space Museum—a silent testimony to a valiant attempt.

↑ This café/bar, located in the heart of Paris, is another reminder of Nungesser and Coli's ill-fated last flight. According to local legend, this establishment—operating under a different name—was a popular 1920s-era watering hole for pilots—perhaps even Nungesser and Coli. *Steven A. Ruffin*

← The only verifiable piece of *l'Oiseau Blanc* still in existence is the landing gear Nungesser and Coli dropped from it soon after takeoff. It is displayed at the French Air and Space Museum, located at the Paris—Le Bourget airport on the outskirts of Paris. The weight and drag saved by shedding the bulky gear was considerable, but not enough to ensure a successful flight. *Steven A. Ruffin*

CHAPTER THREE

THE SPARK THAT ENDED AN ERA

"OH, THE HUMANITY! . . . THIS IS THE WORST THING I'VE EVER WITNESSED."

On the rainy evening of May 6, 1937, a crowd gathered on the sprawling grounds of Naval Air Station Lakehurst, New Jersey. The reporters, photographers, and a host of other onlookers had been waiting for hours to witness the world's greatest airship, the mighty *Hindenburg*, complete that year's first flight from Germany to the United States. One of those in attendance was a young radio announcer named Herb Morrison, whom Chicago's WLS radio station had dispatched to Lakehurst to record the event. As the majestic floating palace finally drifted into sight and slowly inched its way to the seventy-five-foot-high mooring mast, Morrison began a standard description of the approaching aerial giant. Suddenly, his voice took on a frantic tone that quickly became hysterical:

> It burst into flames, and it's falling, it's crashing . . . Oh, my, get out of the way, please . . . This is one of the worst catastrophes in the world. Oh, the humanity! And all the passengers screaming around here . . . I–I can't talk, ladies and gentlemen . . . This is the worst thing I've ever witnessed.

It took just thirty-four seconds for the giant flaming airship to crash to the ground, but Morrison's emotional narrative, along with the vivid, ghastly images, ensured that it would become one of history's most memorable aviation catastrophes. After the smoke had cleared, thirty-six people were dead or dying—thirteen of the ship's thirty-six passengers, twenty-two of its crew of sixty-one, and one ground crew member. The twisted aluminum alloy skeleton of the airship lay crumpled and smoldering on the ground, after the searing flames had consumed most of the remainder of the ship. Although sixty-two of the ninety-seven aboard somehow survived the inferno of exploding hydrogen gas and burning fuel oil, the name *Hindenburg* had become—in a single flash—another synonym for "disaster"—the same flash also brought the golden age of airship travel to a fiery end.

The Zeppelins

The era of the big airships began on July 2, 1900, near Friedrichshafen, Germany. Here, Ferdinand *Graf* (Count) von Zeppelin launched his first airship, which he designated *Luftschiff* (airship) Zeppelin 1, or LZ-1. It was—as all its LZ descendants, including the *Hindenburg*, would be—a rigid airship, having a fabric-covered metal framework with buoyant gas cells contained within. All of Zeppelin's airships used hydrogen gas for their buoyancy, while gasoline or diesel engines driving massive propellers powered them forward. These rigid airships, also called "dirigibles" because they were powered and steerable, shared one other characteristic: they were universally colossal in size. They had to be, since a battleship-size envelope full of hydrogen was required to lift the massive flying machine into the air.

Zeppelin continued his work through the next decade, building progressively bigger, faster, and more reliable airships with ever-increasing payloads. Soon, he started the world's first airline and passenger service. Between 1910 and 1914, Zeppelin airships carried thirty-four thousand passengers all over Germany without a single injury—an incredible accomplishment.

During the First World War, Germany's military forces pressed into service the *Graf*'s airships—or Zeppelins, as they were called. From 1914 through 1918, they flew sea reconnaissance missions and bombing raids over Britain, France, and Italy. Flying at high altitudes in the dark of the night, they indiscriminately dropped bombs on whatever—and whomever—happened to be below them. These raids were not militarily effective, but they caused civilian casualties, including more than five hundred in Britain alone. As a result, the sinister giants became one of the most feared and hated terror weapons of the war.

Graf von Zeppelin died in 1917, but *Luftschiffbau* Zeppelin continued to operate. In October 1924, the head of the company, Hugo Eckener, flew his newest airship, the 656-foot LZ-126, an unprecedented five thousand miles from Germany to Lakehurst, New Jersey. Here, he personally delivered it to the US Navy, who redesignated it the ZR-3—and christened it the USS *Los Angeles*. This outstanding airship would prove to be the Navy's most successful and longest-serving airship.

In 1928, Zeppelin launched what would become the most successful passenger airship ever built, the LZ-127 *Graf Zeppelin*. Over its nine-year period of operation, it logged 590 flights, including, in 1929, history's first passenger-carrying circumnavigation of the earth. In all, it flew more than a million miles, safely carrying thousands of passengers and hundreds of tons of mail and freight all over the world.

The Zeppelin company was so encouraged by its success with the *Graf Zeppelin* that it began construction in 1931 of an even more spectacular airship. For its massive framework, a huge amount of the aluminum alloy, Duralumin, was required. Much of it came from the wreckage of the British airship R-101, which had crashed in France on October 5, 1930, during its first commercial flight. Little did the Germans suspect the apparently jinxed metal would once again come crashing to the ground in a ball of flames.

Luxury Liner Supreme

Superstitions notwithstanding, Zeppelin's newest product was by far the mother of all airships. It took more than four years to build—but was well worth the wait. The mammoth LZ-129, christened the *Hindenburg*, launched in 1936. It is difficult, even in today's world of massive airliners, to imagine the sheer enormity and breathtaking presence of any of the great airships, and this is especially so for the *Hindenburg*. This behemoth was a beautiful, elegant, and complex engineering masterpiece, the ultimate in aeronautical and manufacturing technology, and the world's most luxurious airliner—all rolled into one. Some have called it "the Concorde of its day," but that simply does not do it justice.

It was powered by four state-of-the-art, sixteen-cylinder Daimler-Benz diesel engines, each capable of generating up to 1,320 horsepower and driven by a colossal four-bladed propeller, twenty feet in diameter. The *Hindenburg* had unprecedented endurance, carrying up to seventy-two tons of diesel fuel in its forty-two tanks—enough to fly eight thousand miles nonstop. It was also fast. With a reported cruise speed of seventy-five miles per hour, it could nudge eighty-five at full throttle. These features allowed it to travel from Germany to the United States in less than three

The Zeppelin-built
Airship LZ-129 *Hindenburg* moored
at Naval Air Station Lakehurst, New Jersey.

days—half the time it took the fastest ocean liner, which was the only other option available to passengers. At this time, the *Graf Zeppelin* and *Hindenburg* were the only aircraft in the world flying passengers across the Atlantic.

The *Hindenburg*'s size was unprecedented—it remains, along with its short-lived successor, the *Graf Zeppelin II*, the largest flying machine ever airborne. It stretched an incredible 804 feet in length—nearly a sixth of a mile—and would dwarf even the largest of today's jumbo liners; its internal gas volume of 7 million cubic feet was ninety percent larger than its predecessor, the *Graf Zeppelin*, and gave it a lifting capacity of a whopping 236 tons. Its painted linen fabric covering, if laid out on the ground, would have covered eight acres of real estate. All of this enabled the *Hindenburg* to carry, in complete luxury, up to seventy-two well-heeled passengers, each paying about $450 in Depression-era dollars—equivalent in buying power to $7,500 today—per one-way ticket.

The ride was fast, quiet, clean, and smooth—or as newspaperman Louis Lochner described it, like being "carried in the arms of angels." The *Hindenburg* offered the world's most beautiful panorama, as seen through the slanted observation windows on its port and starboard promenade decks; and with its private staterooms, lounge, formal dining room, reading and smoking rooms, and custom-made aluminum grand piano, passengers enjoyed a degree of splendor that rivaled even the greatest ocean liners.

The *Hindenburg* (left) flying in formation with a US Coast Guard Douglas RD-4 flying boat over Naval Air Station Lakehurst on May 9, 1936. The mooring mast is visible just above the massive Hangar No. 1 seen here. Less than one year later, the giant airship would lie in ruins at the base of that mast. *US Coast Guard*

This massive, elegant "luxury liner of the air," as it was called, could easily have qualified as the Eighth Wonder of the World—and even today ranks near the top of the list of the most magnificent examples of technology that humanity has ever produced.

Most aviation experts of the day also considered the *Hindenburg* one of the safest aircraft ever produced. After all, the Zeppelin company had been flying passengers in its airships for nearly three decades without a single injury. The potential for disaster, however, was inherent: the *Hindenburg* relied on highly flammable hydrogen gas for its buoyancy. The explosive potential of this gas, when allowed to combine with air, was no secret; other airships from around the world had demonstrated this vividly and tragically by exploding in flames. Zeppelin fully recognized the danger and originally designed the *Hindenburg* to use helium—a safe, inert gas—instead of hydrogen. However, in the 1930s, helium was available only in the United States, which refused to export it because of restrictions imposed by the Helium Control Act of 1927. In spite of Zeppelin's best efforts, it was unable to obtain any of this precious gas. Even if they could have circumvented the law, the Germans did not help their case by emblazoning huge black Nazi swastikas on the great airship's vertical tail fins. Highlighted on a white circle surrounded by a brilliant red rectangle, they were all too visibly emblematic of the distasteful regime already ill-reputed in the United States.

The Germans thus had no choice but to fill the cells of the *Hindenburg* with the only buoyant gas they could get: hydrogen. Though not as safe as helium, it was cheaper and more buoyant. Most important, it was available.

Hugo Eckener was—to his credit—anything but a good Nazi. He had fallen into disfavor with his country's fascist leaders by naming his newest supership after Germany's beloved late President, Field Marshall Paul von Hindenburg. Nazi Propaganda Minister Joseph Goebbels had wanted to name it the *Adolf Hitler*, after his *Führer*. Though Eckener prevailed over the name, he could not escape other Nazi demands for his airship—especially since the German government had helped finance its construction. The *Hindenburg* would thus serve as an instrument of propaganda and would carry the swastika insignia of the Nazi party—and Nazi agents—everywhere it flew.

Hugo Eckener, famed airship commander and chairman of the German airship company, *Luftschiffbau* Zeppelin. He was one of the few prominent anti-Nazi Germans to survive World War II and die of old age. *Library of Congress*

Tragedy at Lakehurst

The *Hindenburg* soon began transatlantic passenger travel. By the end of 1936, it had safely crossed the Atlantic thirty-four times. Its first 1937 flight to North America began on the evening of May 3, when it departed Frankfurt, Germany, under the command of Capt. Max Pruss. The flight was uneventful, except that strong headwinds extended the flight time an additional ten hours; then, thunderstorms passing through Lakehurst further delayed the airship's arrival. Finally, at just after 7:00 p.m. on May 6, the giant airship slowly descended and began maneuvering toward the mooring mast, located in the middle of Naval Air Station Lakehurst's vast open landing field. Shifting winds forced Pruss—by now, feeling significant pressure to get the much-delayed airship on the ground—to make two tight turns to keep it lined up. He did not want to make a second approach and cause further delay.

At about 7:25 p.m., the *Hindenburg* dropped its mooring lines to the ground in preparation for landing. Suddenly, a tiny flame appeared just forward of the top tail fin. In seconds, explosive flames engulfed the entire tail and spread rapidly toward the front of the airship. The burning tail section crashed to the ground, tipping the giant airship almost vertically. It all came crashing to the ground "like a giant torch," as the next day's issue of the *New York Times* put it, sending the 231 line handlers below scurrying for their lives. There had been no warning, no time for preparation, and no time to react. In thirty-four seconds, the world's greatest airship was reduced to a crumpled mass of wreckage. Within a minute and a half, the hydrogen had burned itself out, leaving nine tons of spilled diesel fuel to continue burning on the ground for hours more.

Many of those aboard perished when they jumped from the airship to escape the flames. Others died of burns, smoke inhalation, and trauma suffered during and after the crash. Several who remained aboard survived, including Capt. Pruss, who stayed at his station in the control car suspended beneath the ship. Their survival was in part thanks to the heroic efforts of rescuers on the ground.

Conspiracy or Accident?

Why the world's greatest airship burst into flames at this particular moment was something that both German and American authorities very much wanted to know. No one either in the airship or on the ground had even the slightest clue as to what had gone wrong. The investigation board that convened to determine the cause eventually arrived at a conclusion, but it was no more than an educated guess. Almost eighty years later, it is still a matter of debate. Three possible explanations have received the most attention.

The *Hindenburg*, moments after exploding into flame on May 6, 1937, at Naval Air Station Lakehurst. It took only thirty-four seconds for the hydrogen-fed inferno to reduce the world's largest aircraft to a pile of smoldering ruins. This scene helped seal the fate of airship travel.

Sabotage — This was near the top of everyone's list. The aerial giant, which prominently displayed the Nazi colors everywhere it went, was a highly visible symbol of the world's most hated government—one with enemies everywhere, including within Germany itself. A. A. Hoehling, in his 1962 book *Who Destroyed the Hindenburg?*, contends that one of the airship's crew who died in the crash, a rigger named Eric Spehl, was associated with a woman with strong Communist and anti-Nazi connections. Hoehling speculates that Spehl, an amateur photographer, used flashbulbs and a dry cell battery to set the airship afire. This explanation gained greater public popularity when producers adopted it for the plot of the 1975 movie *The Hindenburg*. However, no one ever proved Spehl's guilt, and critics maintain that the dead rigger was little more than a convenient scapegoat. In the end, no definitive evidence of sabotage on the *Hindenburg* ever emerged.

Incendiary-Paint Theory — In 1997, a former NASA scientist named Addison Bain proposed this theory. He argued that the fabric covering the *Hindenburg*'s Duralumin framework was the precipitating cause of the explosion—not the hydrogen inside. It is true that the fabric contained a coat of a flammable doping lacquer impregnated with iron oxide and aluminum powder. The fact that these two highly reactive substances can combine to form an explosive reaction, and that they are often used in explosives and solid rocket fuels, has prompted some—including Bain himself—to overstate that the *Hindenburg*'s outer skin was "painted with rocket fuel." Critics argue that the amounts and ratios of these substances as used on the airship's fabric were not in any way dangerous, and that the fabric was simply not combustible enough to spontaneously ignite.

Static Spark Theory — This is probably the most plausible cause for the accident, and the one that both the investigation board and Eckener himself advocated. This theory holds that a spark ignited hydrogen that had leaked from one of the airship's sixteen gas chambers and combined with air to make an explosive mixture. Neither the source of the spark nor the leak was ever determined. The fact that the *Hindenburg* was tail heavy as it approached the mooring mast suggests that some of the highly buoyant hydrogen gas may have been leaking from the rear of the airship. This would have resulted in a loss of lift there and caused the tail section to droop lower than the rest of the ship. Proponents of this theory hypothesize that the surface of the airship became electrically charged while passing through the humid air that evening. In flight this would not normally be a problem, but when the damp mooring lines contacted the rain-soaked earth, they grounded the metal frame of the airship. This caused a discharge of static electricity between the frame and skin, resulting in a spark that ignited the lethal hydrogen-air mixture. The gas leak could have resulted from an intentional hydrogen release in conjunction with the landing, a faulty gas valve, or perhaps a punctured gasbag. If the latter, some have speculated that structural wires snapped and punctured an envelope during the tight turns Capt. Pruss hurriedly made to get the airship aligned for landing.

⊜

No one will ever know whether the *Hindenburg* crashed because of sabotage, reactive paint, a static spark igniting leaked hydrogen, or something else entirely. The German government retrieved its burnt and twisted metal skeleton and shipped it back to Germany, where they melted it down once again and used it for yet another lost cause: warplanes for Adolf Hitler's growing Nazi aerial armada. The same fate also awaited the *Hindenburg*'s famous predecessor, the *Graf Zeppelin*, as well as its successor, the *Graf Zeppelin II*. Germany was, for the first time in forty years, out of the airship business—and so was the rest of the world.

The *Hindenburg* disaster was not singular among the great airships of this era. The number of spectacular fatal airship mishaps occurring in the 1920s and 1930s is remarkable: *Akron*, *Dixmude*, *Shenandoah*, *Italia*, *Roma*, R-38/ZR-2, and R-101, to name a few. Surprisingly, the *Hindenburg* was only the fifth most deadly—the US Navy Airship *Akron* was the worst, with 73 fatalities. However, the *Hindenburg*'s demise was the most visible. For this reason alone, it is still the best remembered—and as history would prove, the one that marked the end of the rigid airship.

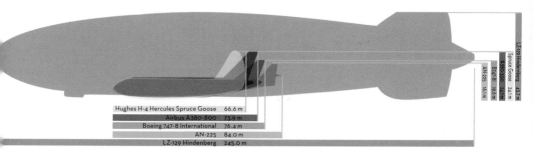

The incredible size of the *Hindenburg* is graphically demonstrated by this scale overlay diagram, which compares it to four of the largest winged aircraft ever built: the Hughes H-4 Hercules, Airbus A380-800, Boeing 747-8, and Antonov AN-225. *Clem Tillier*

The public's desire to ride in airships evaporated in the wake of the awful images and newsreels of the *Hindenburg*'s fiery crash. Besides, fixed-wing aircraft development had progressed to the point where large multi-engine airplanes and flying boats would soon make transoceanic air travel faster and more affordable. Thus, the great airships were no longer the future of air travel that many visionaries of the day predicted they would be, and never again would they cast their giant cloudlike shadows across the earth below.

Today, visitors at Naval Air Station Lakehurst can still see the massive Hangar No. 1 rising up above the landscape. The Navy sheltered and maintained the *Hindenburg* in this structure during each of the German airship's ten previous visits to Lakehurst, and it is where it would have rested on the night of May 6, 1937. Out on the barren field in front of the hangar is a monument shaped like an airship gondola, marking the spot where the burning *Hindenburg* crashed to the ground. A small bronze plaque there reads: ON THIS SITE – MAY 6 1937 – 7:25 P.M. 36 PEOPLE PERISHED

The airship landing area at Naval Air Station Lakehurst, as it appears today. In the foreground is a memorial marking where the gondola of the doomed *Hindenburg* crashed to the ground. The large building in the background is Hangar No. 1, where the giant airship was sheltered and maintained during its visits to Lakehurst. *Steven A. Ruffin*

CHAPTER FOUR

LADY LINDY'S FLIGHT TO ETERNITY

"I HAVE A FEELING THAT THERE IS JUST ABOUT ONE MORE GOOD FLIGHT LEFT IN MY SYSTEM . . ."

On July 2, 1937, a twin-engine Lockheed Model 10E Electra took off from the airport at Lae, a city located on the eastern coast of New Guinea. The two crew members aboard—pilot and navigator—were aiming for a tiny uninhabited coral island in the middle of the vast central Pacific Ocean, 2,556 miles to the east. The flight, which roughly followed the line of the equator, was the longest leg of what the two fliers intended to be a record-breaking circumnavigation of the globe. Yet the airplane never arrived at its destination, and no one to this day knows what happened to it or its occupants.

More than three-quarters of a century later, this disappearance is as much a mystery as it was in 1937. It is also just as intriguing, for the pilot of the Electra was famed American pilot Amelia Earhart. Since her disappearance, dozens of books and films, and hundreds of articles have chronicled the last flight of the world's most famous aviator—and, at this writing, a Google search for "Amelia Earhart" produces more than 1.6 million entries. Clearly, her fate continues to be one of history's greatest and most compelling mysteries.

Lady Lindy

They called her "Lady Lindy," and with good reason. Her unparalleled flying achievements qualified her as the counterpart to the world's most famous male pilot—the great Charles A. Lindberg—who in 1927 became the first pilot to fly solo from New York to Paris. The two famed aviators even bore a striking physical resemblance to one another, making comparisons between them almost unavoidable.

Earhart was born in Atchison, Kansas, on July 24, 1897. After learning to fly in 1921, she bought her first airplane, a Kinner Airster. Within the next few years, she set nearly a dozen major aviation records, gaining her international acclaim and universal recognition.

Amelia Earhart was the rock star of her era. Wherever and whenever she appeared in public, crowds of adoring autograph seekers, photographers, and newshounds flocked around her. She was impossible to miss, since her face appeared nearly everywhere—in newsreels, newspapers, and magazines—almost on a daily basis. She inspired and endorsed product lines of clothing and luggage, and stylish women around the world tried their best to imitate her tomboyish "mop head" look. She was a bestselling author, an enthusiastic aviation advocate, and a vocal activist for women's rights. She hobnobbed regularly with the world's elite and was wined, dined, and courted on a regular basis by the rich and powerful. Eventually, she married her wealthy publisher, publicist, and promoter, George P. Putnam. He adored her and doted on her every whim, while his publicity machine made sure to keep the world up to date on her exploits. In just about every respect, "AE" had a star quality equal to that of the most glamorous screen idols of the day.

Earhart came by her fame honestly. Before the age of forty, she had accumulated a long list of flying accomplishments matched by no other woman—and only a few men—before or since. In June 1928, she became the first woman to cross the Atlantic Ocean in an airplane. However, she did not make the crossing as a pilot, but rather as a passenger . . . or as she put it later, "just baggage, like a sack of potatoes." On this flight, she rode from Newfoundland to Wales in the back of the Fokker F.VII trimotor *Friendship*, crewed by pilot Wilmer Stultz and navigator/mechanic Louis Gordon. Although Earhart's contribution to this successful crossing was slight, it was an important first that earned her international fame and a White House reception with President Calvin Coolidge. Amelia Earhart was now in the national spotlight—and on the radar for much bigger things to come.

In 1929, she placed third in the First Women's Air Derby, and in 1930 she set several women's speed records. On May 20, 1932, she once again

An informal shot of the photogenic Amelia Earhart, as she walks past her Lockheed Electra.

crossed the Atlantic Ocean—this time as a pilot, flying solo. She took off from Harbour Grace, Newfoundland, in her all-red Lockheed Vega single-engine monoplane and landed fifteen hours later in a field in Northern Ireland. Later that same year, she became the first female pilot to fly solo across the North American continent and back—in the process, setting a women's transcontinental speed record. These feats earned her the Gimbel award as the "Most Outstanding Woman of America for 1932" and her election as the first president of the women's aviation group, the Ninety-Nines.

Earhart set yet another major milestone in January 1935, again flying her Vega. She became the first pilot—male or female—to fly solo from Honolulu, Hawaii, to Oakland, California. Three months later, she added her name once again to the record books by becoming the first person to fly from Los Angeles to Mexico City; and three weeks later, from Mexico City to Newark, New Jersey.

Within five years, Amelia Earhart had set a dozen speed, altitude, and distance records. She was at the top of her game.

Round the World

Earhart now set her sights on even more distant horizons. Her new goal would be to fly completely around the world the longest way possible, following the equatorial route. She would complete the journey as a series of separate legs, the aggregate of which would be the longest airplane flight ever. For this, she would need the additional safety and power of a twin-engine airplane, the best possible navigational and radio equipment, and a top-notch navigator. She would also have to step up her own skills as a pilot.

Amelia Earhart was the most famous and accomplished female pilot in the world, but she was not necessarily the best, technically speaking. Some historians have suggested she was only average in ability and that

Amelia Earhart posing in front of her Lockheed 10E Electra. It was one of the most advanced civilian airplanes of its day. *NASA*

↑ Earhart's Lockheed Model 10E Electra at Ford Island, Oahu, on March 20, 1937. Later that day, she lost control of it while taking off on the second leg of her first round-the-world attempt. She would attempt another circumnavigation two months later, with even worse consequences.

← Amelia Earhart at Wheeler Field, Oahu, Hawaii, March 18, 1937. She had just completed the initial leg of her first round-the-world attempt.

her fame came mostly from her husband's promotional efforts. Over the course of her flying career, she had experienced several mishaps, and on a few occasions displayed a lack of either practical knowledge or judgment. In fairness to her, these accidents—all minor—were probably more or less par for anyone who flew as much as Earhart did during this pioneering era of aviation; nevertheless, they provided fodder for those who questioned her abilities as a pilot.

The most famous of her mishaps occurred during her first unsuccessful attempt to fly around the world. She began the adventure on March 17, 1937, by flying without incident from Oakland, California, to Honolulu, Hawaii. The airplane she chose was a twin-engine Lockheed Electra Model 10E, one of the most powerful and advanced civilian flying machines of its day. Built to transport ten passengers, it was large enough to carry the fuel and equipment she required. With her were not one, but two, well-qualified navigators, Capt. Harry Manning (who was additionally a skilled radio operator) and Fred Noonan. Also aboard—though only for this first leg—was a high-profile technical advisor and copilot, famed Hollywood stunt pilot, Paul Mantz.

The four arrived safely at Wheeler Field early on the morning of March 18. Two days later, as Earhart and her two navigators attempted to take off from Ford Island's Luke Field on the second leg of their journey, the big, overloaded twin-engine Lockheed accelerated down the runway and skidded into a ground loop. The landing gear collapsed and the airplane ground to a halt amidst a shower of sparks. No one was injured, but the Electra sustained substantial damage. Once again, Earhart's competence became a topic of discussion. Whether a blown tire or other mechanical problem caused the accident or—as some, including Mantz, believed—she had simply lost control of the airplane was never conclusively established. Whatever the cause, she abandoned the attempt and shipped her airplane back to California for repairs.

Earhart's second and final shot at circumnavigating the earth began two months later. This time, instead of flying east to west, she would fly from west to east, hoping to optimize prevailing weather patterns. She would also carry only one navigator, Fred Noonan. Captain Manning might have been Earhart's first choice, but a three-month leave of absence from his job had expired. In addition, as he later confided to friends, he had lost confidence in Earhart's piloting skills. Noonan, though rumored to have a serious drinking problem, was nevertheless an excellent navigator and well qualified for the task.

Earhart and Noonan began their journey on May 21 by flying an unannounced first leg from Oakland, California, to Miami, Florida. Before

Earhart's wrecked Electra after she lost control while taking off from Ford Island's Luke Field. Before day's end, Amelia was on a ship heading back to California. This accident caused some to question her competence as a pilot.

leaving Miami, Earhart publicly stated, "I have a feeling that there is just about one more good flight left in my system, and I hope this is it."

Flying more than twenty legs over the next month, with stops on the continents of South America, Africa, Asia, and Australia, they finally landed at Lae, New Guinea, on June 29, 1937. They had flown twenty-two thousand miles from one end of the earth to the other, and although they had "only" seven thousand more to go, they were exhausted. They also knew that the remaining miles would be the toughest—nearly all of them over a remote section of the Pacific Ocean, where precise navigation would be critical, and the chances for rescue in the event they had to ditch, slim.

Lost at Sea

On the morning of July 2, 1937, Earhart and Noonan lifted off from the airport at Lae. The Electra was loaded to its maximum weight with radio and navigational equipment, emergency gear, and enough fuel and oil for approximately twenty hours of flight. After straining to become airborne, they pointed the sleek silver airplane towards their next refueling stop. It was a dot in a sea of blue on Noonan's map so small he could hardly see it: Howland Island.

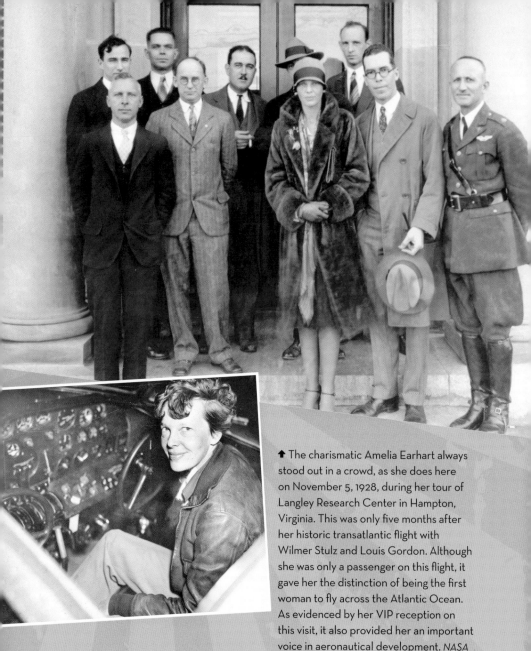

⬆ The charismatic Amelia Earhart always stood out in a crowd, as she does here on November 5, 1928, during her tour of Langley Research Center in Hampton, Virginia. This was only five months after her historic transatlantic flight with Wilmer Stulz and Louis Gordon. Although she was only a passenger on this flight, it gave her the distinction of being the first woman to fly across the Atlantic Ocean. As evidenced by her VIP reception on this visit, it also provided her an important voice in aeronautical development. *NASA*

⬆ Earhart seated in the cockpit of her Electra, in which she and navigator Fred Noonan disappeared. They took off from Lae, New Guinea, on July 2, 1937, en route to Howland Island, but never arrived. *Library of Congress*

This tiny flat strip of land, which barely protrudes from the surface of the Pacific, is less than a square mile in size—just big enough to land an airplane. It is 2,556 miles northeast of New Guinea, and situated all alone in the vast ocean with few visible reference points around it. Finding it using the conventional navigational techniques that existed in 1937 was a daunting task. On a flight this long over open sea, where checkpoints were virtually nonexistent, celestial navigation was essential; even the tiniest error could translate into a miss of several miles, enough to be catastrophic. Earhart's and Noonan's lives depended on locating Howland Island, and there was no margin for error.

Both pilot and navigator fully realized the importance—and difficulty—of locating Howland. Consequently, they had taken extra measures to ensure it did not slip past them. Earhart had pulled strings to get the US Navy to position ships in the Pacific Ocean to assist, if needed, and the US Coast Guard cutter *Itasca* was stationed close to Howland to transmit radio signals to guide her to her destination. In

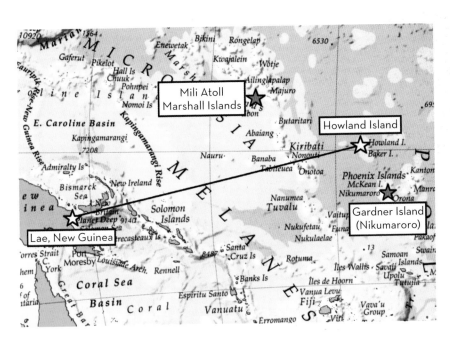

The approximate course Earhart and Noonan followed from Lae, New Guinea, to Howland Island. The 2,556-mile journey was a difficult navigational undertaking. They may have ended up near Gardner Island or somewhere in the Marshall Islands but no one yet knows for sure.

addition, she had installed in the Electra specialized radio equipment to improve communications.

At about eight hundred miles into the flight, they overflew the Nukumanu Islands and radioed their last known position; soon after, the weather turned sour and further communications became sporadic. Eighteen hours into the flight, Earhart and Noonan approached where they thought Howland Island should be, but nothing appeared anywhere on the horizon.

By this time, the Electra was low on fuel and both pilot and navigator were undoubtedly bone tired. After eighteen hours of flying with no rest, it is nearly certain that they were not at full mental capacity at this most critical point in the flight—and it did not help that neither was particularly skilled in the relatively new art of radio navigation. Consequently, things quickly began to unravel for the two fliers. For some reason, Amelia apparently did not receive most of *Itasca*'s radio transmissions to her, even though some of hers reached *Itasca* loud and clear. As far as she and Noonan could tell, they were transmitting into thin air.

The growing concern Earhart was feeling was apparent in her 7:42 a.m. transmission: "We must be on you, but cannot see you—but gas is running low. Have been unable to reach you by radio. We are flying at one thousand feet." A few minutes later, *Itasca* received its strongest transmission from her, indicating she was close—very close. In response, *Itasca* sent out signals to allow her to take a radio bearing. She received them but was unable to pinpoint the direction from which they came.

Her last intelligible transmission came at 8:43 a.m.: "We are on the line 157-337. We will repeat message. We will repeat this on 6210 kilocycles. Wait." Earhart and Noonan apparently believed they had drifted to either the north or south of Howland and had decided to turn and fly a north-south course perpendicular to their original one, hoping to intercept the island. *Itasca* operators, however, had no way of knowing exactly where the 157-337-degree vector that they were flying was located, so they were unable to determine the Lockheed's location. The men of *Itasca* sent up a smoke signal, desperately hoping the lost fliers might see it, but to no avail. When it became obvious that the Electra's fuel was exhausted, the Coast Guard officially listed them as lost at sea.

Newspaper headlines screamed, AMELIA EARHART MISSING. The loss of America's flying sweetheart dominated the news and conversations throughout the country for weeks to come. One of Amelia's more influential friends and admirers, President Franklin D. Roosevelt, immediately ordered a massive coordinated US Navy and Coast Guard search, consisting of nine ships, sixty-six aircraft, and four thousand men; however, no trace of them or their silver bird was found anywhere within the 250,000-square-mile search area. No wreckage or oil slicks ever appeared, and though radio operators from various locations picked up several SOS calls, they were unable to verify that any of them actually came from Earhart. George Putnam continued the search at his own expense after the Navy and Coast Guard called it quits on July 18, but he, too, eventually gave up. Amelia Earhart was declared legally dead on January 5, 1939.

A Debatable Disappearance

So, what went wrong on Amelia Earhart's final flight? Some have suggested that her high-tech radio equipment did not live up to expectations—or that she and Noonan simply did not fully understand how to use it. The frequencies they chose may not have been the best for direction finding, and they may not have had the low-frequency equipment they really needed for *Itasca* to get an accurate fix on her. Others contend that she had removed a critical antenna—accidentally or on purpose—before the flight. It is also possible that Earhart had not properly coordinated with the *Itasca* the time zone and frequencies she would be using, thus further confusing communications between the two. Whatever the cause, the radio navigation system the two fliers relied upon to find Howland Island simply failed.

Obviously, there were also navigational problems. Perhaps undetected wind changes or a minor miscalculation threw the Electra off course, and the overcast conditions they encountered most likely prevented Noonan from taking accurate celestial fixes. Researcher Elgen Long, in his book *Amelia Earhart: The Mystery Solved*, has even suggested that the particular map they were using was inaccurate. He contends that it showed Howland Island at a position several miles from its actual location. This alone could have been enough to seal their fate, even if Noonan's navigation had been perfect.

Many theories have emerged over the years, attempting to explain the fate of the two lost fliers. Most have elements of credibility, but none has yet been proven—or disproven.

"Crash and Sank" — The most widely held belief is that Earhart and Noonan searched for Howland Island until they ran out of fuel and crashed into the Pacific. Some theorize that after passing the Nukumanu Islands, the two got on a wrong heading that took them as much as one hundred miles northwest of Howland Island—much too far away from the tiny island to locate it visually. When they decided they had flown far enough east, they flew back and forth to the north and the south looking for the island that was just not there.

Castaway — Ric Gillespie of the International Group for Historic Aircraft Recovery (TIGHAR) has spent several years and many resources searching for Earhart. He has theorized that she and Noonan managed to land safely on an uninhabited island they came upon while searching to the north and south of their primary heading. Here, they apparently died while awaiting rescue, after which giant coconut crabs may have partially or completely consumed their bodies, leaving little for searchers to find. The SOS calls reported from various sources after the two fliers went missing support this supposition. Since the origin of these calls seemed to converge around Gardner Island (now called Nikumaroro), located about four hundred miles southeast of Howland, this could be where they ended up. Searches of the island from 1940 to the present have revealed metal scraps that may or may not have come from the Electra, a 1930s-era cosmetic cream jar and other artifacts, and even human bone fragments. In 2013, TIGHAR released sonar images they recorded off the coast of Nikumaroro that might be of Earhart's Electra, and in 2014, they claimed that a piece of metal found on Nikumaroro definitely came from Earhart's Electra. As of this writing, however, no one has yet provided definitive proof that any of these findings are linked to Earhart.

Japanese Prisoners — One of the most intriguing hypotheses that has survived over the years is the idea that Earhart and Noonan landed somewhere in the Marshall Islands and were imprisoned by Japanese military authorities. Fred Goerner, in his book *The Search for Amelia Earhart*, as well as other researchers, presented evidence from eyewitnesses who reported seeing the lost fliers land. According to them, they were taken into custody near Mili Atoll, located several hundred miles northwest of Howland. One witness even claimed to have treated the injuries of a male and female American aviator, the latter of which went by the name Amelia. Other witnesses place the two fliers in a prison on Saipan during World War II. One former US Marine even claimed to have found Earhart's passport in a Japanese military safe on Saipan, although it later mysteriously disappeared. Most of these witnesses agree that the ultimate fate of the two was death, either by execution or from disease. Goerner even alleged that Fleet Admiral Chester W. Nimitz, Commander in Chief of the US Navy in the Pacific, privately admitted that the Japanese really had captured the two fliers in the Marshall Islands. If this is true, however, then why all the secrecy?

Earhart, the Spy — Perhaps there was a reason for the Navy's apparent reluctance to discuss the disappearance of Earhart other than avoiding bad press. An even more bizarre version of the castaway theory, as has been proposed by several different researchers, contends that Earhart and Noonan's flight was actually a cover for a spy mission they were conducting for the US government, possibly in exchange for funding and logistical support. They may have even agreed to make an "emergency" landing in the Japanese-held Marshall Islands, in order to give the US Navy an excuse to come to her rescue. This would afford them the opportunity to gather as much intelligence as possible on the increasingly hostile Japanese presence. Instead of the planned rescue, however, the two were arrested as spies. Randall Brink, in his book *Lost Star: The Search for Amelia Earhart*, even gives credence to the rumor that Earhart broadcast Tokyo Rose–like anti-American propaganda during the war. The US Navy did ask the Japanese for permission to search the Marshall Islands, but never received it. Little else of this theory can be substantiated, although Earhart's own mother believed her daughter died while on a secret mission for the US government.

Alive and Well in New Jersey — As if the cloak-and-dagger mystery of Amelia Earhart's disappearance was not already far-fetched enough, there was yet another twist. In 1970, authors of the book *Amelia Earhart Lives* claimed that Earhart survived the war and returned to the United States as a New Jersey housewife named Irene Bolam. Mrs. Bolam promptly sued them for this scandalous allegation and settled the case out of court. Bolam did resemble Earhart, but forensic comparisons proved inconclusive.

✈✦✈

Amelia Earhart's name still crops up in the news on a regular basis. Marine explorers have spent a considerable amount of time, money, and energy in recent years trying to find evidence of her airplane on the bottom of the ocean using sonar devices. Likewise, archeological teams, including TIGHAR, are still following various leads on the islands around Howland in search of some trace of the lost fliers. To date, however, there is no ironclad evidence that could shed any definitive light on their fate.

Someone may eventually solve the mystery of Amelia Earhart—or she may remain forever lost. Either way, the life, career, and disappearance of Lady Lindy must certainly rank as one of the most fascinating stories in aviation history. Nearly eight decades after her disappearance, Earhart's legacy lives on.

A display at the National Air and Space Museum, in Washington, DC, showing a sampling of the theories, legends, and rumors surrounding the mysterious disappearance of Amelia Earhart. *Steven A. Ruffin*

She wrote in a final letter to her husband, the contents of which appeared in the 1996 book *Last Flight*, "Women must try to do things as men have tried. When they fail, their failure must be but a challenge to others." Women aviators have certainly met this challenge in the years since she wrote those words. Today, one can find women in the cockpits of every kind of flying machine in existence—from small single-engine trainers, to airliners, to fighter jets, to spaceships. From whatever island in the sky Amelia Earhart might be watching, she can only be proud of the advancements that resulted, in part, from her amazing example.

CHAPTER FIVE

THE BANDLEADER'S LAST GIG

"WHAT'S THE MATTER . . . ?
DO YOU WANT TO LIVE FOREVER?"

On the foggy English afternoon of December 15, 1944, two US Army officers boarded a small, single-engine transport plane at an obscure Royal Air Force flying field north of London. One of the officers was a tall, slender, somewhat unmilitary-looking major, wearing glasses. The airplane, a Noorduyn UC-64A Norseman, also had a distinctly civilian look to it. The Canadian-built bush plane was one of roughly 750 of its type that the US Army Air Forces had drafted into wartime service.

Just before 2:00 p.m. the airplane, with two passengers and US Army Air Forces Flight Officer John R. S. Morgan at the controls, lifted off, bound for Paris, some 250 miles to the southeast. The Norseman climbed its way past London and toward the murky skies hovering over the English Channel. As it left the British coast and faded into the misty and overcast English Channel, air controllers lost contact with the plane. Neither they nor anyone else ever saw or heard from it again.

Given the enormity of US casualties throughout World War II, the loss of one light transport and three men normally would not have even raised eyebrows. However this case was different. The tall major aboard the Norseman that dreary afternoon was Alton G. Miller—better known as Glenn Miller, the world-famous bandleader. The death of this American patriot and musical icon would have a terrible impact on not only the Allied troops with whom he served, but also his millions of fans back home.

While his disappearance was painful, it was also impossible to explain. Exactly what caused Miller, fellow passenger Lt. Col. Norman F. Baessell, and Flight Officer Morgan to vanish has remained a mystery. Given the far-reaching effects of his disappearance and the intrigue that still swirls around it, Glenn Miller's "last gig" remains one of history's most memorable unsolved mysteries.

King of the Big Band

Glenn Miller was still at the peak of his career when he vanished. Born on an Iowa farm in 1904, the college dropout quickly gained fame as a trombonist, composer, and arranger. By 1938, he was the leader of one of the most popular swing bands of his day. The unique woodwind sound he developed with the Glenn Miller Orchestra propelled him, the band, and their songs to the top of the charts. From 1939 to 1942, they scored an incredible seventy Top Ten hits—thirty-one of these in 1940 alone—earning the bandleader a reported $800,000. These earnings—equivalent to more than $13 million today—were staggering. In 1942, he won the first gold record ever presented for his smash hit "Chattanooga Choo-Choo," which sold 1.2 million copies. Other huge hits included "In the Mood," "Moonlight Serenade," "Stardust," and numerous other tunes now considered classics. The band broke attendance records at ballrooms and concerts and topped the ratings in radio broadcasts that aired three times weekly. Miller and his band even appeared in Hollywood movies.

The December 7, 1941, Japanese attack on Pearl Harbor suddenly thrust the United States into war. As a result, Miller—along with thousands of other patriotic young Americans—rushed to volunteer for the nation's military forces. At the age of thirty-eight, he knew he was too old to fight, but he felt he could still serve his country in a meaningful way by doing what he did best: playing music. He sold himself to the Army by vowing, as he wrote in an August 12, 1942, letter to US Army Brig. Gen. Charles Young, to "put a little more spring into the feet of our marching men and a little more joy into their hearts." The US Army commissioned Miller a captain in the US Army Air Forces, and in short order, he formed the fifty-piece 418th Army Air Force Band, which he took to England in the summer of 1944.

Over the next six months, Miller—by now promoted to major—stayed busy. He and his band of select professional musicians gave dozens of live performances and teamed up with the British Broadcasting Company to send his special brand of music to Allied forces stationed throughout

Famed bandleader Glenn Miller as a major in the US Army Air Forces. *US Air Force*

Major Glenn Miller conducts his 418th Army Air Force band during a 1944 outdoor concert in England. *US Air Force*

Major Glenn Miller (the trombonist on the right) and his band entertain troops at Steeple Morden, Cambridgeshire, England, on August 12, 1944. *US Air Force*

Europe. They even recorded propaganda programs for broadcast deep into the heart of Nazi Germany. The positive effect Miller and his band had while serving in England during the latter half of 1944 was immeasurable. General James H. "Jimmy" Doolittle—famed leader of the daring 1942 raid on Japan, and by 1944 a three-star general in command of the US Eighth Air Force in Europe—fully recognized Miller's contributions. On July 29, 1944, he publicly stated near the end of a Miller concert at High Wycombe, England, that "next to a letter from home, your music is the greatest morale builder in the European Theater of Operations."

A Bad Day to Fly

But even this high praise from one of the nation's true heroes rolled off of the unassuming bandleader's back. He did not take his band to Europe to earn kudos; he went to serve the troops who were fighting and dying there. As Allied victories pushed the war further east, he wanted to move his band with it. He believed the best way to support the troops serving on the front lines was to be there near them. This philosophy prompted him to schedule a Christmas concert in the recently liberated Parisian music hall the Olympia. As soon as he had the date booked, he began looking for transportation to Paris. He needed to arrange for the band's arrival and upcoming concert.

In the hectic confusion of wartime England, securing a hop across the English Channel was no easy task. This was especially so when the weather was not conducive to flying—which was often. Therefore, on the evening of December 14, 1944, when Lieutenant Colonel Baessell—an army staff officer acquaintance of Miller's who had secured a flight to Paris the next day—offered Miller a seat on the Norseman, he jumped at the chance. Most routine flights had been grounded because of the prevailing poor visibility, so this was a lucky break for Miller, who was anxious to get concert preparations underway.

The next day, Miller and Baessell stood on the foggy Twinwood Farm RAF airfield, located in Bedfordshire, a few miles north of London. As they prepared to board the Norseman transport, bearing the tail number 470285, bystanders overheard Miller asking Baesell, "Hey, where the hell are the parachutes?" He was not a fan of flying in the first place, and the small Canadian bush plane did not seem like a safe bet over water, in wartime, and in weather conditions of near-zero visibility. For that matter, perhaps it was not such a good idea to be flying in *any* airplane under those conditions. Baessell replied, "What's the matter, Miller? Do you want to live forever?"

470439

↑ Noorduyn UC-64A Norseman, similar to the one in which Maj. Glenn Miller and two other officers disappeared over the English Channel on December 15, 1944. *US Air Force*

← The Noorduyn UC-64A displayed at the National Museum of the US Air Force. The Norseman was a Canadian bush plane prior to being drafted into the military. *National Museum of the US Air Force*

The US military did not launch a comprehensive search for the missing airplane. This might have caused an outcry, had it been made public—but it was not. Besides, authorities had their reasons for not going to great lengths to find it. It was certainly not the first to disappear mysteriously into the treacherous English Channel, and so everyone assumed the worst when Miller's plane failed to arrive in Paris—or anywhere else. The chances of any of the three men surviving a Channel ditching in a high-wing, fixed-gear airplane such as the Norseman were remote. It would have likely flipped on impact and sunk before they could escape. And even if they

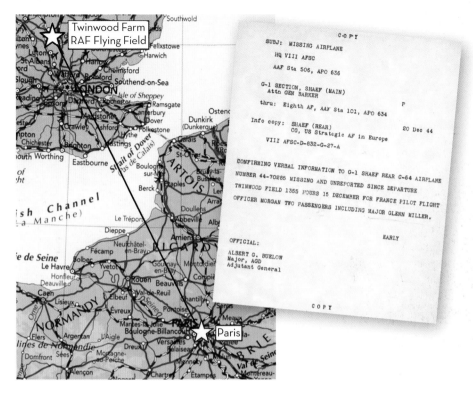

Twinwood Farm
RAF Flying Field

Paris

COPY

SUBJ: MISSING AIRPLANE
HQ VIII AFSC
AAF Sta 506, APO 636

G-1 SECTION, SHAEF (MAIN)
Attn GEN BARKER

thru: Eighth AF, AAF Sta 101, APO 634

Info copy: SHAEF (REAR)
CO, US Strategic AF in Europe
VIII AFSC-D-632-G-27-A

20 Dec 44

CONFIRMING VERBAL INFORMATION TO G-1 SHAEF REAR C-64 AIRPLANE
NUMBER 44-70285 MISSING AND UNREPORTED SINCE DEPARTURE
TWINWOOD FIELD 1355 HOURS 15 DECEMBER FOR FRANCE PILOT FLIGHT
OFFICER MORGAN TWO PASSENGERS INCLUDING MAJOR GLENN MILLER.

OFFICIAL:

ALBERT G. BUELOW
Major, AGD
Adjutant General

EARLY

COPY

⬆ The approximate course of Miller's plane from Bedfordshire to Paris on the day he disappeared. It would have been a routine flight in good weather, but flying over the English Channel in limited visibility could be deadly.

⬆➡ An official document, dated December 20, 1944, confirming that Maj. Glenn Miller and two others had been missing since December 15. *US Air Force*

survived the crash, their prospects of remaining alive in the icy December waters of the English Channel long enough for rescue were virtually nil. Besides, with a war going on, the resources needed for a thorough operation were simply not available.

The day after the Norseman vanished, the massive and bloody Battle of the Bulge began in mainland Europe, diminishing further any inclination to mount a search for a single missing airplane. Miller, Baessell, and Morgan were just three of what were to be 47,000 Eighth Air Force casualties suffered during World War II. Consequently, a little more than a week after they disappeared, the Army officially listed Miller and his two flying companions as missing and presumed dead.

Conspiracy Theories Galore

The official US Army Air Forces explanation for Miller's loss is still probably as reasonable as any other. It held that the Norseman went into the Channel after experiencing icing or engine failure, or after the pilot became disoriented in the dense fog and lost control of the airplane. The airplane would undoubtedly have disintegrated upon impact, and been dragged to the bottom of the Channel by the heavy engine, taking its occupants with it. To this day, nothing definitive has surfaced to refute this explanation.

This is not to say, however, that there is any shortage of alternative theories for Miller's mysterious demise. The official explanation may not tell the whole story. After all, no airplane parts nor bodies ever turned up, and the Army conducted only a cursory search for the missing plane and its occupants. Not only might the official cause have been wrong, it could even have been a cover-up for something more sinister. Therefore, as is typical in such high-profile disappearances, the absence of facts has translated to a surplus of widely diverse theories. Each has attempted in its own unique way to explain Miller's disappearance.

Knocked out of the Sky by Jettisoned Bombs — Bombs dropped by Royal Air Force (RAF) bombers returning from an aborted mission may have knocked the low-flying Norseman out of the sky. On that day, 138 Lancaster bombers returning from an aborted mission to Germany jettisoned their bombs over a ten-mile circular area in the English Channel, designated the South Jettison Area. Bomber crews routinely employed this procedure to get rid of bombs they had been unable to drop on a target. This avoided the hazardous prospect of landing with armed bombs still on board. RAF navigator Fred Shaw, along with fellow crew members aboard one of the bombers that day, recorded in their flight logbooks seeing a small single-engine monoplane fitting the description of a Norseman tip over and crash into the water below. Had the Norseman inadvertently strayed in the foul weather into the forbidden jettison zone, and been hit outright by a falling bomb or blown out of the sky after one exploded upon impact with the water? Shaw and his fellow crew members failed to report their observation at the time, so there was no follow-up. The incident remained mostly unknown until 1984, when Shaw finally decided to report what he had observed on that mission to the British Ministry of Defense. The press quickly learned of it and his story appeared in newspapers worldwide. Historians and other authorities have generally taken this story seriously, although some have questioned certain aspects of it, such as the time and jettison area's location.

Killed in a Crash on the Coast of France — In 1999, another former military man provided a different explanation to Miller's death. Fred W. Atkinson Jr., in an article on his website entitled "A World War II Soldier's Insight Into the 'Mysterious Disappearance' of Glenn Miller," stated that not only did Miller's plane crash, the Army recovered his body. Atkinson served with the Paris-based 320th Air Transport Squadron, which operated Norseman aircraft like the one in which Miller disappeared. He indicated that the Army primarily intended them for short air evacuation flights. They were therefore not equipped with sophisticated navigational instruments and thus were generally grounded in bad weather. According to Atkinson, in spite of the dismal weather conditions, a high-ranking officer issued orders for a flight to bring Major Miller to Paris. The Norseman subsequently crashed near the coast of France, killing all aboard. Atkinson asserted that one of those killed was Miller, as verified by dog tags and identification papers found on the body. He further implied that because the order for Miller's flight in such weather conditions was tantamount to criminal negligence, the Army might have covered up the entire incident by leaving Miller listed as "missing in action."

Shot Down by Antiaircraft Fire — Another explanation appeared in a 2006 book written by Clarence B. Wolfe. The former US antiaircraft gunner serving with Battery D of the 134th Antiaircraft Battalion contends in *I Kept My Word* that his gun battery accidentally downed Miller's plane near Folkestone, England, as it flew over. The only problem is that he claimed the downing occurred in September 1944—more than three months before Miller was declared missing. Did this really happen, but perhaps on a different date?

Miller the Undercover Agent — Another interesting explanation for Miller's disappearance came from a 2009 book written by a former US Army intelligence officer named Hunton Downs. In *The Glenn Miller Conspiracy*, Downs contends that Miller's death was a cover-up for a failed secret mission authorized by Eisenhower. According to Downs, Miller's assignment was to convince key senior German officers to help expedite the war's end by collaborating with the Allies; instead, Nazi intelligence agents captured and executed him. Downs suggests that the US Army fabricated the story of Miller's disappearance over the English Channel to avoid embarrassment and prevent the revelation of sensitive information. This book—fifty years in the making—was a serious effort, although critics have questioned some of its facts, conclusions, and sources.

Died of Cancer — Another unsubstantiated but widely repeated version of Glenn Miller's death is attributed to his brother, Herb Miller. He allegedly revealed in 1983 that his brother did not die in a plane crash over the English Channel, but rather in a hospital from lung cancer. He contended that Glenn took off on the fateful flight as described in the official explanation, but later landed and entered a military hospital, where he died the following day. The crash story was fabricated so that the world would remember him as a fallen hero—not, as Herb allegedly said, someone who had died "in a lousy bed." This version, like some of the other alternative theories, would explain why authorities never conducted an extensive search for the downed airplane. There is other evidence, as well, that Glenn Miller was not in the best health during his time in England. His executive officer and band manager, Don Haynes, wrote that he was losing weight. Miller's radio director in England, George Voutsas, related that Miller had once said, "You know, George, I have an awful feeling you guys are going to go home without me."

Other Theories — Other explanations for Miller's disappearance, proposed by various authors over the years, range from far-fetched to utterly unbelievable. The Germans shot down his plane, and a horribly disfigured Miller remained hidden away in a hospital out of public view. He died in Ohio in 1945 after arriving there with gunshot wounds. His fellow passenger, Baessell, was involved in the black market, and after murdering Miller and Morgan, landed the airplane himself somewhere in France. The US high command discovered that Miller was a German spy and "eliminated" him. US agents killed him because he threatened to expose a group of homosexual US officers. A US military policeman in Paris accidentally shot him. A German assassin downed his airplane. Miller made the flight to France safely, but died in the arms of a French prostitute. Insufficient evidence exists to prove any of these explanations.

Glenn Miller's disappearance on that foggy December afternoon in 1944 is still a mystery. In all likelihood, it will remain that way. To this day, his memorial headstone at Arlington National Cemetery lists him as "MIA"—missing in action.

As for Miller's Army Air Forces Band, it soldiered on without its esteemed leader. Under the direction of Jerry Gray, it played the 1944 Paris Christmas concert Miller died trying to arrange, and the band continued playing until war's end. Its final performance was in Washington, DC, on November 13, 1945—just ten weeks after the war had ended and less than a year after

Miller's disappearance. President Harry S. Truman, accompanied by generals Dwight D. Eisenhower and Henry H. "Hap" Arnold, was in attendance. These VIPs took the opportunity to honor the band—and specifically, its fallen leader—publicly. But the real tribute to Miller was the band itself.

Glenn Miller's legacy continued to grow in the years following his disappearance. It has included a Jimmy Stewart movie; a US postage stamp; numerous books, articles, and documentaries; a museum; and several additional musical awards including, in 2003, a Grammy Lifetime Achievement Award. However, the legacy he probably would have cherished the most is the modern-day descendent of his band: the acclaimed US Air Force jazz ensemble, Airmen of Note. The Air Force created the band in 1950 to continue the tradition of Miller's famous dance band, and it still entertains audiences today.

Glenn Miller left behind a wife, two children, a large fortune, a successful career, and a future full of promise. Though he is long gone, the man, the patriot, the bandleader—and of course, his unique sound—will never be forgotten.

⬆ Display at the National Museum of the US Air Force, honoring famed bandleader, Glenn Miller. *National Museum of the US Air Force*

➡ Major Glenn Miller's summer uniform cap and spare eyeglasses, displayed at the National Museum of the US Air Force. *Steven A. Ruffin*

SECTION II
LAPSES IN JUDGMENT

CHAPTER SIX
THE NIGHT CAMELOT ENDED

"LIKE HIS FATHER, EVERY GIFT
BUT LENGTH OF YEARS."

On the dark, hazy Friday evening of July 16, 1999, a thirty-eight-year-old pilot took off from Essex County Airport, near Caldwell, New Jersey. He was flying a Piper PA-32R-301 Saratoga II—a sleek, dependable, retractable-gear, single-engine light plane. The pilot's wife and her sister also joined him on the flight. Their destination was Martha's Vineyard, the resort island off the southern coast of Massachusetts.

Just before takeoff, the pilot acknowledged tower clearance for a right downwind departure from runway twenty-two. After lifting off at about 8:40 p.m., the Piper climbed for altitude and headed out over Long Island Sound toward the Vineyard, some two hundred miles to the northeast. Air traffic control (ATC) received no further radio transmissions from the pilot, but everything appeared normal as his airplane vanished into the early evening haze.

The Saratoga II and its occupants should have reached their destination in just over an hour, but they never arrived. Soon, news agencies learned that an airplane was missing, and that the pilot was none other than the son of the thirty-fifth president of the United States—in his own right, one of the most famous men in the world—John Fitzgerald Kennedy Jr.

An Ill-Advised Flight

When "John-John," the son of slain US President John F. Kennedy Sr., was only three years old, he became America's darling. On November 25, 1963, the brave little boy stood in front of the entire nation and saluted his father's flag-draped coffin. From that moment, he remained America's favorite "first son." Wealthy, intelligent, likeable, handsome, and the scion of a prominent American family, he was the complete package. It was a surprise to no one when *People* magazine named him 1988's "Sexiest Man Alive." Well before the age of forty, he had established his own identity as an assistant district attorney and, later, co-founder of the political-culture magazine *George*. He was no longer John-John—he was John F. Kennedy Jr. With such a unique thoroughbred pedigree, it seemed certain that he was destined for greater things.

Kennedy had only recently earned his pilot's license, but he was not a total beginner. He had accumulated more than three hundred hours of flight time—far more than the license required, and fifty-five of them at night. However, the Federal Aviation Administration (FAA) classifies the Saratoga II that he flew—by virtue of its power, speed, retractable gear, and other advanced features—both a "complex" and a "high-performance" airplane. Consequently, it is a lot of airplane for a relatively inexperienced pilot to manage. John had logged roughly thirty-six flight hours in it, but only three of these were without a flight instructor. Perhaps most significantly, he had less than one hour of solo time at night in the Saratoga II. Still, his instructor considered him competent enough to handle it and had recently signed him off.

A Piper Saratoga II, the type in which John Kennedy Jr. made his last flight. Its relatively high performance makes it a demanding airplane for an inexperienced pilot to fly. *Steven A. Ruffin*

John F. Kennedy Jr., during a visit to Kennedy Space Center. His uncle, Senator Ted Kennedy, later described him as having "every gift but length of years." *NASA*

Although Kennedy lacked experience in the airplane, he was familiar with the route he was flying that evening. He had flown it, in one direction or the other, some thirty-five times previously. Several of these flights were at night, though this was the first time he had flown it after dark in the Saratoga II. It was a warm, hazy summer evening with little or no overcast, and weather reports indicated that visibility met the FAA Visual Flight Rules (VFR) minimum of three miles; consequently, the flight did not legally require an instrument flight plan. Otherwise, Kennedy would have had to either cancel the flight or take along an instructor, since he did not have an instrument rating.

These facts considered, it seems safe to conclude that John had the requisite ratings, training, skills, and meteorological conditions to make this flight—at least from a technical and legal standpoint. Whether he had the experience and overall competence to complete it *safely* under those conditions proved another matter.

After departing the Essex County Airport, Kennedy climbed to an altitude of 5,500 feet and headed northeast toward the Vineyard. Navigation was simple enough, as he followed the southern Connecticut and Rhode Island shoreline for all but the final leg of the trip. His wife, Carolyn Bessette Kennedy, and sister-in-law, Lauren Bessette, accompanied

The course Kennedy flew from Essex County Airport, New Jersey, before he crashed into the Atlantic Ocean on July 16, 1999. He was only a few miles short of his destination at Martha's Vineyard.

him. Kennedy intended to drop Lauren off at Martha's Vineyard and then fly with Carolyn the additional twenty-five miles up to Hyannis Port, where they planned to attend a wedding the next day.

Kennedy eventually left the coastline and headed out over the dark thirty-mile stretch of the Atlantic Ocean off the western coast of Martha's Vineyard. As he began his descent for landing, things began to go wrong.

What happened next was only determined later from ATC radar images recorded that night. They showed his airplane making a series of unexplained maneuvers and altitude changes that culminated in a steep, high-speed descending turn. The rate of descent quickly accelerated to an alarming vertical drop of nearly 5,000 feet per minute. This scenario suggested only one thing: the airplane had fallen into a dangerous downward spiral. The last position recorded was at 9:40 p.m., when the airplane was about seven miles off the western coast of Martha's Vineyard, at an altitude of 1,100 feet. Then, it simply disappeared from radar.

Unknown to anyone at the time it was happening—perhaps even including the three doomed occupants of the airplane—was that Kennedy had lost control of the airplane. It hit nose first at a speed well in excess of two hundred miles per hour. The effect of hitting the water at that speed was the same as hitting a slab of granite. All three occupants almost certainly died instantly, even before the crumpled mass began to sink to the ocean floor.

When the airplane failed to arrive at Martha's Vineyard, members of the family became concerned and started making phone calls. The hope was that Kennedy had simply changed his plans at the last minute—or perhaps had some minor mechanical or weather-related problem—and landed elsewhere. After authorities ruled out that possibility, they pinpointed the area off the coast of Martha's Vineyard where radar had last tracked the Saratoga II, and initiated a search.

Family members of the missing fliers, along with just about everyone else in the country, anxiously watched and waited through the days to come. Hopes dwindled by the hour that the three might still somehow be clinging to a piece of wreckage floating in the ocean or sitting high and dry on some remote shore. On July 20—four days after they had gone missing—the American public finally learned the gut-wrenching truth: divers from the US Navy salvage ship USNS *Grasp* had located the wreckage of Kennedy's airplane about 120 feet below the surface of the Atlantic Ocean. In short order, they recovered the bodies. It was all too obvious that for all aboard there had been no chance for survival.

A Deadly Dose of Disorientation

As is often the case with aircraft accidents, the cause of the crash that killed John F. Kennedy Jr., his wife, and his sister-in-law was as much an educated guess as it was a scientific finding. The NTSB investigated the wreckage and reviewed stacks of documentation—reports, statements, and interview transcripts. Finding no obvious deficiencies in either the airplane or the pilot, they concluded that the probable cause of the accident was "the pilot's failure to maintain control of the airplane during a descent over water at night, which was a result of spatial disorientation." The haze and darkness, which prevailed at the time, were contributing factors.

Unfortunately, this demon—spatial disorientation—is an all-too-common occurrence in aviation. It has claimed countless other pilots since the earliest days of powered flight. Pilots learn, almost from day one of training, that when unable to see the horizon or other reference points around them—as can occur over water at night and in situations where visibility is limited—they *must* trust only their instruments and not their senses. This is because the senses easily become confused and convey to the pilot false information, while instruments normally do not lie. John apparently lost his sense of spatial awareness on that hazy night when he could not see anything around him on which to focus; consequently, he literally lost the ability to distinguish the difference between up and down. Because of the various forces affecting him in his moving airplane, a dive might have felt like a climb, or a right climbing turn may have given the same sensation as flying straight and level. Due to his state of spatial confusion, he unknowingly fell into a rapidly descending turn—or spiral. The sound of his engine racing during the rapid descent was probably the only indication to him that things were not right. Had he relied on his instruments or autopilot, he could have avoided the situation or even recovered after getting into it, but he obviously failed to do that. The result was a rapidly accelerating and tightening spiral that ended only when the nose of the Saratoga II smacked, right wing low, into the dark waters of the Atlantic Ocean. It was an all-too-easy mistake for even a seasoned pilot to make, and nearly always a deadly one—hence the macabre nickname "graveyard spiral." Several factors may have contributed to John Kennedy Jr.'s tragic end:

Visibility — This was probably more of a concern that hot, hazy July evening than Kennedy's preflight weather briefing led him to believe. Although it was technically above the VFR minimum of three miles all along the route, it was not much more than that. Airports along the coast reported visibilities of between five and eight miles, while at least one other pilot flying over the water in the vicinity that evening reported no visual horizon at all because of the haze. Most prudent non-instrument-rated pilots would avoid flying at night in conditions such as those. John may have found himself in trouble before he even realized the danger he was in.

Nighttime Experience in the Saratoga II — Although Kennedy was legally qualified to fly his high-performance Piper that evening, the amount of flight time he had in it without an instructor at night was minimal—less than an hour—and he had only one single unsupervised nighttime landing in it. Perhaps additional night experience in this airplane would have made enough difference to save him and his passengers.

Late Departure — Kennedy had planned an earlier departure that day, but the heavier-than-usual Friday afternoon traffic that he and his passengers encountered on the way to the airport delayed takeoff. The original plan had been to leave at 6:00 p.m. and arrive at Martha's Vineyard before dark, but it was past sunset when they finally took to the air. This delay made the difference between day and night—and, as events proved, between life and death.

Injured Ankle — John had fractured his left ankle while paragliding about six weeks earlier, which required surgery to repair. On the evening of the flight, a witness observed him using crutches as he loaded his airplane. His physical therapist stated later that Kennedy's foot still did not have a full range of motion. In addition, two different flight instructors with whom he had recently flown stated that they had to assist him in manipulating the rudder pedals. This may have contributed to his inability to pull the airplane out of its death spiral.

Distracted by Personal Problems — It was widely reported that John and Carolyn were experiencing marital problems at the time of the flight. On top of that, his magazine, though initially successful, was no longer financially sound. Given such issues, it would be reasonable to suspect that John might have had other things on his mind that night, and was perhaps not as attentive to flight details as he should have been. Christopher Andersen, in his book *The Day John Died*, lends credibility to this idea. He contends that Kennedy nearly collided with an American Airlines jet earlier that evening after he inadvertently flew into its path.

The Curse

The nation was shocked. Yet again, fate had prematurely snatched one of its favorite sons. The so-called "Kennedy Curse" is legendary—and not without foundation. Many have cited as evidence of its existence the numerous tragic incidents that have afflicted this famous family over the latter part of the twentieth century. Foremost among these were the assassinations of President John F. Kennedy Sr. in 1963 and, five years later, that of his brother, senator and presidential candidate Robert F. "Bobby" Kennedy. The trend goes well beyond those two tragedies, however—from automobile, aircraft, and skiing accidents to stillbirths and serious illnesses to the tragic consequences of bad behavior.

The family's ill fortune in airplanes, however, was the aspect of the curse on which John should have focused. If he had, he might have reconsidered ever taking flying lessons.

Joseph P. Kennedy Jr. — US Navy Lt. Joseph Kennedy was President Kennedy's older brother and the uncle that John Jr. never met. Joe, a World War II naval aviator, had volunteered to participate in a dangerous program called Operation Aphrodite, which involved the use of one of the earliest precursors to today's unmanned aerial vehicles. On August 12, 1944, Joe took off from a base in England in a modified Consolidated B-24 Liberator bomber that was loaded to the gills with explosives. The plan was simple: soon after he had the big plane safely in the air, he and his copilot—the only two aboard—were to bail out. The flying bomb would then proceed to its heavily fortified target, guided by remote control, and crash directly into it. Instead, Kennedy's airplane exploded prematurely before he and his copilot could bail out, killing them both instantly. The cause of the spontaneous explosion was never definitively established.

Kathleen Agnes Kennedy Cavendish — Kathleen was President Kennedy's younger sister and another family member that John Jr. never had the chance to meet. On May 13, 1948, she and three others—including her fiancé, Peter Wentworth-Fitzwilliam, eighth Earl Fitzwilliam, who was not yet divorced from his previous wife—died when their airplane crashed in southern France during a storm. Kathleen was twenty-eight years old.

Senator Edward M. Kennedy — An airplane accident occurring only seven months after the assassination of the president, his older brother, was just one of several misadventures in the career of this resilient politician.

On June 19, 1964, "Teddy" was winging his way from Washington, DC, to Westfield, Massachusetts. While approaching the municipal airport at Westfield to land, the twin-engine Aero Commander 680 in which he was riding crashed into an apple orchard. The pilot and one of Kennedy's aides died, but Teddy and two others survived. It was a narrow escape for the junior senator from Massachusetts. He would spend the next five months in the hospital recovering—and probably thanking his lucky stars for having survived his family's dreaded curse.

Alexander Onassis — John's stepbrother from the second marriage of his mother, Jacqueline Kennedy Onassis, died in a plane crash near Athens, Greece, on January 23, 1973. While not involving a Kennedy, it was just another manifestation of the curse—this time by sheer association. Christopher Andersen also alleges in *The Day John Died* that Jacqueline Kennedy had a recurring premonition that her son would die piloting his own plane. For that reason, she did everything in her power, until her own death in 1994, to prevent him from becoming a pilot. It is therefore just that much easier for Kennedy Curse proponents to feel that the inevitable had happened once again. Andrew Ferguson, who operated the company that maintained Kennedy's airplane, explained his tragic death this way: "He wasn't reckless. He made a stupid mistake. It's like going through a stop sign. But when a Kennedy goes through a stop sign, there always seems to be an eighteen-wheeler coming from the other side."

Conspiracy Theories

Curses notwithstanding, John Kennedy Jr.'s death unsurprisingly generated a greater-than-usual assortment of conspiracy theories. Although the NTSB report provided a logical and reasonable explanation for his crash, those looking for a more sinister cause can find plenty of ammunition.

Almost immediately after the crash, the tabloids went into high gear. They were encouraged in part by a fake FBI "Preliminary Report" that made the rounds, suggesting that his death was not accidental. Consequently, many publications and websites began to claim that Kennedy's death was the result of a conspiracy. They alleged that there had been a large-scale cover-up, evidence destroyed, and "facts" fabricated.

Many of these conspiracy advocates even went so far as to refer to his death as an assassination. Those supposedly implicated included a variety of high-profile potential political rivals and the secret society known as the Illuminati. Some even pointed a finger at the Israeli intelligence service,

Mossad, which allegedly feared that the probing of John's magazine into the 1995 assassination of Israeli Prime Minister Yitzhak Rabin might reveal incriminating secrets. Rumors also circulated that US Navy pyrotechnics, or perhaps even a nuclear accelerator fired from Long Island, accidentally brought down Kennedy's airplane.

Whether any of the numerous alternate explanations for John F. Kennedy Jr.'s demise have even a shred of credibility is debatable. In the absence of hard evidence to the contrary, the NTSB report remains the most likely scenario: an inexperienced pilot flying a high-performance aircraft over water on a dark, hazy night simply became disoriented, lost control, and spiraled into the sea.

⭐

Regardless of whether John Kennedy Jr.'s death was the result of a curse, a sinister plot, lack of competence, bad judgment, or just plain bad luck, the result was the same: America had lost its beloved John-John. The nation mourned his death, perhaps not so much for who or what he was as for what he had represented to the American people—he was the living legacy of a charismatic young president who died tragically in service of his country.

The family held a memorial Mass for John, Carolyn, and Lauren on July 23, 1999, at Old Saint Patrick's Cathedral in New York. Besides family members, President Bill Clinton and numerous other dignitaries attended. There were an additional four thousand mourners both inside and outside of the packed church. John's Uncle Teddy—US Senator Edward M. Kennedy—gave the eulogy. In so doing, he wistfully noted that John had, "like his father, every gift but length of years."

The fateful decision John F. Kennedy Jr. made to take to the air that hazy July evening in 1999 resulted in the tragic end of three promising young lives. The loss of America's favorite prince also effectively ended any hope of the country ever returning to one of its most memorable eras—the enchanted Kennedy period known as "Camelot."

CHAPTER SEVEN

THE DEATH OF A BUTTERFLY

"OBVIOUSLY A MAJOR MALFUNCTION."

On the cold morning of January 28, 1986, America's next spacecraft to rocket its way into orbit sat majestically poised for launch at Kennedy Space Center, Florida. Space Shuttle *Challenger*, otherwise known by its Orbital Vehicle Designation, OV-099, was the second shuttle—after *Columbia*—that the US Space agency, NASA, had launched into space. With nine missions and several significant firsts already under its belt, in less than three years the 115-ton winged orbiter had already more than proven itself. The highly advanced Rockwell-built space plane and its sister ships were the most high-tech manned flying machines ever built, the epitome of human scientific achievement.

Technical brilliance, however, was not enough. Only seventy-three seconds after launch, and in front of television viewers the world over, the pride of America's space program disintegrated into a million pieces and plunged, with its precious human cargo, into the Atlantic Ocean. It was the worst—and most graphically visible—in-flight catastrophe in the history of manned space flight. It was also a major black eye for NASA that would create years of negative fallout, and bring into question the agency's ethical culture and hard-earned reputation for safety. Worst of all, it was a tragic end for seven courageous human beings. For the first time in NASA history, failure had become an option. It was, by any measure, one of aviation history's most significant flights of no return.

A New Concept in Space Flight

The Space Shuttle was the world's first space plane. The concept was the product of a NASA program created in the late 1960s called the Space Transportation System; hence the "STS" prefix for all shuttle missions. The idea was that a winged spacecraft capable of safely gliding back to the earth from orbit for reuse would significantly reduce the exorbitant cost of space missions. In addition, its spacious cargo compartment and hefty thirty-ton payload would facilitate the transport of satellites, interplanetary probes, scientific equipment, and other space hardware into orbit for future projects.

NASA operated six shuttles as reusable low-earth orbital spacecraft between 1981 and 2011: *Enterprise, Columbia, Challenger, Discovery, Atlantis,* and *Endeavour.* All flew space missions except for the prototype *Enterprise,* which NASA used only for flight-testing within Earth's atmosphere. The amazing accomplishments of the $200 billion Space Shuttle program are a matter of public record. During the program's thirty-year span, its five operational shuttles flew 355 different astronauts, ranging in age from twenty-eight to seventy-seven, on 135 missions. In so doing, they logged more than three and one-half *years* in space, completed twenty-one thousand orbits of the earth, and carried 1,750 tons of cargo into orbit. All shuttle missions launched from Kennedy Space Center, Florida, and all but two ended with a conventional winged landing. The two exceptions were those missions in which both shuttle and crew perished: *Challenger* mission STS-51-L and *Columbia* mission STS-107.

The distinctive Space Shuttle launch complex consisted of three major components linked together—the delta-winged orbiter, which carried the crew and cargo; a massive external tank containing 790 tons of liquid oxygen and hydrogen for the orbiter's three main rocket engines; and two solid rocket boosters, which provided most of the thrust for the first two minutes after liftoff. Astronaut Story Musgrave, the only person to fly all five of NASA's operational shuttles into space, aptly described the setup as "bolting a very beautiful butterfly onto a bullet."

The orbiter jettisoned both boosters and the external fuel tank after they had served their purpose, so that only the orbiter itself escaped Earth's atmosphere. When its mission was over, it reentered the atmosphere and glided down to land at Edwards Air Force Base, California; Kennedy Space Center, Florida; or, in the case of STS-3 alone, White Sands, New Mexico.

By the time *Challenger* was ready for its tenth mission in January 1986, many experts considered the Space Shuttle the safest spacecraft ever flown. *Columbia, Challenger, Discovery,* and *Atlantis* had already successfully completed an aggregate of twenty-four missions with hardly a

A "butterfly" bolted to a "bullet." Successful launch of Space Shuttle *Challenger* on mission STS-6, April 4, 1983. On January 28, 1986, it broke apart at T+73 seconds, killing all seven astronauts aboard. *NASA*

hiccup. In fact, the American public—and perhaps NASA officials too—had been lulled into a sense of complacency about space launches. This was a far cry from the early days of the space program, when gamblers placed bets on whether the next launch would end in a successful liftoff—or a massive explosion on the launch pad. As events would prove, however, launching even the Space Shuttle into orbit was still anything but safe.

A Perilous Undertaking

Space is, without a doubt, the most inhospitable and treacherous environment imaginable. Just getting there requires a wild ride atop a metal tube propelled skyward by a semicontrolled explosion of thousands of tons of highly unstable rocket fuel. On the way up, riders must endure bone-crushing gravitational forces as the rocket quickly accelerates them to a speed high enough to escape Earth's gravitational pull.

Once in space, they are exposed to a multitude of deadly conditions seen nowhere on Earth, starting with temperatures cold enough in the shade to convert the human body instantly into a block of ice, yet hot enough in the sunlight to just as quickly turn that same body into a lump of carbon. Then, there is the airless, body-wrecking total vacuum of outer space that is utterly incompatible with life. Finally, since there is no gravity in space, space travelers must deal with the constant sensation of falling, nausea, and the many other discomforts associated with weightlessness.

Getting back into Earth's atmosphere is even more dangerous than escaping it. When it is time to come home, space travelers must once again withstand extremely high g-forces, this time from rapid deceleration; in addition, extreme precautions must be in place to prevent them from burning to a cinder in the three-thousand-degree heat generated by the friction of a seventeen-thousand-mile-per-hour slipstream of air screaming past the spacecraft. Finally, once safely slowed down and back in the earth's atmosphere, the now-powerless craft, designed primarily for space flight, somehow must find a way to bring its human cargo back to terra firma in one piece. Certainly, no human venture has ever been more technically demanding or fraught with peril than space travel.

Yet, surprisingly, in more than a half century of manned space flight, very few humans have failed to return home safely. This outstanding record is due, in part, to the obsessively meticulous care that space agencies have traditionally taken in producing spacecraft, training crew members, and planning missions. It is also due, at least to some extent, to that other ingredient that is always necessary for flight safety: luck. On

Apollo 1 astronauts Gus Grissom, Ed White,
and Roger Chaffee in front of Launch Complex 34, on which
the Saturn 1 launch rocket sits. The three later died in a preflight fire
on the launch pad, making them the first US astronauts killed in action. *NASA*

those few occasions when either of these essential factors was lacking, the consequences were horrendous.

Up until *Challenger*'s tenth and last mission, there had only been two fatal space missions. Both took place within the Soviet Union's ultra-secret space program. The first occurred in April 1967, when cosmonaut Vladimir Komarov of *Soyuz* 1 crashed to his death in his space capsule. After a trouble-plagued eighteen-orbit flight in a spaceship he angrily called a "devil-machine," he finally managed with great difficulty to reenter Earth's atmosphere . . . only to have the capsule's life-saving parachute fail. He plummeted, unchecked, all the way to the earth, crashing to his death. Then on June 30, 1971, three Soviet cosmonauts from *Soyuz* 11 died during their return from the *Salyut* space station. Their capsule developed an air leak and lost pressure, killing them instantly.

The US Space Program also had its disasters. On January 27, 1967, it lost three Apollo 1 astronauts in a preflight launch pad fire. And in 1970, it had a very close call during the Apollo 13 mission to the moon, when an oxygen tank exploded more than two hundred thousand miles from Earth. So far, however, NASA had managed to avoid any loss of life during a space mission. On January 28, 1986, that perfect record would end in a huge cloud of white smoke.

T+73 to Disaster

A highly trained and extremely competent crew of five men and two women were strapped inside *Challenger*'s crew compartment on pad 39B. Sitting there 195 feet above the ground awaiting countdown were Mission Commander Francis R. Scobee; Pilot Michael J. Smith; Mission Specialists Ellison S. Onizuka, Judith A. Resnik, and Ronald E. McNair; and Payload Specialists Gregory B. Jarvis and Christa McAuliffe. This carefully selected group of highly accomplished Americans appropriately represented a diverse cross-section of the nation—not only in gender and ethnicity, but also in their professional and personal backgrounds.

It was rookie astronaut Sharon Christa Corrigan McAuliffe, however, who was the media darling of the crew. Although this was only her first mission, her special distinction was that she had been selected from a pool of eleven thousand applicants to participate in a new NASA program called the Teacher in Space Project. As the winner of this nationwide competition, the thirty-eight-year-old high school teacher, wife, and mother of two was to be the first professional educator ever shot into orbit. Because of the widespread publicity surrounding this program, McAuliffe had become NASA's best-known astronaut. Moreover, because she was attractive, articulate, and enthusiastic about space flight, she proved to be an excellent spokesperson for her own profession, as well as for the US Space Program. As she once said on a late-night TV appearance, "If you're offered a seat on a rocket ship, don't ask what seat. Just get on." This is exactly what she did.

The mission, designated STS-51-L, was routine—as space missions go. Mission planners had tasked the crew with a variety of duties, including deploying satellites and performing experiments in space; in addition, they had scheduled McAuliffe to conduct classroom lessons and experiments for the Teacher in Space Project while orbiting weightless 150 miles above the earth. Her first lesson, entitled "The Ultimate Field Trip," was to be a tour of the cabin and a description of daily life aboard the shuttle.

NASA had experienced a particularly difficult time getting STS-51-L off the launch pad. For various reasons, half a dozen delays in the liftoff had occurred in as many days. The latest holdup had happened just two hours before its final launch, due to a problem with the shuttle's fire detection system. Because these delays were complicating a very tight flight schedule, NASA officials were understandably frustrated and anxious to get *Challenger* into orbit. The pressure was even greater due to the fanfare associated with the much-heralded launching of their first teacher-astronaut into space.

The crew of STS-51-L. *Back row, L to R*: Ellison S. Onizuka, Sharon Christa McAuliffe, Greg Jarvis, and Judy Resnik. *Front row, L to R*: Mike Smith, Dick Scobee, and Ron McNair. All died on January 28, 1986, in the *Challenger* accident. *NASA*

NASA astronaut and Teacher in Space Project representative, Christa McAuliffe, experiences the sensation of weightlessness in a Boeing KC-135 Stratotanker. Pilots of the modified refueling aircraft fly a special parabolic pattern that provides brief periods of zero gravity for astronauts in training. It is nicknamed the "vomit comet" for obvious reasons. McAuliffe was destined never to experience this sensation in space. *NASA*

Finally, on Tuesday morning, January 28, 1986, all systems were "go" for launch. The countdown proceeded without interruption. At 11:38 a.m., the 2,250-ton mass of rocketry, explosive fuel, and orbiter filled with precious scientific and human cargo began to detach its umbilical cords to the 290-foot launch tower and inch slowly skyward. Millions of spectators watched on live TV, many of them children in their classrooms, as the first teacher in history headed into space. Thousands more had gathered on site to view the launch, some of them family members and friends of the crew. All gazed in awe as the two massive solid rocket fuel boosters and three main engines fired up simultaneously. The deafening roar, heat, vibration, concussion, and blinding light generated by the five engines, producing an aggregate power of more than six million pounds of thrust, was something they would never forget.

The spectacle of the mountain of machinery slowly moving skyward appeared exactly as it should have to onlookers and controllers alike. They watched as it soared higher and higher into the blue Florida sky. Unknown to anyone, however, something terrible had already occurred. As a result, at T+73 seconds, the shuttle assembly—still accelerating, and now approaching a speed of Mach 2—suddenly appeared to explode. Dense white smoke appeared, contrasting sharply against the deep blue sky, and rocket parts seemed to spew off in a hundred different directions. Awe turned to horror.

TV news correspondent Tom Mintier was describing the launch for CNN—which by now was the only national news station still broadcasting live. When he saw the explosive eruption, he became silent and for the next few seconds was at a complete loss for words. Forty seconds later, NASA public affairs officer Steve Nesbitt, watching from Mission Control Center in Houston, publicly announced what would become one of the great understatements of all time: "Flight controllers here looking very carefully at the situation. Obviously a major malfunction. We have no downlink." A little later, he tersely added, "We have a report from the Flight Dynamics Officer that the vehicle has exploded." *Challenger* and its crew were no more. What could have gone so terribly wrong in only seventy-three seconds?

What Went Wrong?

Subsequent analysis revealed that *Challenger* did not really explode— it broke apart. What no one noticed during the first second of liftoff was obvious enough on the launch film, which analysts later carefully scrutinized. Clearly visible were ominous little puffs of smoke coming from a field joint on the right solid rocket booster. It was innocuous

← The graphically violent end of Space Shuttle *Challenger*, January 28, 1986. *NASA*

enough at the time to go unnoticed, but by T+60 seconds, an intense plume of flaming gases had replaced the smoke. It soon burned a hole in the adjacent 535,000-gallon external liquid fuel tank. Within seconds, the solid rocket booster broke loose from the strut attaching it to the external tank, shoving the shuttle laterally into an unusual attitude. Since it was now traveling at Mach 1.9—well over one thousand miles per hour—this created a catastrophic aerodynamic load on the orbiter. Thus, at seventy-three seconds after launch and at an altitude of forty-eight thousand feet, *Challenger* simply flew into pieces.

It was at that precise moment that Pilot Michael Smith uttered his last recorded words: "Uh-oh." It was the last recorded statement by any member of the crew and the only one indicating that they were even remotely aware of a problem. After *Challenger* dissolved in a massive puff of white smoke, only the sturdily built crew cabin—with its human occupants still strapped inside—remained intact, as it shot outward and upward from the rest of the debris. It continued to ride its Mach 1.9 momentum skyward for another twenty-five seconds. After it peaked at an altitude of sixty-five thousand feet, it slowly began its agonizing twelve-mile death plummet toward the Atlantic Ocean below. The doomed crew had no way to escape the sealed compartment.

All seven astronauts were probably still alive during the entire two-minute, forty-five-second plunge to the sea. Whether or not they were conscious is another matter. If the cabin maintained atmospheric pressure after the break-up, they may well have been aware of their impending death right up to the moment when they smashed into the water at a speed of 207 miles per hour. The resulting 200g-plus deceleration force they experienced upon impact was many times in excess of any human survivability. The forces completely crushed the reinforced aluminum cabin, and anyone inside still alive died instantly.

Further investigation would soon determine the root cause of the accident, and accusing fingers of blame would point directly to the highest echelons of NASA leadership. Meanwhile, the shuttle program would remain in limbo for the next thirty-two months.

A Flawed Decision

The key to *Challenger*'s destruction was determining the cause of the telltale gray-black wisps of smoke during liftoff. This, as it turned out, required very little detective work. They resulted from a defect that NASA engineers had known about for nearly a decade. The puffs of smoke were indicative of a failed joint between the two lower segments of the right solid rocket booster. The joint failed because of two faulty quarter-inch-thick rubberlike O-rings. Though the innocuous-looking gaskets were anything but high-tech, their role was critical: they were the only barrier preventing burning gases from leaking through the joint when the rocket was firing. When they failed, a fatal seventy-three-second chain of events ensued that ended in the obliteration of *Challenger*.

Managers from both NASA and the company that built the solid rocket boosters, Morton-Thiokol, Inc., were well aware of the problem with these seals. Nevertheless, since the O-rings had not failed catastrophically in any of the previous missions, NASA decision makers continued to consider them an acceptable risk. For this particular launch, however, lower-level engineers had expressed a different view. In a two-hour teleconference on the evening before *Challenger*'s final launch, Morton-Thiokol engineers had argued passionately to NASA managers that the uncharacteristic freezing weather predicted for Kennedy Space Center on launch day would cause the O-rings to harden and lose their elasticity. This would greatly increase the chance of a catastrophic malfunction. For this reason, they urged NASA to halt the launch—something that impatient, and perhaps politically pressured, NASA bosses did not want to hear. One of these was George Hardy, the Deputy Director of Science and Engineering at Marshall Space Flight Center. He stated emphatically, according to witnesses present at the meeting, that he was "appalled" at their recommendation to delay the launch. Witnesses further testified that during that same meeting, another NASA bigwig—Lawrence Mulloy, who headed Marshall's Space Shuttle Solid Rocket Booster Program—exclaimed, "My God, Thiokol, when do you want me to launch, next April?" Both Hardy and Mulloy later complained that their remarks were taken out of context, but one glaringly incriminating fact remained: they ignored the warnings and the adamant recommendation to scrub the mission. Not surprisingly, no one outside of inner NASA circles learned of any of this until much later.

As predicted, the temperature early on the morning of the launch dipped to well below freezing and by launch time, it was still only thirty-six degrees Fahrenheit. This was fifteen degrees colder than any previous launch and even further below the contractor-recommended minimum of fifty-three degrees. However, NASA officials had a schedule they felt compelled to keep, so they pressed on with the launch.

After the accident, questions remained that NASA officials could not or would not answer. What was the cause of this catastrophe and how could they have prevented it? Was it safe to proceed with the shuttle program? When it became obvious that answers were not forthcoming, President

Ronald Reagan appointed a special commission to investigate the accident. He chose former Secretary of State William P. Rogers to head it up. NASA officials at first did their best to gloss over the circumstances leading up to the disaster. Some at the space agency, however, took exception to this. One of these was Richard C. Cook, the lead resource analyst for the solid rocket boosters. He even went so far as to accuse the agency of an orchestrated cover-up. To prove his point, he leaked documents to the *New York Times* that engineers had sent to NASA management warning of the dangers of launching *Challenger.* Management's disregard of these warnings, along with the other incriminating findings of the Rogers Commission, incited a storm of controversy.

The commission was scathingly critical of NASA officials for making what its report called a "flawed" decision to launch on that day, even though they knew there was a significant risk. NASA spin masters, in turn, did their best—using an array of self-serving rationalizations—to justify their decision; but with the damning evidence presented and seven dead astronauts, their excuses had an exceedingly hollow ring.

In the end, NASA got the message and made more than two hundred changes to the shuttle during the thirty-two-month flight suspension that followed the *Challenger* accident. These included the addition of an escape system—a feature that might have saved the *Challenger* crew had it been available to them. In addition, the agency grudgingly examined its own safety and ethical culture. To improve its decision making, it adopted a more stringent, safety-based flight preparation process for all future flights. Both George Hardy and Lawrence Mulloy voluntarily retired from NASA within months following the disaster.

Finally, on September 29, 1988, the Space Shuttle program resumed operations with the launch of *Discovery* on mission STS-26. With the new operating procedures in place, space flight would be safer.

In spite of the hard lessons learned from the loss of *Challenger,* history was destined to repeat itself on February 1, 2003. Space Shuttle *Columbia* was reentering the earth's atmosphere at the completion of mission STS-107. Only minutes shy of landing at Kennedy Space Center, it broke up over eastern Texas and western Louisiana. Once again, seven astronauts were lost . . . and once again, NASA had allowed a fatal accident to occur because of a problem they already knew about—and should have corrected. The loss of *Columbia* and its crew resulted from a piece of thermal insulation foam from the external tank that had broken loose during launch. It blew back, damaging the orbiter's left wing, which during reentry led to the disintegration of the entire orbiter.

Like the defective O-rings that destroyed *Challenger*, pieces of insulation foam breaking off during launch had been a known and persistent problem of which NASA engineers and management were well aware. This issue caused severe damage to the Space Shuttle *Atlantis* in 1988 during STS-27. But as with the O-rings, the foam had not yet destroyed a shuttle, so officials considered it an acceptable flight risk—or in NASA lingo, an "expected anomaly"—that those in management were willing to accept. The price for this policy of Russian roulette once again proved to be devastatingly high.

With both *Challenger* and *Columbia*, NASA had—in the words of its own official history—"overlooked the obvious, allowing two tragedies to unfold on the public stage."

✈★✈

Divers finally recovered the mortal remains of the *Challenger* crew on April 21, 1986—nearly three months after they fell into the Atlantic Ocean and sank in ninety feet of water. Americans will always justifiably remember them as heroes who gave their lives for the cause of space exploration. If not for two faulty O-rings and one "flawed" decision, they might all have lived to tell their grandchildren about the day they rode a butterfly into space.

The remains of the seven *Challenger* crewmembers being transferred to a Lockheed C-141 Starlifter transport at Kennedy Space Center's Shuttle Landing Facility. *NASA*

CHAPTER EIGHT

THE DAY THE BARON FLEW TOO LOW

"I THINK HE HAS SEEN DEATH TOO OFTEN."

On the morning of April 21, 1918, a youthful German pilot strapped himself into the cockpit of his fighter plane in preparation for a combat patrol. His mount was an all-red Fokker Dr.I triplane, bearing the serial number 425/17, and he was flying from a large open field on the outskirts of the French town of Cappy. It was less than seven months before World War I would finally end, but on that day, the brutal four-year conflagration still raged as violently as ever.

According to legend, as the young *Flieger* prepared to take off, a member of the ground crew hesitantly stepped up to the cockpit and said, "Herr *Rittmeister*, may I have an autograph?" Although the timing was odd, the request was understandable. This particular pilot with the close-cropped blond hair also happened to be Germany's greatest hero and the world's most successful fighter ace. He was *Rittmeister* Manfred *Freiherr* von Richthofen. The famous ace laughed good-naturedly at the unlikely autograph-seeker and asked, "What's the hurry? Are you afraid I won't come back?"

This incident may or may not have actually occurred, but if so, one could only hope that the *Rittmeister* signed the autograph. It would be of great historical value, for he would never sign another. In a matter of minutes, the pilot known worldwide as the "Red Baron" lay dead on the ground—after making one of history's most controversial flights of no return.

Rittmeister Manfred *Freiherr* von Richthofen. The eighty-victory German ace wears at his throat the coveted *Pour le Mérite* ("Blue Max"), the German Empire's highest award for bravery. *National Museum of the US Air Force*

The Red Baron

Manfred von Richthofen was born in 1892 near Breslau, Lower Silesia (now Wrocław, Poland). The young aerial warrior was a Prussian nobleman—hence the title *Freiherr*, or Baron. He was also the highly esteemed commander of Germany's first and foremost fighter wing, *Jagdgeschwader* I. The German ace's greatest claim to fame, however, was his unprecedented success against enemy aircraft: with eighty official kills to his credit, he was the highest-scoring and most highly regarded fighter ace of World War I.

The bold and innovative *Rittmeister*—a rank that equates to a captain in the cavalry, where Richthofen began his career—also had a flair for the dramatic. To make himself more visible to both friend and foe, he flew an airplane painted from stem to stern a brilliant blood-colored red. This earned the notorious ace the nickname by which most people remember him today.

Because of his accomplishments, he was—at the age of twenty-five—a living legend, the superstar of his day. Respected by friend and enemy alike, admirers mobbed him everyplace he went, and his image appeared in newspapers, magazines, and films and even on postcards. He already had all of the German Empire's highest decorations, including the most coveted of them all: the Pour le Mérite, also known as the Blue Max. Accounts of his many thrilling exploits appeared everywhere, including in a bestselling autobiography he had recently completed; and as his country's preeminent war hero, he received daily bags full of letters and packages from adoring fans throughout Germany. Some were perfumed and lace-decorated epistles from love-stricken *Fräulein*, both young and old. A few even boldly sent to the handsome and heroic aristocratic ace enticing pieces of highly personal apparel, along with offers of marriage—and anything else he might desire. It was good to be a famous flying ace in the First World War. That is, until the day when the Grim Reaper made his unwelcome appearance.

A Very Long Shot

For Manfred von Richthofen, the angel of death came on the Sunday morning of April 21, 1918. As to what ultimately happened to the celebrated ace, there is no mystery. He took off that morning, accompanied by pilots of *Jagdstaffel* (*Jasta*) 11, one of the four fighter squadrons he commanded. A few minutes after takeoff, they became embroiled in a fierce dogfight with an aggressive formation of Sopwith Camel biplane fighters from British

← Manfred von Richthofen, in cold-weather flying gear. In the background is a Fokker Dr.I (*Dreidecker*) triplane. *Courtesy Peter Kilduff*

Royal Air Force No. 209 Squadron. During this aerial "dance of death," Richthofen managed to maneuver his aircraft onto the tail of an inexperienced Canadian pilot, Lt. Wilfrid R. "Wop" May. The young Canadian glanced behind and saw the dreaded all-red Fokker triplane attached like a leech to his tail. Though still a rookie, he immediately grasped the gravity of the situation. He was in deep trouble.

Lieutenant Wilfrid R. "Wop" May, the young Canadian pilot that Richthofen was furiously pursuing on the morning of his death. May survived the war to enjoy a long and distinguished aviation career.

The Canadian frantically began throwing his highly maneuverable little Sopwith all over the sky. He somehow had to avoid the deadly hot steel slugs that would soon be streaming from the triplane's twin Spandau machine guns—and possibly boring into his unprotected back. His maneuvers were so extreme, they would have been comical under different circumstances, but they accomplished their intended purpose. Richthofen—though a marksman second to none—was unable to get a good bead on the terrified novice who was flying in such an unorthodox manner. Uncharacteristically, the German ace—undoubtedly becoming frustrated—stubbornly stayed with his quarry, even though they had by now crossed over into Allied lines and were getting dangerously low to the ground. This risky scenario was one that even the Red Baron normally avoided. The chance of being hit by enemy ground fire was too great and, if forced to land in enemy territory, his career would end as a prisoner of war.

Meanwhile, Lieutenant May's commander, fellow Canadian and former schoolmate Capt. Arthur Roy Brown, was watching intently from above, all too aware of the fledgling pilot's deadly dilemma. Brown quickly turned his Camel toward the red Fokker seemingly glued to the tail of May's twisting Sopwith. Unlike May, he was no beginner. An experienced and highly accomplished nine-victory ace, he knew exactly what he was doing. As he

Fokker triplane Dr.I 425-17, the fighter
in which the Red Baron died on April 21, 1918.
To this day, no one knows who shot him down. *Courtesy Peter Kilduff*

Sopwith F.1 Camel of the type Lt. "Wop" May and Capt. Roy Brown were flying on the
day that Richthofen died. *National Museum of the US Air Force*

dived from above and behind, he began to overtake the red triplane.

Brown fully realized that May was running out of time. If he did not do something immediately, his young friend and compatriot was doomed. For this reason, Brown—though still well out of range for an accurate shot—squeezed off a long and erratic burst of fire from the two Vickers machine guns mounted in front of his cockpit. The bullets streamed like water from a hose in the direction of the determined German ace. From that distance, Brown could not hope to hit anything vital, but perhaps the arrows of smoke in the sky created by his tracers would at least distract the German away from May.

Royal Air Force Capt. Arthur Roy Brown, the only person ever officially credited with shooting down Manfred von Richthofen. Despite this, most historians believe that a gunner on the ground fired the fatal bullet. Brown died in Ontario, Canada, in 1944.

As luck would have it, Brown's strategy worked. In fact, it worked far better than he could have imagined. The red Fokker abruptly disengaged from the terrified Lieutenant May and descended to a crash landing in a clearing below, near the town of Corbie. The relieved Captain Brown probably marveled at how he had managed to score a decisive hit on the red triplane. It was, without a doubt, a lucky shot; but any combat pilot knew that luck was a big part of success—and he was not complaining.

The blood-red triplane glided—apparently still under control—into the ground directly in front of the Allied troops fighting there. The men cheered loudly as the small fighter hit hard and skidded to a halt in a rough open field. They ran over to the airplane to capture the seemingly uninjured enemy pilot but instead found him taking his last breath. He died of what was later determined to be a single .303-caliber slug through the chest.

The news spread like wildfire: The Red Knight of Germany was dead! Captain Brown put in his claim and quickly received official credit for downing the famous ace. Lucky shot or not, the airplane at which Brown had been firing had gone down. Numerous witnesses both on the ground and in the air saw him shooting at Richthofen just before his red triplane crashed in Allied territory. No one could dispute that Brown was the victor—especially since there was no one else in the vicinity to counter his claim. Or was there?

It is at this point that the controversy begins. It soon became apparent that there had been others—dozens of others—shooting at the bright red airplane, but they were not Camel pilots. They were the Australian riflemen and machine gunners stationed in the vicinity of where Richthofen had skimmed the ground in pursuit of the hapless Lieutenant May. At the same time Brown had been shooting *down* at the low-flying red triplane, the Australian ground gunners were furiously firing *up* at him. The

The field, as it appeared recently, where the Fokker triplane flown by *Rittmeister* Manfred *Freiherr* von Richthofen came to rest on April 21, 1918. *Steve Miller*

ammunition they used was .303 caliber—identical to Captain Brown's. At least three of these ground gunners believed that they had the most legitimate claim to the biggest prize of the war, and they continued to believe it for the rest of their lives.

Who Fired the Silver Bullet?

The question has remained unanswered for nearly a century: Who shot down the Red Baron? Like all good mysteries, the solution is complicated and the truth anything but clear-cut. Practically everyone with any interest in the topic has an opinion—and opinions vary widely—but the truth is that no one really knows. This is in spite of the great lengths to which numerous historical and analytical researchers have gone since 1918, attempting to arrive at the correct answer.

Captain Brown immediately comes to the forefront as the fatal shooter. He was, after all, the only pilot to claim credit for shooting down the German ace. For that matter, he was, in all likelihood, the only flier even to fire at Richthofen that morning. Both Brown and May were convinced that he had fired the fatal shot, and he is still the only person ever officially credited with killing the Red Baron.

Assignment of official credit, however, did nothing to settle the controversy. Doubters have long claimed that Brown's desperate attempt was—both literally and figuratively—a long shot. Brown, in his frantic attempt to distract Richthofen from blasting the struggling Lieutenant May out of the sky, fired all of his rounds not only from well out of range, but also while in a steep high-speed dive. Under the circumstances, it would have been little short of a miracle had he actually gotten a slug into the famed German ace.

But in aerial combat, unlikely occurrences are not unknown. Richthofen himself had already fallen victim to one such fluke only nine months earlier. On July 6, 1917, an anxious gunner in a British observation aircraft opened up on the Baron when he was still ridiculously far out of range. As Richthofen derisively watched the frightened observer's pitiful waste of ammunition, he received a sudden, unanticipated, and crushing blow to the head that knocked him senseless. One of the gunner's slugs had somehow found its way to Richthofen's skull. It was a glancing blow, but a serious one, and he barely got down alive. It was proof positive that even a chance hit from a mile away could be dangerous. Perhaps Brown had also been lucky enough to fire off a "silver bullet" that day, which managed to find its way to the unfortunate German ace.

Perhaps, but probably not. Unfortunately for Brown, the forensic evidence suggested otherwise. The trajectory of the fatal bullet wound in Richthofen's body indicates that it hit him not from above and behind, where Brown was blasting away, but rather from the lower right. Just as important, Richthofen continued flying apparently unfazed for some time after Brown fired at him. With the severity of his wound—a bullet ripping through the chest from right to left, destroying vital organs and major blood vessels—he could probably not have remained conscious for more than a few seconds. These two facts would seem to eliminate even a very lucky Roy Brown as the fatal shooter.

The preponderance of evidence indicates that it was someone on the ground who killed the Red Baron. While chasing Lieutenant May, Richthofen hedgehopped at ground zero for a considerable distance—at one point narrowly missing the church steeple in the French village of Vaux-sur-Somme. As he flew over the Morlancourt Ridge overlooking the river Somme, dozens of enemy ground troops were firing up at him. Any one of these might have proper claim to the Baron's scalp.

One of the most interesting and novel attempts to determine the real shooter was a re-enactment conducted by the producers of Discovery Channel's popular series *Unsolved History.* They employed a team of experts from several different specialty areas to determine who shot the Red Baron. Using computer flight simulation—along with data collected from an authentic .303-caliber rifle, Vickers machine gun, and rotary engine—they reconstructed gunfire trajectories from Brown's Camel to Richthofen's triplane. The researchers diligently factored in rate of fire, relative speeds and distances, engine vibration, and aerodynamic considerations. Their conclusion: the likelihood of Brown scoring any hits at all was somewhere between slim and none.

In the second part of their experiment, they traveled to France to the actual site of Richthofen's last flight. Substituting a modern airplane of similar speed to Richthofen's, and laser beams for real bullets, they re-enacted the last two minutes of the famous dogfight, down to the minutest detail. As the airplane flew over, replicating Richthofen's exact flight path, the investigators on the ground "shot" at it from the known positions that Australian machine gunners had occupied. After comparing their findings to pertinent documents, they concluded that a gunner named William "Snowy" Evans had most likely fired the fatal shot. This was in disagreement to other past researchers who have favored machine gunners Cedric Popkin or Robert Buie as the most likely Richthofen killers. Though this realistic re-enactment was compelling, any conclusive answer to the mystery is as elusive as ever.

Fatal Decision

Another remaining question is why Richthofen choose to ignore his own rule and follow Lieutenant May down to the deck behind enemy lines. One of the key points from his own manual that he wrote regarding air combat operations was that a pilot should never stubbornly pursue his adversary far behind enemy lines. He had always followed that rule, and he strictly forbade his own pilots from such practice. Still, for reasons unknown, he did just that . . . and paid for the transgression with his life.

Manfred von Richthofen was a complex, rather peculiar individual. Although the many books, articles, and documentaries about him would fill a library, little is really known about his inner self. Undoubtedly, he was confident, charismatic, and generally well liked; however, he tended to be somewhat distant in nature. Few, if any, of Richthofen's comrades qualified as close friends other than perhaps his own brother and fellow ace, Lothar. Nor did he apparently have any close female relationships, in spite of the unlimited opportunities his unique status afforded him—and in spite of rumors to the contrary.

One thing that seems certain is that Richthofen was suffering from what amounted to combat fatigue—or, in modern terminology, post-traumatic stress disorder (PTSD). Three and a half years of dangerous wartime service, the latter half of which involved almost continuous aerial combat, had stretched his nerves to the breaking point. He was tired, depressed, and in need of a long rest. In addition, he was still suffering from the severe head wound he had received the previous July. Part of the bone from his skull was still exposed, causing him severe pain. Given his physical and mental state, it seems clear that he should not have even been on flying status the day he died. As translated by Frank McGuire in his book *The Many Deaths of the Red Baron*, Richthofen grimly wrote shortly before his death:

> I feel terrible after every air battle, probably an after-effect of my head wound. When I again set foot on the ground I withdraw to my quarters and don't want to see anybody or hear anything. I think of the war as it really is, not "with a hurrah and a roar" as the people at home imagine it; it is much more serious, bitter.

Just as relevant, though less obvious, was Richthofen's unique cultural mindset. His attitude was perhaps typical of most aristocratic young Prussian military officers of the early twentieth century—especially those who had begun their military careers as early as the age of eleven, as had Richthofen. The importance of courage, perseverance, devotion to duty—and whatever else *Gott und Vaterland* required—was ingrained in him to his very core. Certainly, Richthofen was not one to shirk his duties. Again, as related in McGuire's book, he tellingly wrote near the end of his life:

> Higher authority has suggested that I should quit flying before it catches up with me. But I should despise myself if, now that I am famous and heavily decorated, I consented to live on as a pensioner of my honor, preserving my precious life for the nation while every poor fellow in the trenches, who is doing his duty no less than I am doing mine, has to stick it out.

In spite of his unhealed wound and fatigued mental state, Richthofen would "stick it out" until he could no longer. It mattered little to him that he would have been just as useful commanding and advising from the ground, or that he had already given everything he had for his *Vaterland*. Research psychologists Thomas Hyatt and Daniel Orme, in their 2004 article "Baron Manfred von Richthofen—DNIF (Duties Not Including Flying)," theorized that Richthofen's head wound caused him to suffer from a type of brain dysfunction that compelled him to persist in his flying, even knowing it would soon kill him. Such "mental rigidity" may have also caused the target fixation he experienced when he chased Lieutenant May down low on his fatal foray into enemy territory. Richthofen's mother, however, saw her beloved son in a simpler light. She wrote after her last visit with him, "I think he has seen death too often."

After nearly a century of controversy, no one will ever know conclusively who shot down the legendary German ace. It was most likely a machine gunner on the ground . . . or maybe it was Capt. Roy Brown after all. Perhaps even some unknown rifleman hit the jackpot and never even suspected it. So, despite all efforts to dispel the mystery of Manfred von Richthofen's unforgettable last flight, the mystery lives on—and with it, the remarkable legend of the equally remarkable man they called the Red Baron.

CHAPTER NINE

A MADMAN'S JOURNEY TO NOWHERE

"A STORY UNLIKE ANY OTHER IN THE HISTORY OF AERIAL EXPLORATION."

On July 11, 1897, three adventurous Swedish explorers took off in a balloon from an uninhabited Norwegian Island in the Arctic Ocean. Their grand intention was to fly all the way to the North Pole. If successful, they would be not only the first humans to fly to this frozen sea of ice that constitutes Earth's northernmost region, but also the first to lay eyes on it.

Soon after lifting off, they drifted out of sight into the gray northern sky. No one would ever see them alive again. It would take thirty-three years for unexpected events to reveal their tragic fate. People the world over would then finally learn where and under what circumstances the three adventurers met their end. They would also have the unique opportunity to relive—through the words and eyes of the long-dead explorers themselves—their ill-fated flight and desperate three-month death march to nowhere. This historic flight was only the beginning of a story unlike any other in the history of aerial exploration.

An Impossible Dream

In 1897, getting to the North Pole was about as easy as going to the moon. Over the centuries, explorers had made one unsuccessful attempt after another to reach the mysteriously elusive pole. There were plenty of reasons for their consistent lack of success. The North Pole lies some five hundred miles from the closest human habitation, so virtually nothing was known about it in the late nineteenth century. No one even suspected that, unlike its diametric opposite, the South Pole, it is not a landmass at all. Rather, this geographical northernmost point on the earth is merely a moving accumulation of sea ice floating in the midst of the Arctic Ocean. The only way to get there was to sail through the icy waters as far as possible, and then travel the remaining few hundred miles on foot. This meant weeks of pulling heavy sledges loaded with life-sustaining provisions over the treacherous, ever-changing icy terrain—in some of the worst weather conditions that exist on Earth.

The explorers who were willing to go to such lengths to get to one of the world's most inaccessible and inhospitable places all had their reasons. Some went in search of a so-called Northwest Passage, a northerly trade route connecting Europe to the Far East via the Arctic Ocean; others sought a new world and the possible riches contained therein. But the underlying reason they were willing to risk everything to get to the North Pole—including their very lives—was simply to be the first.

As of 1897, it had proven not only impossible, but also extremely deadly. Hundreds of men had already perished in various past attempts. Some were lost sailing into the dangerous, icy waters encircling the North Pole; others simply disappeared after trudging into the uncharted expanse of the polar ice cap. It seemed that there was simply no way to get to the pole—unless one was able to grow wings and fly there.

To the Pole by Air

Human flight began long before the Wright Brothers' first powered flight of December 17, 1903. Since the first manned balloon flight in 1783, balloons and airships filled with buoyant gases—hot air, hydrogen, or helium—had made hundreds of long-distance flights, soared to great altitudes, and achieved other significant aerial accomplishments. By the end of the nineteenth century, balloon flight had become nearly routine.

It was for this reason that Swedish engineer Salomon August Andrée chose a novel approach to becoming the first man to the North Pole. He would sail there—not through the hazardous icy waters—but above them, soaring on air currents. Andrée, born in 1854, was a graduate of Sweden's Royal Institute of Technology and an official at the Swedish Patent Office. His interest in exploration was aroused in 1882 with his participation in a scientific expedition led by meteorologist Nils Ekholm to the Norwegian island of Spitsbergen. After this, the lust for adventure was in his blood.

Andrée's fascination with ballooning began during a visit to the United States, where he met the famed American aeronaut John Wise.

Andrée eventually learned to fly, and in 1893, he acquired a balloon for his own use. In it, he made nine rather eventful solo flights. In one case, a fierce wind swept him from Sweden across the Baltic Sea and all the way to Finland. He accumulated some forty hours aloft, experimenting with different ballooning techniques and recording a variety of meteorological observations. With his newly developed aeronautical skills, he now directed his attention to his ultimate goal: the conquest of the North Pole.

Andrée calculated that a flight to the pole would require a balloon large enough to carry three men and enough equipment and provisions to survive for four months on the ice. It would have to inflate just before launch, with hydrogen gas manufactured onsite, stay aloft for up to thirty days, and be steerable. These demanding specifications were unprecedented, but Andrée maintained they were possible. In such a balloon, he could be the first human to the North Pole.

He would launch in the summer, when Arctic temperatures were at their most moderate, averaging around thirty-two degrees Fahrenheit. This also gave him the advantage of constant daylight—summer being the season of the midnight sun in the northern latitudes. He and his fellow fliers would drift with the wind northward, while controlling the balloon with a system of guide ropes and sails.

Andrée christened the balloon *Örnen*, or eagle. Built in France, this highly innovative craft featured an envelope made of layers of silk varnished together. It measured about a hundred feet in height and sixty-seven feet in diameter. Andrée designed the balloon with a series of heavy ropes hanging beneath, which would serve both as ballast and as anchors when allowed to drag across the ice. The balloon's other important feature was its three sails, which the aeronauts could angle in flight. When the heavy ropes dragging across the ice slowed the balloon to below wind speed, these sails would allow the breeze to push the balloon sideways in a slightly different direction than that of the wind. With this unproven—and somewhat questionable—system, Andrée hoped to regulate the balloon's ascent, descent, speed, and direction.

Andrée chose as his two flight companions Nils Ekholm—the meteorologist who had led the 1882 to 1883 expedition to Spitsbergen—and Nils Strindberg. Andrée assigned the latter, a handsome twenty-four-year-old physicist at Stockholm University, the task of photographically documenting the expedition. Having just completed balloon training in Paris, Strindberg would also assist in the aeronautical duties.

Even with the best planning and equipment, the mission was by any measure exceedingly bold, perilous, and—in the opinion of many at the time—outright foolhardy. Many prominent scientists of the day

The Andrée expedition launching point at Dane's Island (Danskøya). This uninhabited Norwegian island lies just off the coast of Spitsbergen. Both are islands in the Svalbard archipelago, located in the Arctic Ocean some six hundred miles north of Norway. *Library of Congress*

scoffed at Andrée's proposed attempt as a stunt, rather than a serious scientific expedition. They did not believe such a mission was possible, given then-known Arctic meteorological conditions and the limitations of existing balloon technology. One called it "a madman's journey." Andrée, the consummate engineer, was determined to prove to these naysayers that, with technology, all things were possible.

Up and Away!

Andrée's first attempt to fly to the pole in the summer of 1896 never got off the ground. An uninhabited Norwegian island in the Svalbard archipelago called Dane's Island (Danskøya) was his launching point. This tiny island, located in the Arctic Ocean more than six hundred miles north of the coast of Norway, was as close to the pole as practically possible. As Andrée and his fifty-one-member expedition departed Sweden, a cheering crowd of forty thousand saw them off, expecting great things from the newly appointed national heroes.

When the 1,800-mile voyage to Dane's Island was complete, Andrée disembarked with his team and began constructing housing for the balloon. Here they would assemble, inflate, and service the balloon in a protected environment. Accompanying his expedition was a sizable entourage of reporters and tourists, which gave the scientific event an almost festive atmosphere.

When the balloon was ready for flight, the three aeronauts waited for the wind that would carry them northward to the pole. After six weeks, however, the wind never came. At summer's end, the disgraced would-be

The three members of the ill-fated Andrée expedition. *From L to R*: Knut Frænkel, Salomon August Andrée, and Nils Strindberg.

explorers packed up and returned to Sweden, as one cynic wrote in a contemporary newspaper article, "with their balloon tucked between their legs." They would have to wait for the following summer.

Andrée faced more problems after returning to Sweden. Crew member Ekholm had begun to express doubts about the mission. Among other concerns, he questioned whether the balloon could retain enough hydrogen to complete the flight. Eventually, he backed out altogether. To replace him, Andrée chose an athletic twenty-seven-year-old engineer named Knut Frænkel. Like his fellow crew member Strindberg, Frænkel prepared for the upcoming flight by taking instruction in the art of ballooning. Even so, between the three men who would attempt to balloon their way across the Arctic Ocean to the North Pole, they totaled only twenty-seven flights.

In June 1897, the Andrée expedition returned to Dane's Island for the second—and last—attempt. Once more, they inflated the completely untested balloon, prepared for flight, and waited for the wind. It had to be strong enough to push them northward all the way to the pole, but not so strong as to destroy the balloon during the launch. Andrée estimated, perhaps naively, that with the right conditions they might arrive at the pole within two to three days; but in case it took longer, he assured the public the balloon was capable of remaining aloft for at least a month. While the aeronauts waited, they continually applied varnish to plug recurring gas leaks in the balloon—a red flag they seemed unwilling to acknowledge. They had come too far to back out now.

Finally, on July 11, 1897, a favorable—though sporadic—wind arose over the waiting expedition. Andrée was not convinced, but upon urging from his two impatient young traveling companions, he finally agreed that conditions were minimally acceptable. He realized this might be the only chance they would ever get, and he did not intend to return to Sweden, as before, without at least an attempt. Consequently, the three balloonists donned their flying clothes, loaded last minute items, and climbed into the basket suspended below *Örnen*'s inflated envelope. At 2:30 that afternoon, Andrée ordered the restraining ropes cut. The balloon rose from the shelter and up into the wind.

Observers saw it rise rapidly to several hundred feet and then just as quickly descend back to the water over which it was flying. The basket in which the men were riding dipped into the bay while the three occupants furiously dumped sand ballast. The balloon abruptly ascended again, shearing off the ends of the all-important guide ropes, and drifted away. The three intrepid aeronauts were last seen fading into the northeastern sky. It had been a very rocky launch—an omen of things to come—but they were finally on their way to the North Pole.

Lost!

Days passed while followers the world over held their breaths. One of the carrier pigeons Andrée had taken along turned up four days after their departure, landing in the rigging of a seal-hunting ship operating near their launch site. The boat's captain, anticipating fresh fowl for his evening meal, shot the bird—but it fell into the water, so he proceeded on without it. When he later learned it might have been one of Andrée's pigeons, he sailed back and retrieved the dead bird still floating on the surface of the water. The attached message, which Andrée had written two days after the balloon's departure, stated that all was well. His coordinates indicated they had traveled 170 miles northeast at an average speed of about four miles per hour. This proved to be the only one of Andrée's thirty-six pigeons that ever appeared.

In the ensuing months, false reports about the three missing explorers came from all corners of the world. "Andrée pigeons" seemed to turn up everywhere—someone even reported one in downtown Chicago. There were balloon sightings and word of strange noises on deserted islands in the Arctic area. It was variously reported that the explorers had crossed the North Pole; landed in Siberia; died at the hands of hostile Eskimos; or had fallen into an abyss at the pole and were now at the center of the earth.

Searchers combed all the likely areas that they were able to access but found no trace of the lost balloonists. It was as if they actually had fallen to the center of the earth. After several months, it became obvious that regardless of where they landed or how well equipped they were, they must by now be dead. The years rolled past, and in time, Andrée and his ill-fated expedition faded into distant memory . . . that is, until a fortuitous discovery three decades later put his name back in the headlines.

Ghosts Arisen from the Past

On August 6, 1930, walrus hunters from the Norwegian ship *Bratvaag* climbed onto an uninhabited strip of ice and rock in the Arctic Ocean called White Island (Kvitøya). This tiny, barren easternmost member of the Svalbard archipelago lies approximately 250 miles east of Dane's Island, where Andrée and his two comrades had launched thirty-three years earlier. What the hunters discovered there was far more significant than walrus—on a rocky clearing on the southwestern corner of the island, they stumbled upon what had once been a human campsite. It soon became apparent to the hunters that they had discovered the final resting place of the long-lost Andrée expedition.

The hunters found a multitude of artifacts strewn around the area: tools, scientific instruments, guns, ammunition, items of clothing, a boat, sledges, a still-functional camp stove containing fuel, and a variety of written records. The most significant find, however, was the frozen skeletal remains of two human bodies—Andrée's and Strindberg's, as it turned out. At least it was now known where two of the three doomed Swedish explorers had ended their lives, but other questions remained: How did they die? Under what circumstances did they land their balloon and arrive at this depressing little spot in the middle of nowhere? And where was the third member of the expedition, Knut Frænkel?

It did not take long to find the answer to the last question. A group of journalists on the island investigating the campsite discovered the body of Frænkel, lying frozen into the ice some distance from the other two bodies. At least now, they could account for all three members of the expedition. But what about the other unanswered questions?

The artifacts and remains of the three lost explorers were brought home on the *Svenskund*—the same ship that had taken them to Dane's Island in 1897. It arrived in Stockholm, escorted by a flotilla of warships, two hundred civilian boats, and an aerial formation. The bells tolled throughout the city as Sweden's King Gustav V personally accepted their bodies "in the name of the Swedish nation." Four days of military salutes and memorials followed, after which, the mortal remains of the three heroes were cremated. By now, news of the discovery of the lost Andrée expedition had made headlines throughout the world.

Among the various records the three men kept of their activities were logbooks, letters, maps, journals, and diaries. The most descriptive of these was the account Andrée faithfully maintained to the very end. Another auspicious find supplemented this: several canisters of undeveloped film containing images that Strindberg had shot during the expedition. Amazingly, after thirty-three years in the harsh Arctic environment, photo experts were able to develop ninety-three of these exposures. The shadowy, ghostly images that appeared, together with the lost explorers' own written words, effectively brought them back from the dead. What emerged was a story unlike any other ever known.

Ordeal on the Ice

After their tumultuous takeoff at Dane's Island, the three balloonists drifted northeastward. Eventually they entered fog, which cooled the balloon's buoyant hydrogen gas and caused it to descend to the ice. The balloonists dumped sand, anchors, tools, even food—but for hours, their basket continued to bump heavily across the uneven ice through the fog, tossing the occupants about mercilessly.

By the morning of the third day, July 14, the flight was finished. The slowly deflating balloon had alternated between flight and bumping along the ice for sixty-five and one-half hours; still, it was three hundred miles short of its polar destination. When the three men stepped out onto the ice, they sadly accepted the realization that they were as close to the North Pole as they would ever be. They had failed, and now—hundreds of miles from anywhere—they had to find some way to survive. They took the next few days to reorganize and pack their remaining 1,600 pounds of gear into sledges. On July 22, they began manhandling them southeastward toward a pre-arranged depot in the Franz Josef Land archipelago.

Slowly and laboriously, the three grounded aeronauts began what was to be their death march, dragging their sledges—each weighing several hundred pounds—across what Andrée described as "dreadful terrain." They struggled through frigid temperatures, snow, rain, and fog, and over the slowly drifting, but ever-changing and treacherously uneven, ice floes. They alternately skirted around, climbed, or hacked their way through walls of ice, and crossed the endless leads of water running between them. Repeatedly, they had to fish one another out of the water after falling in. On some days, they managed only a few hundred yards. They slept on the ice and supplemented their diet whenever possible with meat from the bears, seals, and gulls they were able to shoot.

The summer days were literally endless, with the sun still hanging above the horizon at midnight. This, however, would not continue much longer. After a few weeks, the cold unending days would give way to much colder and equally endless nights. Racing against the oncoming winter, the three men had to find a safe haven. Meanwhile they suffered bitterly as they inched southward, fighting for their lives: snow blindness, skin sores, frostbite, diarrhea, bruises and dislocated joints, viral infections, and muscle cramps.

After two weeks of this torturous travel, they discovered to their utter dismay that the ice on which they were traveling was drifting west faster than they were walking east. They therefore changed directions and headed southwest toward a different cache of provisions on Seven Islands (Sjuøyane) at the northernmost part of the Svalbard archipelago. Again, however, the unpredictable movement of the ice thwarted their plan. It began drifting them away from their only lifeline. With life-saving provisions located to the east and west, they were traveling almost due south—and ever deeper into no man's land. On September 1, Andrée saw the sun "touch the horizon at midnight." The polar summer was about to end; a long, cold, dark—and depressing—winter would soon begin.

Salomon Andrée and Knut Frænkel, soon after their balloon *Örnen* (eagle) was forced down onto the ice. The third member of the expedition, Nils Strindberg, snapped the picture. The quality of Strindberg's photographs is remarkable, given that the film from which they were developed lay hibernating in the polar wilderness for thirty-three years.

Two weeks later, the three men—by now, half-dead from injury and exhaustion—sighted land for the first time in sixty-eight days. It was White Island. It took until October 5, for the ice on which they drifted to bring them close enough to struggle ashore. They started to set up camp and began collecting driftwood to build a shelter but got no further. On October 6, Andrée made his last legible diary entry, and within days, all three were dead.

It remains a mystery why the three explorers, who had so tenaciously managed to travel this far, suddenly gave up. They had made it to dry land and still had enough life-sustaining provisions to survive the winter. Researchers have suggested various scenarios for their demise: attacks from marauding bears; lead or carbon monoxide poisoning; vitamin A overdose from eating toxic bear livers; trichinosis contracted from bear meat; botulism from tainted seal meat; scurvy—and even murder-suicide. Any of these is possible, but perhaps the real reason was something less clinical. Maybe they simply surrendered to the mental depression and utter exhaustion they felt after nearly three months in the frozen hell, the prospect of a long winter of mind-numbing cold and eternal darkness, and the hopeless despair of imminent doom that must have pervaded their very souls. No one will ever know.

Frænkel and Strindberg posing with
a polar bear they had just shot. Fresh game would be
an important source of nourishment for the three lost explorers.
It may have also been a contributor to their demise.

An excellent view of how the three downed balloonists spent their last days on
earth. For more than two months, they dragged sledges like this one, each packed
with hundreds of pounds of life-saving provisions, across treacherous ice floes and
over and through walls of ice. Soon after arriving at White Island (Kvitøya), all three
men died—for reasons still unknown.

Andrée's native country honored him as a hero. His audacious attempt stimulated nationalistic pride like few other events in Sweden ever have. More recently, however, some have come to view his ill-advised attempt in another light: Andrée, though undoubtedly a courageous visionary, was also a victim of self-deceit. He almost certainly realized that the expedition had little if any chance to succeed. He was well aware of the permeability of the balloon's envelope, the unproven nature of its steering mechanism, and the unpredictability of the Arctic winds. However, in light of his previous failure, the hero's sendoff his nation had given him, and the many prominent contributors—including Sweden's King Oscar II—who had helped finance the expedition, he felt obligated to

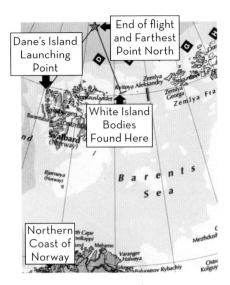

The ill-fated voyage of the Salomon Andrée expedition. The three men drifted an undetermined distance northeast from Dane's Island in their balloon before coming to rest on the ice, well short of the North Pole. Their death march southward ended on White Island.

make the attempt, hopeless or not. Lacking the moral courage to do the only sensible thing and cancel the expedition, he elected instead to save face, thereby dooming himself and his two young comrades to a needlessly cruel and premature death.

A few years after the failed Andrée expedition, two different explorers claimed the honor of being the first to the North Pole: Frederick Cook in 1908 and Robert Peary in 1909. Significantly, neither of them did it by air. It is also noteworthy that there still exists some doubt that either actually succeeded in achieving what they claimed.

No one disputes, however, that Salomon Andrée and his two intrepid comrades were the first to attempt the North Pole by air. They paid for it with their lives. But their "madman's journey" remains one of aviation history's earliest and most memorable one-way flights to eternity.

CHAPTER TEN

THE CONGRESSMEN WHO VANISHED

"SOMETHING TERRIBLE IS GOING TO HAPPEN."

On the foggy morning of October 16, 1972, a small twin-engine airplane with four men aboard lifted off from Anchorage International Airport, Alaska. Their destination was the state capitol, Juneau, some six hundred miles to the southeast. It was a long flight for a light aircraft, especially considering the remote and unfriendly terrain below. But by Alaskan standards, it was routine. In fact, the only unusual thing about this particular flight was that one of America's most powerful political leaders was among the three passengers.

Shortly after takeoff, the pilot of the chartered Pan Alaska Airways Cessna 310C radioed his flight plan to the Anchorage Flight Service Station. He intended to follow the commonly used navigational airway that roughly paralleled the shoreline of the Gulf of Alaska to the coastal town of Yakutat. From there, he would fly a direct course into Juneau International Airport. He estimated the total flying time at three and one-half hours. Those on the ground at Anchorage watched as the small twin slowly faded into the southeastern sky. Neither the plane, nor the four unsuspecting men aboard were ever to be seen again.

A Premonition

Aboard the airplane were Nicholas J. Begich, a first-term Democratic Representative from Alaska, and Thomas Hale Boggs Sr., a Congressional

Thomas Hale Boggs Sr. was a fourteen-term veteran congressional representative from Louisiana. As majority leader of the US House of Representatives, he was the second-ranking Democrat in Congress. He and three other men disappeared during a routine flight from Anchorage to Juneau on October 16, 1972. *Collection of the US House of Representatives*

Representative from Louisiana. The latter also happened to be the reigning majority leader of the US House of Representatives—which made him the second-ranking Democrat in the House. The third passenger aboard the aircraft was Begich's aide, Russell L. Brown. Brown felt fortunate to be on the flight, since another one of Begich's assistants had given up his seat as a favor. They were on their way to a Democratic fundraiser for Begich, who was actively campaigning for a second term.

The forty-year-old Begich was an up-and-coming young politician with a bright political future. He was also a family man, with a wife and six children ranging in age from four to fourteen. He was undoubtedly thrilled and honored to have the prestigious Boggs stumping with him on the campaign trail. It was a powerful endorsement for the well-connected majority leader to travel all the way to Alaska to assist in his campaign.

While Begich's election seemed a sure bet, one of his closest friends and supporters was not so optimistic. Margaret Pojhola had a premonition after seeing him on the evening before his last flight. She confided to her husband that she felt "something terrible is going to happen."

The venerable Boggs was a fourteen-term veteran of Congress. Through the years, he had worked his way up through the congressional ranks to his present position as House majority leader. As such, the fifty-eight-year-old legislator was the most likely candidate to become the next Speaker of the House of Representatives, a position that would have placed him second only to the vice president in the line of succession to the presidency. Boggs was, by any measure, one of the most prominent political figures of his day.

The pilot of the charter plane was thirty-eight-year-old Don Edgar Jonz. He also happened to be the president, chief pilot, and sole stockholder of Pan Alaska Airways, Ltd. By all appearances and credentials, he was an accomplished and highly qualified pilot who possessed all the necessary aeronautical ratings. He was not only a licensed commercial airline transport pilot, but also a certified flight and instrument instructor. From his years of flying as a bush pilot, Jonz had accumulated an impressive seventeen thousand flight hours. As further evidence of his expertise, he had recently authored two magazine articles on flying in the adverse weather conditions he so often encountered in the unpredictable Alaskan skies. There was really only one legitimate criticism of the blond-haired, athletic young pilot: his attitude. He had gained a reputation with colleagues for being arrogant, taking unnecessary risks, and sometimes neglecting to fly "by the book." Overall, however, he seemed eminently qualified to pilot his highly placed passengers anywhere—including the Anchorage-to-Juneau leg over the treacherous Alaskan landscape.

A Cessna 310C, of the type in which congressional representatives Hale Boggs and Nicholas Begich, congressional aide Russell Brown, and pilot Don Jonz disappeared on October 16, 1972. No trace of the men or airplane ever turned up. *Cessna Aircraft*

The airplane Jonz selected that day was also up to the task. A twin-engine Cessna 310C—the type made famous by "Sky King" in the classic TV series of the same name—was a popular plane with an excellent safety reputation. This particular aircraft, which carried the registration number N1812H, was more than ten years old. But it was well maintained, in good operating condition, and considered completely airworthy.

However, Jonz had not equipped this particular airplane with certain items of safety equipment, as verified later by the NTSB investigation. The Cessna did not have an autopilot or an anti-icing system. While neither was required by air regulations, they were useful when flying in the often-inclement Alaskan weather. Also missing were two other safety items that *were* required. The Cessna was not carrying the survival equipment or Emergency Locator Transmitter (ELT) mandated by a newly enacted Alaska state law. In the event of a crash or forced landing in a remote area, the ELT would send out radio signals that rescuers could trace back to the downed aircraft. The need for survival equipment when flying over the remote and rugged Alaskan terrain was self-evident. The importance of these items was such that when Jonz radioed ten minutes after takeoff to file his flight plan, the Anchorage Flight Service Station specialist specifically asked him if he had the required equipment aboard, to which Jonz replied, "Affirmative."

The reason why Jonz lied about having the required emergency equipment is self-evident: to do otherwise would have been admitting that he was flying illegally. The more difficult question is why he failed to take this equipment with him in the first place. They were items he already possessed, so all he had to do was load them onto the airplane. Perhaps he forgot them, or maybe he felt he could not afford the extra weight—the NTSB later estimated that the small airplane, when loaded with the three passengers and their luggage, already exceeded its maximum recommended takeoff weight. No one will ever know for sure why Jonz failed to comply with this safety regulation.

Lost in the Wilderness

Just what happened to the four men and their aircraft after takeoff has never been determined. They may have gone down over mountains, glacier, or water, since their intended route took them over all of this terrain. It seemed that they had simply vanished into the vast Alaskan wilderness. Alaska is almost two and one-half times the size of the next largest US state, Texas—but it has only three percent the number of people. Not only is it mostly uninhabited, the weather is often not conducive to flying and the terrain is typically hostile to even the most basic human existence. The state truly lives up to its official nickname "the Last Frontier."

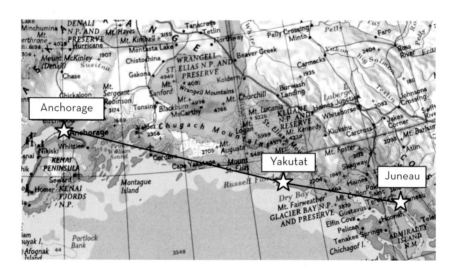

The route that pilot Don Jonz intended to follow from Anchorage to Juneau. No one knows where—or why—he and his three passengers ended their flight.

Many airplanes have disappeared in Alaska's remote skies, waters, and landmasses, never to return. This has prompted some to refer to its vast spaces as Alaska's Bermuda Triangle—a reference to the area of sea lying off the eastern coast of Florida that has similarly claimed numerous ships and aircraft.

Perhaps the earliest well-publicized aviation disappearance in Alaska's immense zone of the unknown occurred in 1937. That year, famed aviator Sigismund Levanevsky and his five crew members disappeared near the Alaska North Slope. Levanevsky, often called "Russia's Lindbergh," was attempting to fly from Moscow to New York City via the North Pole. The final resting place of the six intrepid Soviet fliers and their four-engine aircraft remains to this day a mystery. Likewise, finding Boggs and his missing Cessna in such a massive region made looking for a needle in a haystack seem easy.

An Unprecedented Search

By 1:15 p.m. on October 16, the airplane carrying the four men was forty-five minutes overdue at Juneau. Accordingly, airport authorities notified the US Air Force Rescue Coordination Center at Elmendorf Air Force Base, near Anchorage. Personnel there quickly initiated a search operation, which ultimately became one of the most intensive air, land, and sea searches ever conducted. Though hampered at first by ground fog covering most of southeastern Alaska, dozens of civilian and military ships, airplanes, helicopters, and even high-performance jets, began the search for the missing Cessna. The Civil Air Patrol, Army, Navy, Air Force, and Coast Guard all participated. The Air Force even took the unprecedented action of sending its highly sophisticated and top-secret Lockheed SR-71 Blackbird reconnaissance jet to assist. It was the first time it had ever employed this phenomenal high-altitude spy plane for a search and rescue operation. From an altitude of fifteen miles, its powerful camera was capable of imaging at unbelievably high resolution an incredible ninety thousand square miles every hour, making it ideal for this particular mission.

The hunt continued for thirty-nine days—more than five and one-half weeks. It covered all possible routes that pilot Jonz might have taken. Air searchers flew more than a thousand sorties and logged 3,600 flight hours, as they crisscrossed nearly 326,000 square miles of the rugged terrain. However, in spite of its duration, thoroughness, and intensity, the massive multiservice search operation turned up nothing. Not a single trace of the orange and white Cessna, nor any of its occupants ever appeared, and not a single trace has surfaced to this day. On November 24, 1972, authorities ended the search. All those aboard the ill-fated charter plane were presumed dead.

The NTSB conducted a thorough investigation of the disappearance but was "unable to determine the probable cause of this accident from the evidence presently available." It declined even to venture a serious guess as to what had happened to the lost airplane and its occupants. The report further noted that the investigation would resume whenever the downed aircraft was located. However, as the years unfolded, not so much as a screw, sliver of aluminum, or shard of Plexiglas from the vanished airplane ever turned up.

A Mysterious Tip

In nearly all unexplained high-profile disappearances—such as the Boggs case—the mysterious shadow of intrigue eventually materializes. This one was no exception, although it took twenty years to make itself apparent. In 1992, a Freedom of Information Act request brought to light some amazing and seemingly incriminating FBI documents. These cryptic messages revealed that authorities had received an apparently credible tip revealing the location of Boggs' downed plane only hours after its disappearance.

The telexes from the FBI's Los Angeles office disclosed information never before made public. They revealed that a man in the Long Beach area had contacted authorities to report what he believed was the location of the downed Cessna. He had some undefined connection with a top-secret private electronics firm that specialized in "highly sophisticated, experimental, electronic surveillance." The directions he gave were quite specific, pointing to a spot halfway between Anchorage and Juneau near Yakutat Bay and Alaska's largest ice field, Malaspina Glacier. The informant further revealed they had detected, and were tracking, at least two survivors who had apparently departed the downed plane!

FBI officials considered this information "significant," and forwarded it to their headquarters in Washington, DC. A follow-up telex later verified that they considered the informant—though evasive about his background and the firm that had obtained the information—to be reliable and the information very possibly authentic. All pertinent names in the documents released in 1992 were blacked out, so it has been impossible to learn the identity of this mystery man or the company with which he was associated.

One popular theory alleges that the FBI intentionally kept this potentially life-saving information secret to prevent Boggs' rescue. The FBI actually did have a score to settle with the missing Majority Leader. On April 5, 1971, he had—on the floor of Congress, no less—compared

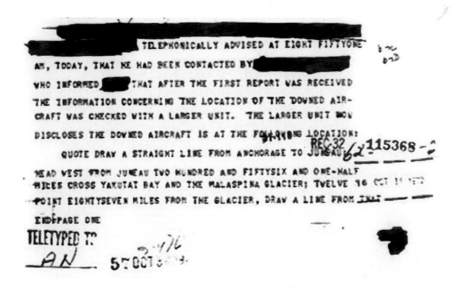

TELEPHONICALLY ADVISED AT EIGHT FIFTYONE AM, TODAY, THAT HE HAD BEEN CONTACTED BY WHO INFORMED THAT AFTER THE FIRST REPORT WAS RECEIVED THE INFORMATION CONCERNING THE LOCATION OF THE DOWNED AIRCRAFT WAS CHECKED WITH A LARGER UNIT. THE LARGER UNIT NOW DISCLOSES THE DOWNED AIRCRAFT IS AT THE FOLLOWING LOCATION: QUOTE DRAW A STRAIGHT LINE FROM ANCHORAGE TO JUNEAU HEAD WEST FROM JUNEAU TWO HUNDRED AND FIFTYSIX AND ONE-HALF MILES CROSS YAKUTAT BAY AND THE MALASPINA GLACIER; TWELVE POINT EIGHTYSEVEN MILES FROM THE GLACIER, DRAW A LINE FROM THAT ENDPAGE ONE

REC 32 115368 -

TELETYPED T:
AN 5 OCT

Part of the heavily redacted FBI telex describing the anonymous tip received about Boggs' missing plane. The mystery caller defined in specific terms where the downed aircraft was located. The next page of the telex states that this information was "immediately furnished [to the] US Coast Guard." Did the Coast Guard act on it? *FBI Freedom of Information Record*

the FBI's surveillance methods to those used by the Soviet Union's KGB and Nazi Germany's Gestapo. He ended his speech by calling for the removal of then-FBI Director J. Edgar Hoover. Hoover died a year later—five months prior to Boggs' disappearance—so he could hardly be blamed for squelching the anonymous tip; however, there probably was enough residual acrimony against Boggs within the bureau for the conspiracy spinners to make their case.

The biggest problem with this theory is that its premise is false. Both FBI and US Coast Guard documents clearly verify that the FBI *did* pass the anonymous tip on to the Coast Guard. Therefore, allegations that the feds kept the information to themselves or ignored it are false. What the Coast Guard did to follow up on the tip is unclear, but in the end, it did not matter. The thirty-nine-day search operation covered all the bases. Tip or no tip, Boggs' plane would almost certainly have been sighted had it been in any way visible. That it remained lost suggests that it was sitting under water or ice, or perhaps spread in a million small pieces across an icy hillside. As for the anonymous tip, no one has yet verified or refuted its legitimacy.

There is at least one other widely held conspiracy theory relating to Boggs' disappearance. It refers to his participation in the highly controversial Warren Commission—the panel tasked to investigate the assassination of President John F. Kennedy. The commission ultimately concluded that there was no conspiracy and that gunman Lee Harvey Oswald acted alone when he fired the fatal shots. Some evidence suggests that Boggs privately had reservations about the commission and its report, and that he may have even been considering reopening the investigation. This, in turn, marked him for assassination by whatever dark unknown force may have been behind the killing of President Kennedy.

In truth, no evidence exists to prove that anyone sabotaged Boggs' flight. No one can rule it out, since the plane was never found, but even Boggs' daughter, noted political analyst Cokie Roberts, has expressed her disbelief that there was ever any conspiracy against her powerful father. However, others see it differently. At least one member of the Begich family has publicly stated that there may have been foul play. It is unlikely that anyone will ever know for sure—at least until the missing Cessna turns up.

A Bad Case of "Attitude"

Yet another scenario for the four men's demise seems more likely. It involves the abysmal weather into which Jonz flew. It failed to meet even the minimum criteria for the Visual Flight Rules (VFR) flight plan he filed soon after takeoff. There was dense fog and drizzle with limited visibility. Jonz filed a VFR plan instead of the more appropriate Instrument Flight Rules (IFR) plan for one simple reason: legally, he could not file IFR. In order to do this for a flight carrying paying passengers, regulations required Jonz to have either a copilot or an autopilot, and he had neither. Still, he was an experienced instrument-rated pilot who was otherwise qualified to fly in such weather, so this may or may not have been a contributing factor.

There was, however, another—and more serious—meteorological challenge for Jonz to contend with that day: icing. This insidious killer strikes fear into the hearts of even the most grizzled aviators. An aircraft flying in icing conditions can simply fall out of the sky. The accumulating ice adds unsustainable weight to the airplane and simultaneously reduces the wings' lifting ability. Failure to initiate effective anti-icing procedures or to escape the condition by changing altitude or direction will quickly result in disaster.

Jonz had recently written an article on this very topic for the highly regarded aviation magazine *Flying*. Ironically, it hit the newsstands in October 1972—the very month he disappeared. The article, entitled "Ice Without Fear," revealed the author's remarkably cavalier attitude towards this deadly hazard. His lead paragraph said it all: "The thought of in-flight structural icing inspires the crazies in a lot of airmen. In my opinion, most of it is a crock." He went on to write, "If you are sneaky, smart and careful, you can fly 350 days a year and disregard 99 percent of the BS you hear about icing."

It is likely that Jonz did encounter icing conditions on his last flight. At least one other pilot flying a similar route that day reported that his airplane had started to collect ice, and that he barely escaped it by quickly climbing for altitude. It is entirely possible that the dangerous condition of which Jonz was so disdainful—coupled with his failure to outfit his airplane properly with emergency equipment—could have been his undoing. The unfortunate decisions this experienced but devil-may-care pilot made that day may have teamed up against him—and cost him and his passengers their lives.

Ultimately, just about the only thing known with certainty about the disappearance of Cessna 310C N1812H and its highly placed passengers is that there still remains plenty of uncertainty.

Both of the missing congressional representatives were re-elected to office in the election that followed less than a month after their disappearance. Their official tenure was, by necessity, short. On December 31, 1972, a presumptive death hearing in Anchorage legally declared Nicholas Begich dead. Three days later, House Resolution 1 of the Ninety-Third Congress officially accepted Boggs' death, as well. A special election that followed placed his widow, Corinne "Lindy" Boggs, into the Louisiana Second Congressional District seat her husband had filled for the previous twenty-eight years. She occupied that position for an additional eighteen years, and later served as US Ambassador to the Vatican.

It is appropriate that the state flower of Alaska is the forget-me-not. Forty years have passed since Majority Leader Boggs and Representative Begich vanished with two other men during a routine trans-Alaskan flight. Yet, there are many from that state—and others, as well—who have still not forgotten their unexplained disappearance in the Alaskan wilderness. It is unlikely they ever will.

CRIMINAL AND OTHER POLITICALLY INCORRECT BEHAVIOUR

CHAPTER ELEVEN
MAD FLIGHT TO OBLIVION

"ONE OF THE MOST MYSTERIOUS AFFAIRS OF WAR."

Shortly after 11:00 p.m. on May 10, 1941, one of the most bizarre and controversial flights of all time came to an abrupt end in a remote area of western Scotland. On this otherwise quiet evening, a loud explosion startled a farm couple who lived a few miles south of Glasgow, near the village of Eaglesham. When David McLean ran to his window, he was shocked to see the flames of a crashed aircraft blazing on the ground nearby. As he looked up into the darkened sky, he could just make out a parachute drifting down onto a nearby moor.

Armed with a pitchfork, the bewildered but wary farmer ran out to the parachutist and demanded to know, "Are ye a Nazi enemy, or are ye one o' ours?" The downed flier, grimacing from the ankle injury he had just suffered, replied in German-accented English that he was not a "Nazi enemy," but instead, a friend of Britain. He further informed McLean that he had an important message for the Duke of Hamilton, whose estate—Dungavel Castle—was located nearby.

The unsuspecting farmer helped the injured pilot into his house, where—as dictated by proper British etiquette—his wife offered him a cup of tea. The middle-aged pilot with bushy eyebrows identified himself as German Air Force *Hauptman* (Captain) Alfred Horn. The McLeans had no way of knowing it, but the visitor who had so abruptly dropped in on them was in reality the third-ranking leader of Britain's mortal enemy—Nazi Germany. "*Hauptman* Horn" was none other than Adolf Hitler's right-hand man and the Deputy *Führer* of the Nazi party, Walter Richard Rudolf Hess.

Thus ended one of history's strangest wartime missions. No bombs were dropped and no bullets fired, but the bizarre and controversial stunt had far-reaching historical and political implications. To this day, Rudolf Hess's infamous flight of no return is one of history's most fascinating.

The Rise of Rudolf Hess

Rudolf Hess was born in 1894 in Alexandria, Egypt, into a wealthy family of German merchants. During World War I, he served with distinction in the Imperial German Army—first as a foot soldier, and then after recovering from a serious chest wound, a fighter pilot with the Royal Bavarian squadron, *Jasta* 35b. After Germany's capitulation, the disillusioned Hess joined the *Freikorps von Epp,* a right-wing, anti-Communist paramilitary organization. Before long, he crossed paths with a charismatic young fellow reactionary named Adolf Hitler. The two ex-soldiers became friends and fellow members of the ultra-extreme fascist organization *Nationalsozialistische Deutsche Arbeiterpartei*—the Nazi Party.

In November 1923, Hitler attempted to overthrow the Bavarian government in Munich with his famous "Beer Hall Putsch." After the somewhat amateurish coup attempt failed, both he and Hess ended up imprisoned together in a fortress located in Landsberg, Bavaria. While incarcerated, the faithful Hess assisted Hitler in writing his infamous blueprint of hate, *Mein Kampf.* After their release, Hess remained with Hitler as his personal secretary. When the Nazis finally came to power in 1933, Hess assumed the position of Deputy *Führer* of the Nazi Party. By 1939, he had become the third-ranking Nazi in all of Germany—answering only to Hitler and his flamboyant air minister, *Reichsmarschal* Hermann Göring.

In spite of Hess's high official ranking in the Nazi party, his influence had been on the wane for years. By 1941, other highly positioned Nazis had already displaced him in all but title. Consequently, Hess may have felt compelled to perform some spectacular feat in order to regain his status with his *Führer.*

Hess's bizarre plan, if successful, would certainly have restored Hitler's confidence in him. Germany was at war with Great Britain, a country that Hitler had never really wanted to fight and one that was proving difficult to defeat. Hess decided—apparently unilaterally—that it would be in both Germany's and Britain's best interests to join forces against what he considered the common enemy of all Western Europe: the Soviet Union. Surely, he thought, Britain would also see the wisdom of such an alliance.

An Old Eagle Takes Flight Again

Rudolf Hess was an aviator at heart, so his secret plan would involve a flight so ambitious it would have challenged the skills of any of the world's greatest

⬆ British military personnel examining the wreckage of Hess's downed Messerschmitt Bf 110 fighter. He parachuted from it, rather than attempt a risky night landing.

⬅ A formal pose of Deputy *Führer* Rudolf Hess in his Nazi uniform.

pilots. He would fly an unarmed high-performance combat aircraft from the heart of Germany across Northern Europe, over the North Sea, and into the heart of his well-defended enemy, the British Isles. He would pass over more than a thousand miles of mostly unfamiliar territory, and he would do it completely alone, at night, and in total secrecy—even from his own country.

The entire flight would take place over hostile territory. Since even the *Luftwaffe* was unaware of his plan, its pilots would also be doing their best to shoot him down. He would therefore have to slip past a double-deadly gauntlet of antiaircraft defenses and night fighter interceptors without being blown out of the sky. Then, if lucky enough to arrive at his destination, he had to find a way to get himself onto the ground safely, in enemy territory, and in the dead of night. If successful, Hess then intended to score a diplomatic coup that would change the course of human history. To improve his chances the superstitious Nazi even consulted his personal astrologer in order to select a night for the flight on which an optimal alignment of the planets would occur. Though he did not lack confidence or ambition, he would need all the help he could muster.

Hess was an accomplished pilot. He had maintained his flying skills in the years since World War I—winning in 1934 an air race around Germany's highest peak, the Zugspitze. Therefore, all that was necessary for him to fly one of the *Luftwaffe*'s fast, modern fighters was a few hours of advanced training. This was not a problem for the Deputy *Führer* of the Third Reich: no one—except for Hitler and Göring—had the authority to deny him this access. And in all likelihood, neither had even a clue as to what he was up to.

Consequently, Hess surreptitiously began visiting Willi Messerschmitt's *Bayerische Flugzeugwerke* (Bavarian Aircraft Works), located at Augsburg, where he could learn to fly one of Germany's premiere high-performance, long-range combat aircraft: the twin-engine Messerschmitt Bf 110 *Zerstörer* (Destroyer). A fast and highly versatile two-seat fighter, it was also widely used for bombing, ground attack, and reconnaissance duties.

Hess made numerous flights from the factory airfield near Augsburg over the course of several months leading up to his secret mission. After making his first few hops with an instructor, he began flying solo. After he had mastered the necessary skills, he claimed one of the fast Messerschmitts, an E/2-N model, as his own personal aircraft. It sat in its hangar, under constant guard and untouched, except by Hess himself.

◆ Rudolf Hess stands on the right next to his leader and comrade, Adolf Hitler. Nazi Minister of Propaganda Joseph Goebbels is visible in the background at the far left.

Messerschmitt Bf 110G-2 at Britain's Royal Air Force Museum, Hendon. This is similar to the aircraft Rudolf Hess used for his infamous flight of May 19, 1941. *Steven A. Ruffin*

Eventually, he had his fighter fitted with wing fuel tanks, which extended its range to well over a thousand miles. He then began making practice flights with the aircraft fully fueled—a tricky undertaking even for the highly experienced test pilots who routinely flew for Messerschmitt.

A Most Mysterious Affair

Hess made a series of false starts in pursuit of his intended diplomatic mission before finally succeeding. Each time, he had his fuel tanks topped off for what appeared to be a long journey. No one at the airfield could even guess where he might be going, and no one dared question the Deputy *Führer*. In each of these attempts, he aborted soon after takeoff for various reasons.

Finally, at a little before 6:00 p.m. on May 10, 1941, Hess once again fueled up his long-range, twin-engine fighter and took off for points unknown to anyone else. This time, he did not turn back. He headed northwest across Germany at more than two hundred miles per hour through the rapidly darkening sky, carefully flying well clear of German fighter interceptor bases, as well as other observation, antiaircraft, and defense stations in and around the Ruhr Valley.

Shortly after Hess's secret takeoff that evening, word of his apparently unauthorized flight somehow leaked out. German *Luftwaffe* ace and fighter group commander Adolf Galland received an urgent phone call at his base in western France. As he relates in his autobiography, *The First and the Last*, the frantic caller at the other end of the line exclaimed, "The Deputy *Führer* has gone mad and is flying to England in a Messerschmitt. He must be brought down!"

The phone call was from none other than the *Reichsmarschal* himself—Hermann Göring, Hitler's number two in command and Galland's ultimate superior. Galland, a distinguished flier and fighter—and not a politician—wondered to himself if perhaps Göring was the one who had gone stark raving mad. Why in the world had Nazi Germany's air minister just personally ordered him to shoot Hitler's own deputy out of the sky?

Galland halfheartedly scrambled a few fighters he had available. It was a token gesture at complying with an incomprehensible order. Meanwhile, he pondered further the question of why Göring would want Hess killed. After all, the "mad" pilot in question was one of Adolf Hitler's oldest and best friends and a powerful and highly regarded leader in the Nazi regime. It made no sense, but it really did not matter, anyway. As night approached, his fighters had little chance of intercepting Hess and even less of shooting him down. Whatever the secretive Deputy *Führer*'s destination, no one in the Third Reich could stop him now. It was, as Galland wrote, "one of the most mysterious affairs of war."

Prisoner of War

As Hess winged his way across Germany and Holland, he carefully evaded the Nazi air defense network. When he reached the Dutch coast, he veered northeast to avoid known enemy air defenses before turning west and heading into British airspace, toward Scotland. Remarkably, he managed to thread his way through this lethal maze of obstacles, and at approximately 11:00 p.m., he arrived at his destination in Scotland.

As he searched the darkness in vain for the small private landing strip situated on the Duke of Hamilton's estate, he began to run low on fuel. Finally, with no alternatives remaining, he unbuckled his seat belt, opened the glass canopy, rolled his fighter upside down, and dropped into the dark unknown. As he floated to earth in his parachute, he watched his trusty Messerschmitt plow into the Scottish moor below him. Before long, he also landed hard, not far from his burning airplane. In a few minutes, he made his acquaintance with the pitchfork-wielding McLean.

After Hess finished his tea, the now-congenial farmer turned his uninvited visitor over to the authorities. While the high-ranking Nazi was in the process of passing from one official to the next, he finally divulged his true identity and dramatically proclaimed that he had come in the name of humanity. He explained to his skeptical captors that he was there as a personal envoy of his *Führer*, Adolf Hitler, to seek a peace settlement between Germany and Britain.

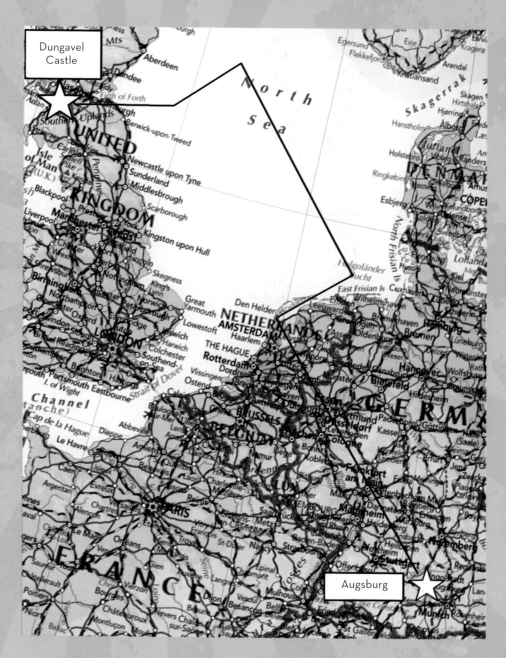

Rudolf Hess's route from Augsburg, Germany, to Dungavel Castle, Scotland. This solo night flight was a considerable achievement in navigation and airmanship. Before even attempting to penetrate Britain's highly capable defenses, he first had to escape those of Nazi Germany.

British authorities, however, decided for reasons of their own that the best course of action was to ignore Hess and his strange airborne peace offering. On May 17, after intensive interrogation and minimal public comment, they locked him in the Tower of London. Three days later, they moved him to Mytchett Place in Surrey, and finally to a prison in South Wales, where he remained a solitary prisoner for the duration of the war. In spite of Hess's adamant demands, British Prime Minister Winston Churchill steadfastly refused even to meet with the captured Nazi leader. The resolute prime minister had no desire to make peace with a regime he wanted only to destroy.

Man without a Country

Back in Germany, Hitler publicly proclaimed that the secret mission of his now ex-Deputy *Führer* was completely unauthorized. Not only did he refuse to sanction the flight in any way, he even went so far as to brand his former friend insane and suffering from "pacifist delusions." German radio immediately announced, "Rudolf Hess, Deputy *Führer*, has flown to England in pursuit of an idea of madness. The *Führer* has removed him from all posts and excluded him from the Party."

The possibility that Hitler may have been in on Hess's risky plan is still a matter of debate. Some historians believe that the two had previously discussed it and that Hitler may even have privately sanctioned the mission. He certainly had plenty of incentive to make peace with Great Britain: he secretly planned to invade the Soviet Union the following month. An alliance with Great Britain would free him from the war on the Western Front and greatly enhance his prospects of defeating the Soviet power to the east. However, no written records have yet materialized that substantiate any such discussion between Hess and Hitler.

Hess had apparently devised his plan—with or without Hitler's endorsement—in order to reach out to a group of influential British citizens he believed to be pro-German. Some of these, who may have even included members of the British Royal Family, were in a position to oppose—or perhaps even depose—the pugnacious Churchill. The man Hess was attempting to contact, the Duke of Hamilton, was a fellow aviator whom he may have briefly met during the 1936 Olympics in Berlin. The Duke was an influential former member of Parliament and current air commodore in Britain's Royal Air Force. Hess apparently considered him the best person to connect him with the right people.

How Hess arrived at such a notion is debatable. Some historians have suggested that the doltish Deputy *Führer* was the hapless victim of an elaborate British plot to lure him to Britain. Others contend that the clandestine Hess affair was not a plot, but rather a sincere attempt by both countries to negotiate a peaceful solution. Unfortunately, after Hess's noisy and somewhat messy arrival in Scotland became a front-page story, no one on either side wanted any more to do with it.

Was Hess really a legitimate part of a plot to overthrow the British government? Or was he simply a British intelligence dupe? Was he Hitler's personal "winged messenger of peace?" Or was Churchill correct when he called him a deranged madman bent on "an act of benevolent lunacy"? It looks as though the jury will remain out pending further credible information.

For reasons unknown, the British government still has many of the documents most pertinent to the Hess affair under lock and key. There they will remain—at least as it stands at this writing—until the year 2017. Until then, the truth behind his historic flight will continue to be one of history's most closely guarded secrets. However, the fact that the British government is still withholding information after nearly three-quarters of a century suggests there may be more to the affair than either lunacy or clumsy diplomacy. It could even be, as John Costello asserts in his book *Ten Days to Destiny*, that Hess's historic mission was "an interlocking sequence of secret British and German peace maneuvers that can be tracked right back to the summer of 1940."

Rudolf Hess (far right) at the Nuremburg Trials with fellow Nazis, former *Reichmarschal* Hermann Göring (left) and *Grossadmiral* Karl Dönitz (center). Hess and Dönitz ended up in Spandau Prison, while Göring avoided his appointment with the hangman by committing suicide. *US Army Signal Corps*

Rudolf Hess left behind a wife, a three-year-old son, and a number of letters. One letter was addressed to Hitler, stating, "My *Führer*, should you not agree with what I have done, simply call me a madman." Hitler was quick to oblige him—and he wasted no time in signing Hess's death warrant in the event he ever again set foot in Germany. Hess's note to his wife explained that she would probably not see him again for a long time. It was an understatement.

Rudolf Hess, languishing in prison in 1945. From the evening of his ill-conceived flight to the end of his controversial life more than forty-six years later, he never enjoyed a single day of freedom. *US Army Signal Corps*

After the war ended, the unrepentant and still sadly misguided Hess stated publicly at the Nuremburg International Military Tribunal: "I am happy to know that I have done my duty toward my people, my duty as a German, as a National Socialist, as a loyal follower of my *Führer*. I regret nothing." Not surprisingly, the tribunal found him guilty of war crimes. Instead of sending him to the hangman, however—like most of his other high-ranking Nazi colleagues—it sentenced him to a lifetime of solitary confinement at Berlin's Spandau Allied Military Prison. Here, he languished for the remaining forty-one years of his life, the latter half of these as the fortress's only guest.

On August 17, 1987, the ninety-three-year-old Hess committed suicide by hanging himself. At least this was the official explanation. Hess's son, Wolf Rüdiger Hess, among others, has alleged that the former Reich Minister did not commit suicide at all, but that agents of the British government murdered him. Others contend that the man who died at Spandau after spending nearly half a century there in solitary confinement, was not really Hess at all, but an imposter.

There is still little certainty regarding Rudolf Hess's fantastic flight, but in the end, his futile mission failed to change the course of the war in any way. In fact, it accomplished nothing at all—other than to terminate his own misguided political career and his freedom, forever.

CHAPTER TWELVE

THE CRIME OF THE CENTURY

"NO FUNNY STUFF OR I'LL DO THE JOB."

On Thanksgiving eve, November 24, 1971, a tall, thin, well-dressed man boarded Northwest Orient Airlines Flight 305, in Portland, Oregon. The scheduled 2:45 p.m. flight was just a short thirty-minute hop due north to its destination of Seattle. The olive-complexioned man wore a suit, overcoat, and dark sunglasses, and he appeared to be in his midforties. He sat near the rear of the cabin in a row by himself.

Soon after the Boeing 727-51 jetliner took off, the mysterious passenger calmly presented a neatly printed note to flight attendant Florence Schaffner. She initially thought it was a request for a date or some other sort of proposal—not an uncommon occurrence for the attractive twenty-three-year-old woman. When she read it, however, she immediately realized it was anything but an innocent flirtation. It read, "Miss, I have a bomb. Come sit by me." When she did, he opened an attaché case he was carrying and briefly displayed its contents. Plainly visible inside were red cylindrical sticks and a battery connected by an electrical wire. It may or may not have been the real thing, but it looked authentic enough for Schaffner to take him seriously. He indicated that he wanted $200,000 in unmarked, "negotiable" bills, four parachutes (two back main chutes and two front reserve chutes), and a fuel truck ready and waiting when they landed at the Seattle-Tacoma airport. The man impressed Schaffner as being polite—and generous: he told her to keep the change after paying for a two-dollar drink with a twenty-dollar bill. Before she left to take the note to the pilot, however, he added ominously, "No funny stuff or I'll do the job."

Northwest Orient Airlines Boeing 727-51 N467US, from which hijacker D. B. Cooper made his famous escape on November 24, 1971. This photograph was taken in March 1967 at Cleveland's Hopkins International Airport. Cooper chose the 727 because of its distinctive rear boarding steps (which are retracted in this photo). *Bob Garrard, with permission*

Thus begins the strange saga of skyjacker "D. B. Cooper." The high-altitude scheme he orchestrated for himself that Thanksgiving eve was either the heist of the century—or the biggest blunder in criminal history. To this day, no one knows which.

Out into the Night

Nearing Seattle, the crew of Flight 205 immediately notified authorities on the ground of the hijacker's demands. FBI agents quickly assembled ten thousand twenty-dollar bills and four parachutes while the airliner circled above Seattle, waiting to land. The bills were unmarked, as specified by the hijacker, but with serial numbers prerecorded to facilitate future identification. Mercifully, throughout the unfolding drama, the other passengers on the flight remained oblivious to the crime in progress. The pilot explained the delay by announcing that it was due to a minor mechanical problem.

After landing, the mysterious sky pirate accepted delivery of his two main and two reserve chutes, and a large bundle of greenbacks. He then allowed all the passengers, along with flight attendants Schaffner and Alice Hancock, to exit the aircraft. Soon, he ordered the remaining four crew members, Capt. William Scott, 1st Officer William Rataczak, 2nd Officer Harold Anderson, and flight attendant Tina Mucklow, to take off. His instructions were to head the now-empty airliner toward Mexico City, via Reno, Nevada, for another refueling stop. Soon after takeoff, for reasons unknown at the time, the hijacker ordered the pilots to climb to an altitude of ten thousand feet, drop the landing gear, and lower the flaps to an angle of fifteen degrees.

When the crew had complied with these instructions, the skyjacker ordered all four of them into the cockpit and then lowered the rear outside stairway of the jet. He had obviously selected the Boeing 727 as the vehicle for his crime specifically because of this distinctive feature. Donning a main and reserve parachute, Cooper then tethered the heavy parcel of money to his body, using some nylon rope from one of the extra parachutes. He did this in order to keep it from being lost during what was sure to be a wild descent into the equally wild night. As he was doing that, he probably wished he had specified hundred-dollar bills. The bulky bag of twenties weighed twenty-one pounds, while C-notes would have weighed only four.

At about 8:00 p.m., a cockpit warning light alerted the pilots that the airliner's rear door was ajar. When they asked the skyjacker via the intercom if he needed any assistance, they got a resounding "No!" It was the last word they—or anybody else—heard the mysterious criminal utter. A few minutes later, the audacious jumper made his way down the airliner's rear stairway, parachutes and money attached, and jumped into the two-hundred-mile-per-hour slipstream and the dark unknown that lay beyond. He was still wearing nothing more substantial than his loafers and business suit. All he left behind were the two unused parachutes, a thin black J. C. Penney tie with a pearl tie tack, eight cigarette butts, and a few mostly unreadable fingerprints.

The FBI later pieced together what little they could about this eventful four-hour period. The man in question wore sunglasses, drank bourbon and soda, and chain-smoked filter-tipped Raleigh cigarettes. In the forty-some years since the enigmatic man who came to be known as "D. B. Cooper" hijacked Flight 305 and jumped into immortality, almost nothing else has been learned about him.

A Legend Is Born

To this day, one of the few certainties about this legendary mystery man is that, ironically, he never referred to himself as "D. B. Cooper." The only time he ever mentioned a name at all was while purchasing his airline ticket from Portland to Seattle. He paid for it with a twenty-dollar bill and gave the name "Dan Cooper" for the passenger manifest. By most accounts, the origin of the misnomer, "D. B. Cooper"—by which he is universally remembered—stemmed from a mistake. One of the early suspects included a Portland man named Daniel B.—or "D. B."—Cooper. The press keyed on this name and widely reported it as that of the hijacker. Authorities soon cleared the real D. B. Cooper of any wrongdoing, but the catchy name stuck. The world would forever afterward remember the infamous skyjacker— incorrectly—as "D. B. Cooper."

Just as this was not his real name, it is almost equally certain that it was not Dan Cooper, either. In 1971, proof of identity was not required to buy an airline ticket, so he could have given any name he wished. In all likelihood, "Dan Cooper" was a pseudonym. It also happened to be the name of a European comic book action hero popular in the 1960s. Some have conjectured that the skyjacker may have been a fan of this cartoon character and decided to adopt his name as a personal joke. To this day, no one has the slightest idea what his real name was.

Equally unknown was where Cooper landed. The exact location was impossible to determine, since the crew—all of whom were up front in the flight compartment—had no way of knowing exactly when he had exited the aircraft. For that matter, they did not know that he actually *had* jumped until the airliner landed in Reno. There, FBI agents, who doubted

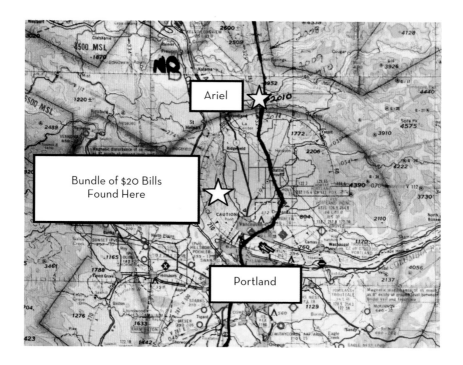

A portion of the aeronautical chart used by the FBI showing the flight path of Cooper's airliner, as it made its way south from Seattle to Reno, Nevada. Cooper jumped at about 8:10 p.m., over the town of Ariel, Washington. The only part of his loot that ever turned up was a bundle of twenty-dollar bills, found more than eight years later—and more than twenty miles southwest of Ariel. *FBI (labels added by author)*

that the hijacker would really be crazy enough to jump, waited to arrest him. Pilots of US Air Force aircraft, who had scrambled to observe and assist, were equally clueless. Even though they shadowed the airliner throughout its flight from Seattle to Reno, they failed to see anyone jump that dark and rainy night. Based on when the rear door light came on, the best guess was that Cooper had jumped at about 8:10 p.m., at which time the plane was flying over a remote area of the lower Cascade Mountains in southwestern Washington.

One of the most intense manhunts in history began on Thanksgiving morning and continued for eighteen days. The elaborate operation—which ended up costing far more than the $200,000 ransom—focused on an area approximately twenty miles north of Portland, near the isolated town of Ariel, Washington. An armada of airplanes, helicopters, and hundreds of law enforcement and military personnel turned up nothing. There was no trace of Cooper, his parachute, or the money. Even now—after nearly a half century of dead-end leads, a thousand suspects, an estimated one hundred thousand interviews, a case file that is dozens of volumes thick, and untold numbers of false accusations and crackpot confessions—authorities are no closer to solving this crime than they were in 1971. To this day, there are only these indisputable truths: no one knows where Cooper landed, what happened to him—or even who the mysterious hijacker really was. It remains the greatest aviation crime mystery of all time.

D. B. Cooper, Cult Hero

This case, which the FBI code-named "NORJAK" (for Northwest Hijacking), has been a never-ending source of aggravation for the nation's top law-enforcement agency. Retired FBI agent Ralph Himmelsbach spent much of his career unsuccessfully chasing down Cooper leads. Even after forty-plus years, his frustration is still apparent when he speaks about Cooper, calling the fugitive outlaw just another "sleazy, rotten criminal

FBI composite sketch of the skyjacker known as "D. B. Cooper." On Thanksgiving eve, 1971, he jumped with $200,000 from the back of a Boeing 727 into a stormy night, ten thousand feet above the wilderness of southwestern Washington. The case remains unsolved, and to this day, no one knows who he really was or if he survived the jump. *FBI*

. . . a loser." Other agents, however—some of whom are still tinkering, at least unofficially, with the case—view Cooper more respectfully, as a more sophisticated and educated man.

Regardless, it seems that the more the authorities searched for the elusive skyjacker, the more he gained in public popularity. His sheer boldness, ingenuity, and prowess in fooling the nation's foremost law enforcement organization made him a sort of cult hero. He committed the perfect crime without hurting anyone else, and he got away with it. Not even famed 1930s gangster John Dillinger—whom many struggling, Depression-era Americans secretly admired—managed to do that. Cooper's crime, occurring as it did near the end of the Vietnam era, successfully bucked the system at a time when "sticking it to the man" was a popular idea. Consequently, the gutsy skyjacker and his daring crime became a part of American folklore.

Over the years, numerous books, songs, TV documentaries, and even a Robert Duvall movie, have honored the legend of D. B. Cooper. In addition, several towns and establishments around the country still hold D. B. Cooper parties. The most popular of these occurs in Ariel, Washington, near where Cooper supposedly landed. Every Thanksgiving, the tiny town celebrates "Cooper's Capers" in honor of its most famous nonresident's only known nonvisit.

Slim Chance of Survival

It is still anyone's guess as to where Cooper landed and what happened to him. Many are convinced that he died during the jump. Some even consider his attempt so desperate that it was tantamount to suicide. It is not difficult to arrive at that conclusion; after all, he jumped while flying over very hostile terrain, from an aircraft traveling at ten thousand feet altitude and two hundred miles per hour, into a dark, cold, and wet night, wearing only a business suit. If not killed outright when his unprotected body slammed into the blast of icy wind, he may have died of exposure during or after the descent or from injuries he received when he blindly parachuted into the trees, rocks, or water below.

If Cooper did somehow beat all the odds and survive the jump, how then could he possibly have escaped to safety in one of the country's most rugged and remote areas and in the midst of one of the most intense manhunts ever conducted? He was obviously not dressed, or in any other way prepared, for a nighttime hike through dense forests and mountains. Logically, the chances that he survived seem nearly nonexistent. Even the FBI eventually admitted that he probably died during the attempt, stating publicly that there was little chance that even an experienced parachutist—which, they concluded, Cooper probably was not—could have survived such a jump.

Still, the FBI never stopped looking for the elusive Mr. Cooper. If he died during the jump, then what happened to his body? The widespread search for Cooper turned up at least two corpses from the past, but neither of these was his. Moreover, the extensive manhunt failed to find even one of the ten thousand missing twenty-dollar bills. Out of the many that must have eventually broken loose and drifted across the countryside, surely some of them would have turned up somewhere—unless the hijacker managed to survive and hang onto them.

Proof that Cooper could have survived this seemingly impossible jump came after the crime: on April 7, 1972, when a copycat skyjacker named Richard McCoy successfully reproduced the feat. He parachuted from the back of a United Airlines Boeing 727 over Utah in the same manner as Cooper, except he took with him a more substantial ransom of $500,000. The FBI thought that they might have found their man, Cooper, but when agents captured McCoy a few days later, they quickly ruled that possibility out. McCoy had an airtight alibi for the night Cooper committed his crime. McCoy went to prison for air piracy—and later died in a police shootout after escaping. Meanwhile, the indomitable D. B. Cooper remained at large.

Not surprisingly, these two skyjackings prompted airports around the country to institute more stringent security measures. In addition, Boeing retrofitted its 727 jetliners with a lock on the back door to prevent anyone else from opening it in flight. This so-called "Cooper Vane" put a stop to any further sky-jumping hijinks.

A Significant Breakthrough

More than eight years later, just when the legend of D. B. Cooper was beginning to fade, there was an amazing break in the case. In February 1980, eight-year-old Brian Ingram was camping with his family on the Columbia River near Vancouver, Washington, when he uncovered in the sandy bank some bundles of weathered and moldy twenty-dollar bills—290 of them to be exact. A comparison of serial numbers quickly verified that the $5,800 was part of the Cooper loot. This electrifying discovery prompted authorities to initiate a renewed search operation near where the bills were located. Finally, it seemed, the solution to the D. B. Cooper case might be at hand.

However, in spite of a search almost as extensive as the original, Cooper's body was still missing and none of the remaining $194,200 could

Part of the "Cooper Cash" an eight-year-old boy discovered in 1980, buried in the sand near Vancouver, Washington. The 290 twenty-dollar bills were the only ones ever found. *FBI*

be found. Young Ingram's find proved to be the only bills connected with the Cooper case ever to appear, either in or out of circulation.

So, just what did the fortuitous find—more than twenty miles southwest of where authorities originally assumed that Cooper landed—mean? Did the package of money separate from Cooper during or after the jump, fall into the water, and wash downstream? Or did Cooper purposely toss some of the money away, hoping to throw authorities off his track? No one knows. As for the lucky boy who found the bundles of bills in the sand, he received a cash reward in addition to several of the original bills to keep as souvenirs. One of these eventually sold at an auction for more than $6,500.

Other Leads

No more hard evidence for the Cooper case ever surfaced. Over the decades since the crime was committed, law enforcement authorities received thousands of tips from people who thought they had information about Cooper. One was a 1996 claim made by a woman in Florida, who related that her husband had confessed on his deathbed that he was the infamous skyjacker, D. B Cooper. Duane Weber, a seventy-year-old antique dealer, did resemble sketches of the skyjacker, and there were several other bits of compelling, though inconclusive, circumstantial evidence. In the end, however, his DNA did not match that obtained from Cooper's tie.

Then, in 2007, a man revealed that his late brother, Kenneth Christiansen, might have been D. B. Cooper. Before the Cooper skyjacking, Kenneth had been a rather disgruntled employee of Northwest Orient. Then, about a year after the skyjacking, he bought a house and paid for it in cash—an unusual transaction for a person of his means. He also happened to be a bourbon drinker, a smoker, and a former paratrooper—but most important, his photo closely matched flight attendant Schaffner's recollection of Cooper. Christiansen is still the most likely D. B. Cooper suspect, but authorities never definitively connected him to the crime.

In 2011, D. B. Cooper was still making headlines. At that time, the FBI announced it had a "credible" lead on the case. A woman in Oklahoma, who claimed to be the skyjacker's niece, provided a fingerprint investigators hoped might match a possible Cooper print found on the airliner. However, this lead was just like all the ones before it—inconclusive.

⇽★⇾

After more than forty years, the D. B. Cooper case is still unsolved; in all likelihood, it will remain that way. No one will ever know whether he survived the ordeal and lived in comfort to a ripe old age, or whether he died a quick death the instant he stepped off the extended rear stairway of the high-flying airliner.

Either way, no one today doubts that his actions on that dark and rainy Thanksgiving eve two miles above the wilderness of the Pacific Northwest were worthy of the legend they created. His famous jump into immortality remains the only major unsolved domestic skyjacking in US history. Accordingly, this notorious "novel without a final chapter," as one FBI agent recently described it, remains an open case. To this day, the FBI has a standing statement on its official website, requesting anyone with information to contact its Seattle field office.

CHAPTER THIRTEEN

WHEN THE SKIES RAINED TERROR

"ARE YOU GUYS READY? LET'S ROLL."

On the cloudless morning of September 11, 2001, four US airliners took off from three different airports located on the Eastern Seaboard. All of the flights were regularly scheduled nonstop transcontinental hops to the West Coast. They were normal in all respects—except that distributed among the total 232 passengers were 19 suicidal terrorists from the al-Qaeda Islamist militant group. They were armed with both knives and incapacitating chemical agents.

During a two-hour period of utter horror, the fanatical Middle Eastern terrorists, bent on killing themselves and as many innocent Americans as possible, launched four separate but highly coordinated aerial attacks against high-profile targets in the United States. They hijacked and intentionally crashed four commercial jet airliners, loaded with hundreds of passengers and thousands of gallons of explosive jet fuel. Three of them hit America's two most iconic cities, New York City and Washington, DC. In so doing, they either destroyed or substantially damaged two of the nation's most important symbols of wealth and power. Worst of all, they took the lives of three thousand innocent people.

These four flights combined to form history's most devastating terrorist attack. The day we now call simply 9/11 truly was, as President George W. Bush told the American public on that evening, the day "our nation saw evil."

Falling Airliners

The terrorists intentionally chose transcontinental flights, knowing the airliners would be heavily loaded with fuel, and they picked a Tuesday because it is typically a light flying day. These two factors would translate into minimal passenger resistance and maximum explosive power upon impact. At least one terrorist on each flight was a pilot who had trained at a US civilian flight school.

No one can ever know the horror that occurred within the four doomed airliners during these flights, but a great deal of information can be gleaned from evidence recovered on the ground, radio transmissions, and phone calls made by those aboard. The image that emerges from each of the hijacked planes is the same: stark terror, panic, confusion, and heartbreaking sorrow.

Attack No. 1: American Airlines Flight 11 — This flight was the first of the four to take off and the first to crash. The Los Angeles-bound Boeing 767-200ER left Boston's Logan International Airport at 7:59 a.m. with eighty-one passengers, a crew of eleven, and approximately ten thousand gallons of fuel. About half of the available seats were empty.

Approximately fifteen minutes after takeoff, five terrorists seated near the front of the cabin in the business and first-class sections violently seized control of the aircraft. Two of the flight attendants on board, Betty Ong and Madeline "Amy" Sweeney, had the presence of mind to call American Airlines ground offices and inform them of the situation. The terrorists, using knives and a Mace-like incapacitating agent, had stabbed two flight attendants and slashed the throat of a passenger before forcing their way into the cockpit and overpowering both pilots. Mohamed Atta, the thirty-three-year-old tactical leader of the 9/11 operation and son of an Egyptian lawyer, then sat down in the pilot's seat and took over the controls.

Air traffic control (ATC) personnel first became suspicious when the plane's pilots stopped responding to radio messages. Before long, its identifier on the radar screen disappeared, indicating that someone had turned off its transponder. No doubt remained after Atta inadvertently transmitted publicly a message he intended only for the passengers: "We have some planes. Just stay quiet and we'll be OK. We are returning to the airport. . . . Nobody move. Everything will be OK. If you try to make any moves, you'll endanger yourself and the airplane. Just stay quiet."

West of Albany, New York, Atta turned the airliner away from its northwesterly course, and headed south, toward New York City. A few minutes later, the final transmission: "Nobody move, please. We are going back to the airport. Don't try to make any stupid moves."

An ATC official contacted Otis Air National Guard Base, located on Cape Cod, Massachusetts, and stated, "We have a hijacked aircraft headed towards New York and we need you guys to . . . scramble some F-16s or something up there to help us out." After considerable delay, two McDonnell Douglas F-15 Eagle fighter jets launched, each armed with air-to-air missiles and 20mm cannon. They went supersonic—reaching a speed of Mach 1.4—trying to intercept the hijacked airliner, but it was all for nothing. Before they were even airborne, Flight 11 ceased to exist. Even if they could have intercepted the speeding Boeing, the pilots lacked at that time the authorization—or sufficient reason—to shoot down an unarmed airliner full of passengers.

The last communication with Flight 11 came from flight attendant Sweeney: "Something is wrong. We are in a rapid descent . . . we are all over the place. . . . We are flying low. We are flying very, very low. We are flying way too low. . . . Oh, my God, we are way too low!" The phone call ended abruptly.

At 8:46:40, American 11, flying at a speed of 440 miles per hour, slammed into the 93rd through 99th floors of the 110-story North Tower of New York City's World Trade Center complex.

Attack No. 2: United Airlines Flight 175 — At 8:14 a.m. another Boeing 767-200ER took off from Logan International Airport, also bound for Los Angeles. Aboard were fifty-six passengers and a crew of nine. Two-thirds of the available seats were empty. The scenario for this second hijacking of the morning was almost identical to the previous one: about thirty minutes after takeoff, five Arabic-speaking terrorists seated in the business and first-class sections violently took control of the airliner.

The captain and first officer of Flight 175 were already aware that something was amiss with Flight 11, which had taken off from Logan fifteen minutes before them. ATC had advised Flight 175 to be on the lookout for Flight 11 and to steer clear of it; in addition, the Flight 175 crew had heard terrorist Atta's ominous radio transmission. In spite of this forewarning, they were themselves overpowered by the five terrorists onboard, who then turned the jetliner south toward New York City. By now, trackers on the ground were starting to realize that they had not just one, but two, hijackings in progress. Still, no one knew anything about the hijackers' intentions, their destination, the chaos they were creating inside of each plane—or the unspeakable horror that was yet to come.

A Coast Guard rescue team on its way to the scene of the World Trade Center attack, September 11, 2001. *US Coast Guard/PA2 Tom Sperduto*

The Pentagon as it appeared three
days after the devastating 9/11 terrorist attack.
The airliner hit the west wall traveling 530 miles per hour.
All 64 people aboard the airliner died, along with 125 military
and civilian personnel inside the Pentagon. *DOD/TSgt. Cedric H. Rudisill*

A closer view of the damage done to the Pentagon's west-facing wall, as it appeared
the day after the attack. Some conspiracy theorists asserted that a missile caused
the damage, and not an airliner. Security film and numerous eyewitnesses prove
otherwise. *DOD/R. D. Ward*

As with Flight 11, some of those on Flight 175 made phone calls, revealing that the five terrorist attackers carried knives and an incapacitating agent. They had stabbed at least one flight attendant and apparently killed both of the pilots. Then, twenty-three-year-old Marwan al-Shehhi, a citizen of the United Arab Emirates, took over the controls. Passenger Brian Sweeney revealed in a call that he and other passengers were considering storming the cockpit of the erratically flown jet. Another passenger, Peter Hanson, told his father:

> It's getting bad, Dad. A stewardess was stabbed . . . . Passengers are throwing up and getting sick. The plane is making jerky movements . . . . I think we are going down. I think they intend to go to Chicago or someplace and fly into a building. Don't worry, Dad. If it happens, it'll be very fast. . . . My God . . . my God!

The airliner continued southwest, passing to the west of New York City. After narrowly avoiding collision with two other airliners, it turned and approached Lower Manhattan. It descended very rapidly from twenty-eight thousand feet, and at 9:03:02 a.m.—just over sixteen minutes after Flight 11 had hit the North Tower—it flew straight into the South Tower, killing all sixty-five people aboard. It crashed into the 77th through 85th floors, while in a left-banking turn, flying at a speed of 540 miles per hour. Flight 175 had the dubious distinction of being the only one of the four ill-fated 9/11 airliners to crash on live TV, as the entire world watched in horror.

It was now devastatingly clear to everyone that these two horrendous crashes were not accidents. The United States was under attack—and there was more to come.

Attack No. 3: American Airlines Flight 77 — The third doomed aircraft that morning was a Boeing 757-200, which—like the previous two hijacked airliners—was bound for Los Angeles. Like Flight 175, two-thirds of the seats were empty. Only fifty-eight passengers were aboard, along with a crew of six. Again, five armed terrorists sat near the front of the aircraft.

The airliner departed Washington Dulles International Airport at 8:20 a.m. and proceeded west. At just over thirty-one minutes into the flight, the terrorists took over the airliner and turned it back toward Washington, DC, with its transponder switched off. By this time, Flight 11 had already crashed into the World Trade Center and it was obvious that hijackers were in control of Flight 175; it therefore seemed certain to everyone on the ground that Flight 77 had suffered a similar fate. Terrorist Hani Hanjour, a twenty-nine-year-old Saudi Arabian who had obtained a commercial pilot's license in the United States two years earlier, was at the controls.

As with the two other commandeered airliners, some of those aboard Flight 77 were surreptitiously able to make telephone calls from either their personal cell phones or the airliner's seatback phones. Flight attendant Renee May informed her mother that her plane had been hijacked, and that everyone had been moved to the rear of the aircraft. She asked her to notify American Airlines. Passenger Barbara Olson called her husband, US Solicitor General Theodore Olson. She told him terrorists armed with knives and box cutters had hijacked her plane. All he could do was to tell her the upsetting news that two airliners had crashed into the World Trade Center.

At 9:32 a.m., ATC observed "a primary radar target" heading toward Washington, DC, at a high rate of speed. It was Flight 77. Controllers advised the Secret Service that it might be heading toward the White House. Fighter jets from Langley Air Force Base, Virginia, were scrambled, but in the confusion, they were vectored in the wrong direction. It did not matter anyway: it was too late.

At 9:37:46 a.m., Flight 77, traveling at full power in a 530-mile-per-hour dive, slammed into the west-facing wall of the Pentagon, located just outside of Washington, DC. All 64 people aboard perished, along with another 125 inside the Pentagon. The withering fire—fed by 7,500 gallons of jet fuel—reached an estimated two thousand degrees Fahrenheit and took several days to extinguish.

Attack No. 4: United Airlines Flight 93 — This was the fourth and final jetliner deliberately crashed on 9/11. It too was sparsely booked, with passengers in only one-fifth of the seats. However, it differed from the other three hijacked flights in that there were only four terrorists aboard, and its destination was San Francisco. It was also destined to be the only jetliner not to hit any structure on the ground. This was because a group of passengers onboard had the time and courage to rise up against the terrorists and thwart their malevolent plan.

The Boeing 757-200 took off at 8:42 a.m. from Newark Liberty International Airport after a twenty-five-minute delay. The delay could have been a lifesaver for everyone aboard, for by this time, authorities knew about the Flight 11 hijacking. Unfortunately, they neglected to take any precautionary action. Had they immediately stopped all takeoffs, Flight 93 would never have left the ground. Instead, thirty-seven passengers and a crew of seven took off, never to return. Four minutes after Flight 93 was airborne, Flight 11 crashed into the World Trade Center, followed sixteen minutes later by Flight 175.

After Flight 93 reached its cruising altitude of thirty-one thousand feet, the pilots received a message from a United Airlines flight dispatcher, advising them to "beware any cockpit intrusion." It further stated that two aircraft had hit the World Trade Center.

Whatever precautions the Flight 93 crew may have taken were not enough. The aircraft suddenly descended seven hundred feet, after which a strange radio transmission emanated from the jetliner: sounds of struggling, with a voice shouting, "Mayday!" and "Hey, get out of here!"

Controllers were unsuccessfully trying to contact the airliner, now over eastern Ohio, when they heard, "Ladies and gentlemen: Here the captain, please sit down keep remaining sitting. We have a bomb onboard. So, sit."

The airliner, by now over Cleveland, turned back toward the southeast and gained altitude. At least a dozen passengers and crew members managed to make phone calls revealing that knife-wielding terrorists wearing red bandanas had hijacked the plane. They had killed or injured at least three people and had forced everyone to the rear of the aircraft.

One of the passengers, Tom Burnett, called his wife in California and said, "The plane has been hijacked. We're in the air. They've already knifed a guy. There's a bomb on board. Call the FBI." Other passengers and crew members made similar calls, confirming to the world the horror occurring high in the skies over Ohio and Pennsylvania.

By this time, the FAA knew beyond any doubt that terrorists had hijacked four airliners. Consequently, they took the unprecedented action of ordering all 4,500 aircraft in the skies over the United States to land, regardless of destination. United Flight 93, now under the control of terrorists, was one of the few that ignored this order. Terrorist Ziad Jarrah, a twenty-six-year-old from a wealthy Lebanese family, pointed the big Boeing toward Washington, DC.

The phone calls from those aboard Flight 93 indicate that some of them were formulating a plan to retake the aircraft from the terrorists. Knowing that terrorists had already intentionally crashed other airliners, they resolved to go down fighting. Tom Burnett told his wife, "A group of us is going to do something." When she protested, he replied, "If they're going to crash the plane into the ground, we have to do something. We can't wait for the authorities. We have to do something now."

Another passenger, thirty-two-year-old software manager Todd Beamer, spoke and prayed for several minutes on his seatback phone with a telephone supervisor in Chicago. Near the end, she overheard Beamer through the still-open phone line utter perhaps the most memorable words of this tragic day: "Are you guys ready? Let's roll."

Moments later, flight attendant Sandy Bradshaw told her husband, "Everyone's running to first class. I've got to go. Bye." Another caller yelled,

"They're doing it! They're doing it! They're doing it!" Then the line went dead.

At 9:57 a.m., the passenger assault on the terrorists began. The cockpit voice recorder revealed the sounds of the uprising—shouts, thumps, grunts, glass breaking. The struggle continued, while terrorist pilot Jarrah desperately rolled the airplane back and forth trying to knock the attacking passengers off balance. He instructed a fellow jihadist to block the cockpit door while he continued to throw the jetliner around the sky, but the determined impromptu assault continued. At 10:02:23 a.m., with the passengers only seconds away from entering the cockpit, Jarrah rolled the jetliner on its back, while his comrade shouted in Arabic, "*Allahu Akbar! Allahu Akbar!*"—Allah is the greatest! Allah is the greatest!

At 10:03:11 a.m., Flight 93 plunged into a remote field near Shanksville, Pennsylvania—only twenty minutes short of Washington, DC. It hit the ground in a forty-degree inverted dive, at a speed of 563 miles per hour. No one on the ground was injured. The intrepid group of passengers, who fought to the final second, did not succeed in saving their own lives; but by forcing the terrorists to dive the jet into the ground prematurely, they saved countless additional innocent lives and prevented the loss of yet another precious national asset.

A Day of Infamy

Within a space of seventy-seven minutes, four jetliners had been turned into manned, guided missiles and crashed, killing all 265 people aboard. The first three of these had hit targets on the ground, instantly killing many more. However, even this was not tragedy enough for this day of horror. The intense heat generated by the combined twenty thousand gallons of burning jet fuel from American Airlines Flight 11 and United Airlines Flight 175 weakened the structures of the two World Trade Center towers such that at 9:59, the South Tower collapsed, followed at 10:28 by the North Tower. Before this occurred, 200 desperate human beings jumped from the tops of the Twin Towers to certain death more than a thousand feet below. The total disintegration of the two skyscrapers, with thousands of people still trapped inside, brought the total death toll for the day to approximately 3,000. Among the dead were more than 400 heroic emergency rescue workers.

These are the known fatalities from 9/11. No one will ever know how many additional deaths occurred later—and are still occurring—as a direct result of the massive clouds of lethal toxins and carcinogens released by the collapse of the Twin Towers. Equally immeasurable are the pain and

sorrow that families and friends of the victims have had to endure ever
since that day.

A Failure of Imagination

The events of 9/11 may well be the best-documented terrorist attack
in history: audio transcripts, photos, video recordings, and eyewitness
reports; innumerable books, articles, and TV documentaries; and the
voluminous findings of a major governmental investigatory commission.
Even with this unprecedented wealth of evidence, the inevitable conspiracy
theorists soon emerged to present their alternative theories of what "really"
happened that day.

Most center around the strange notion that the attacks were all part
of a vast US government conspiracy. The hijacked airliners were really
remotely flown military aircraft; the Twin Towers were brought down
by explosive charges on the ground; Flight 93 was actually shot down by
another airplane; Air Force fighter jets failed to intervene because they
were ordered to stand down; the Pentagon was not struck by an airliner at
all, but by a missile.

The conspiracy vendors never proved any of these allegations, nor did
they ever make a strong case for why the US government would commit
such atrocities against its own people. Instead, the best-documented—and
most scathing—criticism came from the nation's own self-evaluation,
which is summarized in the 9/11 Commission's Final Report. The attack, it
concluded, was "a failure of policy, management, capability, and above all, a
failure of imagination."

The facts are indisputable. A close examination of the reams of hard
evidence indicates that the terrorist attacks of 9/11 were exactly what
they appeared to be—a well-planned sneak attack by a fanatically suicidal
enemy on an unsuspecting nation.

On that day when airliners full of innocent people fell from the skies—
only to kill more innocents on the ground—a military officer monitoring
the attacks was heard to say, "This is a new type of war. . . ." It was also a
new type of *world*, in which no one was safe anymore. The war on terror
continues, and probably will for years to come. Even so, Americans will
never forget—or forgive—the criminals responsible for those four tragic,
life-ending flights that caused what many still remember as "the saddest
day in US history."

CHAPTER FOURTEEN
GONE WITH THE WIND

"'PIMPERNEL' HOWARD HAS MADE HIS LAST TRIP."

British Overseas Airways Corporation (BOAC) Flight 777-A lifted off from Lisbon, Portugal, on the morning of June 1, 1943, en route to England. The scheduled one-thousand-mile, seven-hour flight would take the Douglas DC-3, its thirteen passengers, and crew of four in a northerly direction across the Atlantic Ocean's Bay of Biscay. Its destination was Whitchurch Airport, located near the southwestern English city of Bristol. Among the more prominent passengers aboard were a Jewish leader with important connections to the British government, a Reuters news correspondent, and two highly placed corporate executives. A slender, fragile-looking, blond-haired Englishman named Leslie Stainer was also aboard the flight; however, just about everyone knew Stainer best by his other name, Leslie Howard, the internationally acclaimed actor who had starred in the blockbuster movie *Gone with the Wind*.

The flight proceeded without incident as the twin-engine transport headed north, up the western coasts of Portugal and Spain, and out over the open waters of the Bay of Biscay. The world was at war, so no area of the European sky was completely safe. This was, however, a regularly scheduled civilian flight over international waters, and it had originated from a neutral country. The pilots hoped that as long as they steered clear of the French coast, hostile aircraft would leave them unmolested.

Just before 11:00 a.m., when the airliner was about two hundred miles off the northern coast of Spain, ground dispatchers in England received a radio distress signal from the crew of Flight 777-A: "I am being followed by

A BOAC-operated Douglas DC-3 airliner sitting on the tarmac at Gibraltar airport, circa 1943. Wartime searchlights silhouette it while the Rock of Gibraltar looms in the background. This could be the same plane that Leslie Howard boarded in Lisbon. *Royal Air Force*

strange aircraft. Putting on best speed. . . . We are being attacked. Cannon shells and tracers are going through the fuselage. Wave-hopping and doing my best." Then, only silence.

Murder in the Air

It was not until later that the world learned how the events of that day unfolded, but a German *Luftwaffe* flight of fighter-bombers on their way home from a submarine escort mission intercepted the airliner. The DC-3 was over the Bay of Biscay, heading north at an altitude of between seven and ten thousand feet. The eight twin-engine Junkers Ju 88C-6s belonged to 14 *Staffel* of *Gruppe* V/*Kampfgeschwader* 40, based in occupied France, near Bordeaux. Almost immediately, two of the Nazi warplanes took aim at the defenseless airliner and opened fire. They quickly set the DC-3 ablaze, after which it plunged into the Atlantic Ocean. The German pilots lingered only long enough to document their victory by circling and taking photographs of the wreckage in the water before it sank. The attack was little more than an aerial firing squad, a mass execution. Those aboard

A captured German Junkers Ju 88D photographed sometime after the war at Wright-Patterson Air Force Base, Ohio. On June 1, 1943, a flight of eight German fighters similar to this one attacked the airliner in which Leslie Howard was riding. *American Aviation Historical Society*

the airliner had no chance to defend themselves and no possibility of surviving. Leslie Howard and sixteen other innocent civilians were dead.

The Lisbon–Bristol flight was a regularly scheduled shuttle that BOAC had been operating since September 1940. The airline employed a half dozen Dutch crews and aircraft that had managed to escape to Britain before the May 1940 German invasion of the Netherlands. The ex-KLM Royal Dutch Airlines craft and crews had successfully completed more than five hundred trips over the previous three years, but the long over-water flights were anything but uneventful. Wartime airspace was constantly contested by Great Britain and Germany—and heavily patrolled by marauding fighters from both sides. Twice in the previous six months, *Luftwaffe* fighters had attacked the same plane in which Howard and his fellow fliers ultimately died on June 3. The DC-3-194, bearing the name *Ibis* and the registration designation G-AGBB, had in both cases sustained significant damage but managed to arrive at its destination. The passengers were undoubtedly aware of this when they boarded the airliner. These were dangerous skies. On that day, they would be deadly.

When *Ibis* failed to arrive at Whitchurch, Royal Australian Air Force 461 Squadron sent out two Short Sunderland flying boats to search for the airplane and any possible survivors. They found nothing—no wreckage, no bodies, no oil slick. The ocean had apparently sucked the DC-3 and its occupants into its depths without a trace. A further search the following day—during which a Sunderland was forced to fend off an attack by another *Schwarm* of eight German Ju 88s—also failed to turn up any sign of the missing airliner. Consequently, all those aboard, including Leslie Howard, were presumed dead. Shortly after, the Germans made it official when they announced that their fighters had shot down a transport plane over the Bay of Biscay. It could only have been *Ibis*.

Both Allied and neutral powers decried the unprovoked attack as a war crime, and BOAC suspended any further daytime flights. Why they had allowed this particular flight to continue in broad daylight without any protection after the previous attacks is a question that remains unanswered. Equally open to conjecture was why the Germans decided to shoot down this particular airliner—which had flown this route on a regular

The Douglas DC-3 *Ibis*, as it appeared when operated by KLM. Here, it sits on the tarmac with engines running, date and place unknown. In 1940, the British Overseas Airways Corporation (BOAC) leased this aircraft from KLM and painted it in brown and green camouflage colors. On June 1, 1943, Leslie Howard and sixteen other innocent civilians died in it when German fighters shot it down into the Bay of Biscay.

Map showing the intended route of Flight 777A from Lisbon, Portugal, to Bristol, England. German fighters downed the unarmed Douglas DC-3 about two hundred miles off the northern coast of Spain.

basis for the past three years—on this particular day. Was it a coincidence, or were they specifically targeting one of the VIPs aboard?

A Talented Patriot

Leslie Steiner—later anglicized to "Stainer"—was born in London on April 3, 1893. After graduating from an exclusive London boys' school, he worked as a bank clerk until the outbreak of World War I, during which he served in the trenches as a subaltern in the British Army's Northamptonshire Yeomanry. After suffering a severe case of shell shock, the Army invalided him out of the service.

Soon, he began to pursue acting, initially as a form of therapy recommended by one of his doctors. Before long, the talented and handsome young British performer, who by now had adopted the stage name Leslie Howard, had become a star of both stage and silent screen in England. It was only a matter of time before he migrated to the United States, where he found even greater success—first on Broadway, and later, in movies. During the 1930s, he made twenty-two films, eighteen of them in Hollywood. Critics still regard several of these, including *The Scarlet Pimpernel* and *The Petrified Forest*, as classics. His work in Hollywood culminated in 1939 with a costarring role, opposite Vivien Leigh and Clark Gable, in the immortal Civil War epic *Gone with the Wind*. Over the course of his illustrious career, Howard received many awards and two Academy Award nominations for Best Actor.

Yet, Howard was not only a talented actor and well-known star—he was a patriot. When Europe went to war again in 1939, he returned at the age of forty-six to his native England and began serving his country by producing, directing, starring in, and even financing anti-Nazi propaganda films. These included *"Pimpernel" Smith*, *In Which We Serve*, *The Lamp Still Burns*, and *The First of the Few*. In the latter movie, which was probably the best of Howard's wartime films, he portrayed R. J. Mitchell, the cancer-stricken designer of Britain's most famous fighter, the Supermarine Spitfire.

Leslie Howard's patriotic activities extended well beyond filmmaking. He participated in wartime fundraising activities and, aided by his fluency in German, made numerous anti-Nazi radio broadcasts. His effectiveness in this regard—along with his Jewish background—made him a focal point of hatred from anti-Semitic Nazi leaders. Nazi Propaganda Minister Joseph Goebbels, whom Howard had personally lampooned in one of his movies, particularly despised him. This loathing was so great that the notorious British traitor and Nazi propagandist William Joyce—better known to the

Leslie Howard signs autographs for fans on February 15, 1943, while visiting US Eighth Air Force personnel at Watford, England. A few months later, the Hollywood idol, propagandist, and patriot would be dead. *US Army Signal Corps*

world as "Lord Haw-Haw"—publicly announced that Goebbels intended to execute Howard if he ever got him in his grasp.

Many have speculated that this political aspect of Howard's career led to his death. They believe he was the primary target of the German aerial marauders that blasted his airliner out of the sky. There is no evidence he really was a spy, as the Germans alleged, but his activities in support of the British government were no secret. The British Council, an organization promoting British culture, had asked Howard in 1943 to travel to neutral Spain and Portugal on a "goodwill tour." When he hesitated, British Foreign Secretary Anthony Eden personally convinced him to go. Officially, he was visiting the two neutral countries to promote his movies, but his underlying purpose was to drum up support for the Allied cause against the fascists.

Consequently, he spent the entire month of May traveling throughout the Iberian Peninsula making public appearances. His efforts were highly successful, even though Spain—technically a neutral country—was controlled by fascist dictator Gen. Francisco Franco. Not only did nearly a thousand cinemas in Spain and Portugal willingly show Howard's anti-Nazi propaganda movies, Portuguese viewers selected his *"Pimpernel" Smith* as film of the year. Howard may also have used his connections to meet with General Franco himself, to lobby for Spain's continued neutrality.

German agents shadowed Howard everywhere he went in Iberia and reported on his activities. Goebbels was furious at the headway the British actor was making in direct opposition to his own Nazi propaganda efforts in the peninsula's two neutral countries. It seems likely that the Nazis were simply biding their time until they could exact revenge on Howard.

Their opportunity came when Howard suddenly appeared with his manager at Lisbon's Portela Airport and bumped two lower-priority passengers to board Flight 777-A, setting the stage for the aerial assassination that was to follow. It is generally assumed that the German Ju 88s intentionally attacked Howard's unarmed airliner and killed all seventeen people aboard just to eliminate him. But was he the real target?

A Case of Mistaken Identity?

The Nazis were exuberant at Howard's tragic death. Goebbels boasted in his propagandist newspaper *Der Angriff*, "'Pimpernel' Howard has made his last trip." Howard's propaganda work had done great damage to the Nazi cause, so the Germans were happy to be rid of him.

But had they done so on purpose? According to another compelling theory, the Germans may have had a different and more important target in mind. Howard's business partner and manager, Alfred T. Chenhalls, was with Howard at Lisbon's Portela Airport prior to their last flight. This busy wartime flying field, located in one of the few neutral European countries that remained, was a major crossroads for international travelers and spies alike. For this reason, Howard and Chenhalls were in plain view of many interested observers as they waited to board their flight. Chenhalls was a portly, middle-aged, cigar-smoking chap who just happened to bear a strong physical resemblance to Prime Minister Churchill. Thus some have speculated that Leslie Howard was not the primary target in the infamous shoot-down at all, but rather Winston Churchill.

Proponents of this theory hypothesize that German agents or sympathizers observed Chenhalls in the airport terminal with Howard and misidentified him as the bulldog-jawed "blood, sweat, and tears" prime minister of Great Britain. Leslie Howard even bore a striking resemblance to Churchill's bodyguard, Detective Inspector Walter H. Thompson, so Howard and Chenhalls may have been mistaken for the prime minister and his bodyguard. The fact that Churchill was known to be in the region at the time, touring North Africa, made it all the more believable and bolstered the possibility that he might have been traveling back to England via Lisbon. In fact, British agents may have intentionally planted this disinformation to mislead their German counterparts. Thus, the mistaken identity theory is not as far-fetched as it may seem. Certainly, the Nazis would have jumped at the chance to intercept the prime minister's aircraft. They would have stopped at nothing—including the atrocity of shooting down an unarmed civilian airliner full of innocent people—if there was the slightest possibility of killing their most hated and most dangerous enemy.

This theory has its drawbacks. First, it seems unlikely that trained German agents would have mistaken a man as well-known as Winston Churchill. Equally important, many—including Churchill himself in his memoirs—have questioned why anyone would even suspect that a powerful world leader, with a great navy and air force at his disposal, would risk his life flying in an unprotected commercial aircraft in broad daylight over enemy-patrolled territory. In truth, the prime minister flew back to England from Gibraltar four days later in his own personal aircraft, an Avro Type 685 York four-engine transport. He was never anywhere near Lisbon.

Other Likely Suspects

Others have speculated that the target for the attack on Flight 777-A was neither Leslie Howard nor Winston Churchill. The Nazis would undoubtedly have liked to send to the bottom of the sea certain other passengers aboard the doomed BOAC transport. Topping the list was Wilfrid B. Israel, a wealthy British Jew and ardent Zionist with important connections within the British government. He was returning to Britain from a two-month investigation into the plight of Jewish refugees in the Iberian Peninsula. His plan for enlisting the British government to help provide them aid and safe passage to Palestine no doubt rankled many of those in the anti-Semitic Nazi regime.

The Nazis might also have been targeting other passengers on flight 777-A—or even someone bumped from the flight at the last minute. Wartime flights were mostly limited to high-ranking diplomats and government officials, military members, and VIPs who had special clearance to fly. For that reason, most BOAC flights between Lisbon and the United Kingdom provided a target-rich environment for enemy assassins. However, if Israel or anyone else on Flight 777-A, other than Leslie Howard, was the object of the heinous attack, no evidence has ever surfaced to prove it.

There remains yet another possible explanation for the downing of Leslie Howard's airliner. Perhaps it was nothing more sinister than a tragic misjudgment on the part of the attacking German airmen. They were five hundred miles from home and getting low on fuel, so the *Luftwaffe* commander of the enemy formation, *Oberleutnant* Herbert Hintze, had to make a quick decision: either shoot the airliner down or let it go. The airliner was civilian operated and carrying civilian passengers, but it was also en route to Britain, the country with which his nation was at war. In addition, the DC-3 carried wartime camouflage colors to make it less visible to other aircraft in the sky. This paint scheme was perhaps a logical wartime precaution, but it may also have suggested to Hintze that the airliner had a military purpose that made it fair game.

The German pilots involved in the Howard shootdown, including Hintze, claimed that this was indeed the case. After the war, they contended—to a man—that the Flight 777-A DC-3 appeared to be an enemy military aircraft, and therefore a legitimate target. They expressed regret at having shot down a plane filled with innocent civilians and claimed outrage at not having been informed of the scheduled civilian flight from Lisbon to England that day. Had they known, they insisted, they would never have attacked it.

Not everyone accepts the German pilots' story. Their version may have been a rationalization to ease their guilty consciences—or an out-and-out fabrication, intended to ward off accusations of war crimes. Ultimately, no hard evidence exists to prove that this despicable action was an intentional attempt to assassinate Leslie Howard, Winston Churchill, Wilfred Israel, or anyone else; nor can anyone say for sure that the shootdown was anything more than a tragic mistake.

⎯★⎯

The circumstances surrounding the killing of Leslie Howard and the other passengers of Flight 777-A remain unclear, even after seven decades of research that have resulted in numerous books, articles, and documentaries. One thing is certain: it was an appalling tragedy for the victims, their families, and friends. It was an especially painful blow to Howard's fans worldwide, who felt a personal bond with the talented and sophisticated idol of stage and screen.

CHAPTER FIFTEEN

A PLANE THAT FELL IN THE MOUNTAINS

"THEY SURVIVED BY BEING RESOURCEFUL."

On October 13, 1972, a Uruguayan Air Force-chartered transport with forty-five souls aboard took off from the airport at Mendoza, Argentina. Its destination was Santiago, Chile, on the western side of the formidable Andes Mountains. Nothing appeared amiss with the Fairchild-Hiller FH-227D twin-engine turboprop as it took off and faded into the distant Andean skies. Yet, it never reached its destination. No one saw where it went, and no one received a single emergency call from it. It simply disappeared. The ensuing search operation, though extensive, failed to turn up any trace of the missing plane. It was as if a towering mountain peak had snatched it and its human cargo from the sky and swallowed it whole.

It would take ten long weeks for the mountains to give up the secret of the missing transport and its passengers, which would prove to be one of history's most incredible survival exploits. The widespread celebration of this inspiring tale of human endurance was, however, short-lived. Admiration would soon turn to revulsion.

A Difficult Flight

Fifteen members of the amateur Old Christians rugby team from Montevideo, Uruguay, had chartered the military transport to take them to a tournament in Santiago, Chile. For the young players, most of whom were

A Fairchild-Hiller FH-227D, painted in the colors of Uruguayan Air Force Flight 571 for the movie *Alive*. It is almost identical in appearance to the one that crashed in the Andes Mountains on October 13, 1972.

also students, the trip would be an exciting, fun-filled excursion to a foreign country—a new experience for most of them. They chose the Uruguayan Air Force (*Fuerza Aérea Uruguaya*) transport because the charter fee, equivalent at the time to $1,600 US, was considerably cheaper than flying commercial—provided they could fill the seats with paying passengers. To help with that, they enlisted family members and friends to come along. On the day of departure, the practically new American-built airliner was at near capacity with forty passengers and a Uruguayan Air Force crew of five.

The transport, designated Flight 571, left Montevideo on October 12 for Santiago, some 850 miles due west. However, bad weather ahead prompted the pilots to divert to Mendoza, Argentina, a city in the eastern foothills of the massive Andean mountain range, 120 miles northeast of Santiago. Here, they prudently decided to wait overnight until mountain conditions had improved.

The experienced captain of the transport, Col. Julio César Ferradas, was well aware of the dangers inherent in flying through the Andes. The mighty mountain chain had claimed more than its share of fliers who dared to challenge its supremacy. It is not only the world's longest continental mountain range, but also the second highest. Because the chain of mountain peaks, or *cordillera*, in this area reaches upward to well above twenty thousand feet, Ferradas felt it advisable to navigate his heavily loaded propeller-driven aircraft from Mendoza to Santiago at lower altitude through one of the established mountain passes. This required weaving below and through a seventy-five-mile wall of seemingly impenetrable snow-covered peaks. Obviously, this could only be accomplished on the clearest of days. Even with optimal weather conditions, Ferradas had yet another hazard with which to contend: the notoriously treacherous turbulent air currents so characteristic of this mighty mountain chain. Some of his impatient young passengers considered him overly cautious for diverting to Mendoza, but the veteran pilot knew things they did not.

The next day, as Ferradas checked weather reports, one of the impatient young rugby players badgered him and his copilot, Lt. Col. Dante Héctor Lagurara, to go ahead and take off. Ferradas' joking reply was tragically prophetic: "Do you want your parents to read in the papers that forty-five Uruguayans are lost in the *cordillera*?"

The young passenger's taunts aside, Ferradas knew that he had to make a decision. Argentinean law required his Uruguayan military aircraft to vacate the country that day, so he had to either continue the journey as planned or return to Uruguay. The latter would mean a sizeable loss in revenue for the already financially strapped Uruguayan Air Force, so he chose to go on. Fortunately, weather reports indicated that one of the aerial trails through the Andes, the Planchón Pass, would be clear enough to navigate by early afternoon. This left only the turbulence to contend with—though at that time of day, it would be at its worst. Still, the experienced military pilot felt he could safely complete the flight. Consequently, at 2:18 p.m. the big transport and its passengers departed the airport at Mendoza. The date was October 13—a Friday.

A Plan Gone Wrong

The flight plan called for a southerly heading from Mendoza to the Planchón Pass. Here the big, high-winged turboprop would turn west and fly through the mountain pass to the town of Curicó, Chile, which lay on the western side of the Andes. At this point, Ferradas and Lagurara would turn north and begin their descent for a landing at Santiago's Pudahuel International Airport, some one hundred miles to the north.

The plan was relatively straightforward, but executing it would be considerably more complicated. As Flight 571 flew into the pass, a thick layer of clouds still completely obscured the terrain below; but it was too late to

Intended route of Flight 571 from Montevideo, Uruguay, to Santiago, Chile. After diverting overnight to Mendoza, Argentina, the military transport flew south to the Planchón Pass and then west through the mountains toward the town of Curicó, Chile. Here, it would have turned north and descended for landing at Santiago, but it crashed in the mountains before reaching Curicó.

turn back. After the pilots weaved their way through the peaks to the location they believed to be the all-important checkpoint at Curicó, they turned and began a blind descent into the clouds. What they could not know is that the tailwind they had last recorded had since become a headwind. With no visible checkpoints to verify groundspeeds or positions, they could only guess where they were. Instead of being over Curicó, they were still in the mountains well east of it. Thus, when they began their descent, they were diving directly into the rocky peaks of the Andes Mountains.

The first indication that anything was wrong was the fierce turbulence that suddenly took away the breath of the plane's occupants as they descended into the mountains below. One unnamed young passenger, in a lame attempt at humor, grabbed the cabin microphone and announced, "Ladies and gentlemen, please put on your parachutes. We are about to land in the *cordillera*." Before anyone could laugh, the aircraft hit a vicious downdraft and plunged several hundred feet, scaring the shtick out of the jokester and everyone else aboard. When this happened yet again, the struggling transport suddenly dropped below the cloud layer and into the clear.

The scene that burst into the view of those looking out their windows was nothing short of nightmarish. Instead of the expected fertile Chilean fields far below, they saw jagged pieces of rock screaming past only ten feet below the wingtip. The pilots immediately shoved the throttles forward for full power and attempted to climb, but it was too late. The right wing smashed into the rocks and immediately sheared off. As the severed wing ripped loose from the plane, it sliced through the tail, tearing it off the fuselage. With it went two crew members and three passengers, all still strapped in their seats. By this time, the left wing too had broken off, leaving the wingless metal canister to plunge like a missile into the snow and rock below. It hit the mountainside at well over two hundred miles per hour, sucking out two more passengers from the now-open rear of the plane. Many of the remaining seats broke loose, crushing bodies, and filling the air with a deafening cacophony of noise—not least of which was the screams of fear and agony from those still alive. The fuselage continued to career down the side of the mountain, like a huge metallic sledge, until it screeched to a stop in a small valley. The air was suddenly very frigid inside the fuselage and for a moment, everything was strangely quiet. Then, all anyone could hear were the hysterical screams. The real ordeal was about to begin.

Situation: Hopeless

Of the forty-five people aboard, thirty-four survived the immediate crash. That *anyone* lived through the wingless airliner's high-speed collision with the mountainside was truly a miracle, let alone three-quarters of the passengers and crew. Those who somehow escaped serious injury eventually regained their senses. They pulled themselves from the wreckage and began to do what they could to help those who had been less fortunate. Many were in shock and suffering agonizing pain from their injuries.

The dead included pilot Ferradas, the seven sucked out of the back of the plane, and three others in the main cabin who died on impact. Another with a severed leg died of blood loss within minutes. Copilot Lagurara was alive, but wedged in the crushed cockpit next to the pilot. He too would soon die.

The surviving passengers assessed their situation. They were stranded—surrounded by dead, dying, and severely injured people—in an open airliner fuselage on a snowy mountain in one of the most remote spots on Earth. They had no idea where they were, and all they could see in any direction was snow and mountain peaks. According to the airplane's altimeter, they were sitting at nearly twelve thousand feet—more than two miles—above sea level. In this air, any exertion caused shortness of breath and fatigue, and the temperatures could dip to well below zero degrees Fahrenheit. With no source of heat, it was as bitterly frigid inside the thin aluminum walls as it was outside. To add to the misery, there was little of use in the tailless, wingless aircraft cabin. Virtually no food, water, medical supplies, fuel, blankets, or extra clothing were available—and none of those aboard had dressed for anything cooler than an evening stroll in downtown Santiago.

Yet another casualty of the crash was the plane's radio transmitter. This meant the survivors had no way of contacting the outside world for help. Finally, as a crowning touch to the perfectly miserable state of affairs, snow began to fall minutes after the crash. The rapidly accumulating flakes on and around the light-colored fuselage shell rendered it all the more invisible from the air. It was in all respects an utterly hopeless situation for the survivors of Flight 571. They had every reason to envy those who had died instantly and suffered no more.

As darkness began to fall, the crash survivors settled in for the longest, coldest, and most painful night of their lives. All suffered from varying degrees of emotional and physical injury and all were freezing in the subzero, high-altitude environment. They huddled together and took turns pummeling each other to keep their blood circulating. Even so, many of them suffered debilitating injury from frostbite. The only relief they might have had was sleep, but circumstances denied them even that. The bitter cold and the screams of the injured did not permit it. A few were delirious, while others were fortunate enough to be unconscious. Those who escaped injury included three medical students who tried to help those in pain, but without even the most basic medical supplies, they could do very little. If there was any merciful aspect of these darkest hours, it was that none of the survivors had any inkling of what was to come. They were better off not knowing how many more hellish days and nights they would have to endure before rescue—or death—freed them from their misery. Death claimed three more by morning, and many others would perish in the days to come.

Obtaining drinking water was the first order of business for the survivors. As they gasped to breathe in the arid, high-altitude environment, they quickly became thirsty. Fortunately, there were mountains full of H_2O all around them, in the form of snow—but they quickly found that sucking on ice while freezing to death was a distinctly unpleasant way to stay hydrated. They soon devised a way to melt the snow in a makeshift container atop the sun-heated metal fuselage. They now had all the drinking water they needed.

A much bigger problem was the almost total lack of food. When the already-hungry survivors inventoried their meager supplies, they found only a few snack items. Even with the most severe rationing, these would last only a few days. Their new high-altitude home was in reality a subzero desert, completely unfit for human or animal habitation. It offered nothing but several feet of snow under which were only a few inedible lichens. It was an environment so inhospitable that even wild animals avoided it. Even had there been any other living creatures available to serve as food, the survivors had no way to catch them.

The Chilean Aerial Rescue Service launched a major search operation immediately after the Uruguayan transport failed to arrive in Santiago. It continued, as weather permitted, for ten days. The desperate survivors repeatedly saw and heard planes in the sky, but help never came. The light-colored, snow-covered metal fuselage was invisible to those overhead. The stranded passengers had been able to get bits and pieces of information on a transistor radio that had survived the crash, and when they eventually heard the devastating news that authorities had suspended the search, their spirits sank. They resigned themselves to remaining on the snowy mountain until they died of exposure or starvation.

The days continued to pass slowly and painfully. The starving survivors grew weaker, more irritable, and more depressed. Some were dangerously close to hysteria. They were also steadily becoming fewer in number. One after another of the more severely injured died, in most cases after a protracted period of excruciating pain.

Then, with the situation seemingly as bad as it could possibly get, disaster struck again. On October 29, the seventeenth night of their ordeal, a freak avalanche fell onto the open-ended fuselage and its beleaguered inhabitants, dumping tons of snow on them as they slept. Eight of them smothered to death before the others could disinter them from their snowy grave. The living now numbered only nineteen. In the days to come, this number would dwindle further, leaving a final contingent of sixteen frightened young men.

Dying for Something to Eat

It had become obvious to the survivors that help from the outside world was out of the question. They resolved somehow to take control of their fate. This, however, would require physical strength and endurance, which in turn required adequate nourishment. Most of the few food items they had salvaged from the crash were long gone, and nothing edible existed in their frozen, lifeless world. As they grew weaker and more desperate by the day, only one solution remained. One of the starving survivors, Fernando Parrado, was the first to verbalize it. He stated perhaps jokingly that if necessary, he would "cut meat from one of the dead pilots—after all, they got us into this mess." Before long, the discussion took on a more serious tone.

The starving survivors could no longer ignore the obvious. They needed food, not only to stay alive, but also to maintain enough strength to find help. Yet, there was only one source of protein available to them—the flesh of their dead comrades, lying preserved in the snow and ice all around them. Though sickened by the thought, they eventually came to realize, one by one, that the unspeakable was their only salvation. They began eating the raw flesh of their deceased fellow passengers.

Cannibalism is, with a few exceptions, taboo among the human race. However, "survival cannibalism"—eating human flesh out of necessity to remain alive—is more common. One of the most notorious instances of this occurred in the American West during the winter of 1846 to 1847. A group of eighty-one American pioneers, known as the Donner Party, became stranded in the snowy Sierra Nevada Mountains while traveling by wagon train to California. To avoid starvation, some of them resorted to devouring the flesh of those who had died. The Flight 571 survivors found themselves in a similar predicament. Not surprisingly, they responded in a similar fashion.

Expedition to Civilization

The days and weeks in the freezing aluminum fuselage shell passed slowly for the remaining sixteen survivors as they learned to cope with the brutal conditions. Thanks to the nutrition, they slowly regained some of their lost strength. They elected a few of the fittest and strongest to venture out on an expedition to find help. Those selected received extra rations and an exemption from their daily duties so that they might rest and gain strength.

Finally, on December 11, traveling conditions were right. It had been nearly two full months since the unscheduled arrival of Flight 571 at its final resting place on the mountain. Even the supply of human food was running low. It was now or never. They had previously launched a number of local excursions, none of which turned up any signs of civilization. This time, however, the selected team of three resolved to keep going until they either found help or died trying.

A few hours after departing, the three explorers decided that one of them should hand over his provisions to the other two and return to the airliner. The extra food the remaining two carried would increase their range significantly—perhaps enough to make all the difference. The remaining two, Roberto Canessa and Fernando Parrado, continued on, doggedly. They climbed, waded through snow up to their hips, and slipped and slid up one mountain slope and down another. One of the peaks they traversed towered to an altitude of nearly fifteen thousand feet. With nothing to lose, they kept going.

After seven days, they staggered over a ridge and saw before them a river and patches of green. As they continued on, they came upon cows, an empty soup can, and a horseshoe—all signs of human habitation.

Finally, after ten brutal days and forty-three miles of slogging up and down icy peaks, they made contact with Chilean cattlemen on the far side of a small stream. The note Parrado wrote and tossed over to them began, "I came from a plane that fell in the mountains . . ."

After ten weeks of icy hell on earth, the ordeal was almost over. Authorities quickly initiated a coordinated rescue operation, and by December 23, all remaining survivors were back from the mountain and reunited with their families. The press dubbed it a "Christmas Miracle." Seventy-two days had elapsed since the doomed military transport crashed onto the mountainside. Of the forty-five people originally aboard, only sixteen were still alive.

Aftermath

The world embraced the young heroes who had returned from the dead, but the sixteen survivors carefully avoided any discussion of the act they had committed to stay alive. The fact that nearly all required immediate hospitalization was fortunate, in that it served to isolate them from the throngs of onlookers, well-wishers, and reporters.

All the young men were dirty, unshaven, and emaciated—having lost anywhere from thirty to eighty pounds each. Many of their crash injuries still had not healed, and they suffered from a variety of ailments: hypertension, irregular heartbeat, skin infections, sunburn, conjunctivitis, and more. Still, it was evident to their doctors that after ten weeks with no food, they should have been in even worse condition. The truth finally emerged that they had survived by eating human flesh.

This shocking news created a furor. How could educated young Christian men have committed such a horrible sin? One Chilean newspaper even printed their story under the headline, "May God Forgive Them." Others, however, understood the necessity of what they had done. Among these was the Catholic Church, to which most of the survivors belonged. Church leaders compassionately decreed that the survivors' cannibalistic practice was no more of a sin than receiving an organ transplant—it was just another way for the dead to donate tissue to the living.

Noted archeologist Dr. Julie Schablitsky wrote of the cannibalistic Donner Party, "They didn't survive by eating each other; they survived by being

Flight 571 crash site memorial, as it appeared in 2006.

resourceful." The same is true of the Andes crash survivors. These young men, with a burning desire to live, did what they had to do. They survived because of their resilience, and because of the self-discipline, teamwork, and ingenuity they displayed under the worst conditions imaginable. As for the act they committed to remain alive: would anyone else, suddenly and unexpectedly thrust into a similar situation, behave any differently?

Regardless of how one chooses to view the actions of the Andes survivors during their brutal ten-week ordeal of death and misery, theirs was one of the most amazing feats of human survival ever recorded. The fact that they *did* survive to live full lives was a testament to them and a tribute to the twenty-nine who remained forever on the mountain.

SECTION IV

INTO THE TWILIGHT ZONE

CHAPTER SIXTEEN

A HAUNTING DISTRACTION

"HEY, WHAT'S HAPPENING HERE?"

On the dark, clear evening of December 29, 1972, Eastern Airlines Flight 401 departed New York's JFK International Airport for Miami. The nearly new Lockheed L-1011 TriStar wide-body carried 163 passengers and 13 crew members. The two-hour flight was without incident until 11:34 p.m., when it approached Miami. The captain ordered the landing gear lowered, and immediately noticed the glaring absence of the green nose gear indicator light. This meant one of two very different things: the indicator light had simply malfunctioned, or else the nose gear was actually not down and locked. The pilot-in-command, Capt. Robert Loft, a thirty-year veteran with nearly thirty thousand flight hours, now had to determine whether he had a true in-flight emergency, or simply a burned out light bulb. After advising Miami Approach Control of the situation, he climbed out of the pattern to two thousand feet and turned onto a westerly heading away from the airport to troubleshoot the problem.

At 11:41, the Miami controller became concerned. He noticed that the airliner had descended from its already low altitude to only nine hundred feet above the ground. He immediately radioed the airliner, asking, "[H]ow are things comin' out there?" Capt. Loft, apparently satisfied by this time that their only problem was a faulty indicator light, advised that they were returning to the airport to land. Seconds later, the big Lockheed vanished from the radar screen. Unknown to the controller, it had just plunged into the swampy Florida Everglades and shredded into a million pieces, killing or fatally injuring 101 of the 176 people aboard.

Eastern Airlines Lockheed L-1011-385-1, registration number N310EA. On December 29, 1972, this airliner crashed into the Florida Everglades, killing or fatally injuring 101 of the 176 people aboard. Eastern had only acquired the new "Whisperliner" the previous August. © *Jon Proctor Collection, with permission*

The crash of Flight 401, though horrendously tragic, was far from the deadliest in US history. It is, however, unique because it was one of the most preventable aviation accidents ever to occur—and it initiated a series of ghostly in-flight airline encounters that rocked the commercial airline industry.

A Moment of Inattention

NTSB investigators were fortunate in having a wealth of information relating to the crash of Flight 401. At their disposal were records of all radio communications, survivor interviews, evidence from the crash scene, and data collected from the cockpit voice recorder and flight data recorder. From all this, they were able to piece together an exceptionally clear picture of the events leading up to the crash. That picture was not a pretty one.

The Flight 401 crew faced a serious issue. They had to determine whether the TriStar's nose gear was down and locked, as it should have been. The answer to this question meant the difference between a routine landing and a nose-down, potentially deadly belly slide to a screeching stop.

Determining the gear's status was difficult since it was not visible from any vantage point inside the jetliner. The only way to check it was for a crew member to climb down into the forward avionics bay below the flight deck and visually verify, through an optical sighting device, the proper alignment of the nose gear indices. Captain Loft had assigned the flight engineer, Second Officer Don Repo, to that task. Unfortunately, it was so dark down there that Repo was unable to make a definitive determination. Therefore, the copilot, First Officer Albert Stockstill, began working on the other possible culprit—the nose gear light indicator assembly. If it was found to be defective, they would assume that the gear was functioning properly and proceed with a normal landing.

Thus, two of the three crew members responsible for flying the big jet, skimming just above the ground at a speed of 227 miles per hour, were engaged in other activities. Only Captain Loft, who was becoming increasingly impatient at the delay, was still at the controls. Soon, he placed the big jet on autopilot and turned his attention, as well, to the stubborn indicator light with which Stockstill was still struggling. Now, no human was in control of the giant airliner streaking just two thousand feet over the Florida Everglades on that moonless night. Consequently, no one noticed the altitude-warning chime that sounded in the cockpit at 11:40:38. If either of the pilots had heard it, they would have known that the jet had just dropped 250 feet. Now, they were flying at an altitude of only 1,750 feet . . . and still heading down.

Eventually, the captain and first officer decided that the light was indeed malfunctioning, as they had suspected, and that the gear was in all likelihood down and locked. Exactly one second after the pilots advised approach control that they were heading back to the airport to land, Stockstill was recorded as saying: "We did something to the altitude," to which Loft replied, "What?"

Stockstill then asked, "We're still at two thousand, right?" Loft then spoke the last words of his life: "Hey, what's happening here?" He then shoved on full throttles.

Five seconds later, at 11:42:12, the giant airliner crashed into the marshy ground. It hit with sufficient force to scatter the wreckage over eleven acres. Littered among the pieces were its 176 former occupants, 101 of whom were dead or dying. Among the latter were Captain Loft, First Officer Stockstill, and Second Officer Repo.

A Most Unsterile Cockpit

The question with which investigators concerned themselves was relatively straightforward: why did the big Lockheed descend to the ground undetected when its Autoflight autopilot system had been set for two thousand feet? The NTSB crash investigators considered several possibilities and concluded that when Captain Loft turned to speak with Second Officer Repo, he may have inadvertently bumped against the control yoke. This would have disengaged the "altitude hold" function of the jet's Autoflight system, and put it into a slow descent to the ground. By the time the distracted pilots noticed that they had been losing altitude, it was too late.

As for the nose gear issue that precipitated the fatal series of events, post-crash analysis verified that the nose gear warning light lens assembly had malfunctioned. Investigators never determined if the nose gear had been in a down and locked position, but in all likelihood it was in perfect working order, and the landing would have been uneventful. The entire tragedy thus began because of nothing more significant than a faulty $12 light bulb. It was the inattentiveness of the crew—coupled with a series of unlucky coincidences—that doomed the giant airliner and the lives of 101 people.

That an entire flight crew of seasoned professionals could become so distracted from their primary duties as to allow their aircraft to fly into the ground seems too unlikely to believe. However, this was exactly what happened in the case of Flight 401. The highly experienced and otherwise competent crew members temporarily forgot the cardinal rule of airmanship that instructors drill into every student pilot from day one of flight training: "First, fly the airplane!" This means that no matter what other issues are occurring in the cockpit, the pilot must above all else maintain control of the aircraft. Failure to heed this rule renders all other issues instantly and completely irrelevant.

Human factors researchers from the FAA and NASA have long considered flight-deck distractions an important area of concern. Their focus over the past decades on this subtle killer was inspired in large part by the Flight 401 tragedy—a crash involving a crew so distracted that they allowed their perfectly airworthy aircraft to crash. One of the regulations resulting from this research was the so-called "Sterile Cockpit Rule," enacted by the FAA in 1981. This prohibits flight crews from engaging in nonessential activities during takeoffs, landings, and at other critical times during flights.

Unfortunately, even with this and other such rules in place, cockpit distractions continue to plague the aviation industry. One highly publicized example of this occurred on October 21, 2009, when a Northwest Airlines Airbus A320 flying out of San Diego with 149 people aboard overflew its destination of Minneapolis–Saint Paul by 150 miles. The two pilots of Flight 188 had apparently become so involved with their laptop computers that they lost track of time and of where they were. Air traffic controllers were unable to contact the pilots, making the entire scenario seem suspiciously like a hijacking. Consequently, aviation authorities alerted the White House, while the Air National Guard readied fighter jets for takeoff to intercept the wayward airliner. The very embarrassed

An excerpt from the NTSB report on the Eastern Airlines Flight 401 crash. The impeccable qualifications of the three flight deck crewmembers were not enough to prevent this tragedy.
NTSB

The following is a listing of pertinent flightcrew information:

Item	Capt. Loft	F/O Stockstill	S/O Repo
Age	55	39	51
Date of birth	3/17/17	6 9/33	5/10/21
Time L-1011	280 hrs.	306 hrs.	53 hrs,
Total time	29, 700 hrs.	5,800 hrs.	15, 700 hrs.
Certificates	ATR	ATR & FE	FE, A&P & Commercial
Numbers	ATR-464-38	ATR-1311877 FE- 1547248	FE-1752585 Comm. -13278 A&P-291 795
Ratings	AMEL, DC-3-4, 6, 7, 8, M202, 404, L-49, L-188 L-1011 B-751/720 CW-46	AMEL, DC-3 Comm. Priv. ASEL. FE - DC-7, L-188 B-727	Comm. Priv. ASEL & Inst. F E - Recip. Turbo Prop & Turbo Jet
Hours flown 24 hrs. prior this flight	2:25	2 25	5:00
Hours flown this flight	2:22	2 22	2:22

pilots only turned the Airbus back to the airport when controllers finally managed to contact them and advise them of their blunder. The plane eventually arrived safely at its destination—seventy-four minutes late—but both pilots were suspended and their licenses revoked. The captain and first officer of this aircraft had more than thirty thousand flight hours between them, proving once again that experience is not enough to protect a pilot from distractions in the cockpit.

The events that occurred in the cockpit of Flight 401 that dark night cost the lives of 101 people, including all three members of the flight crew whose responsibility it had been to prevent such a horrendous accident. The blame for this needless tragedy rested squarely on their shoulders. It could even be that the intense sense of guilt and regret, which they would undoubtedly have felt had they lived, caused two of them to return and try to make amends . . . in the afterlife.

Flying Ghosts

In the months after the crash, numerous reliable witnesses reported seeing extremely lifelike ghostly images of Captain Loft and Second Officer Repo. Most of the sightings occurred on Eastern L-1011 airliners fitted with parts salvaged from the wreckage of Flight 401. One senior Eastern Airlines captain reported seeing Repo "sitting there clear as day" in the jump seat of his airliner during a flight. When the captain turned away and then looked back, the apparition was gone. On another occasion, a passenger called a flight attendant to check on a man sitting next to her wearing an Eastern Airlines pilot uniform who appeared to be ill. He disappeared before her eyes, but she later identified him from a photo as Repo.

Passengers and crew reported other sightings of Repo, in some instances with him performing tasks aboard the aircraft and warning of impending trouble. Credible witnesses also reported similar sightings of Captain Loft's ghost. They saw his image appear on different occasions and then vanish. These alleged sightings circulated as rumors throughout the airline community. When word leaked out, they quickly became legendary—and the subject of a bestselling book and made-for-TV movie. They even inspired the song "The Ghost of Flight 401," which appeared on the 1979 Bob Welch hit album *Three Hearts*.

Author John G. Fuller collected a great deal of anecdotal evidence from seemingly legitimate sources in support of these sightings and presented them in his book *The Ghost of Flight 401*. Not everyone, however, was receptive to such paranormal activities occurring on Eastern Airlines aircraft. Company president Frank Borman reportedly called it "a bunch of crap," and the company threatened employees with either dismissal or referral for psychological evaluation if caught spreading ghostly rumors. Likewise, some family members of the alleged ghosts were not pleased. One of them sued author Fuller over some of the assertions made in his book.

As is the case with just about all of history's ghost sightings to date, the validity of the Flight 401 apparitions can never be proven—or disproven. However, reported ghost sightings in aviation did not originate with those of Flight 401. The world of flight has long had its fair share of ghostly appearances, unexplained events, phantom aircraft, and messages from the beyond. One of the earliest and most enduring of these originated at a desolate Royal Flying Corps airfield near Montrose, Scotland. There a young RFC pilot died in 1913 when his sloppily repaired airplane fell apart in the air. Over the ensuing years, numerous pilots stationed there routinely reported seeing his image in various places around the base.

Another eerie and much-publicized series of supernatural events occurred in relation to the October 5, 1930, first—and last—passenger-carrying flight of the British airship R-101. On its maiden voyage, the 777-foot-long dirigible crashed and burned in France, killing forty-eight of the fifty-four people aboard. As related by John G. Fuller in another of his books, *The Airmen Who Would Not Die*, famed psychic Eileen Garrett had, before

R-101's last flight, a vision of a great airship crashing in flames. She voiced her premonition to the Director of Civil Aviation, Sir William Sefton Brancker, who laughed it off as nonsense. He of all people should have listened, as he was one of those destined to die in the crash. A second warning about R-101 came, purportedly, from the spirit of a famed British pilot named Raymond Hinchcliffe, who had disappeared in a 1928 transatlantic attempt. The dead pilot's spirit reportedly appeared during a séance, to warn one of his friends serving on R-101 that the new airship had serious structural problems.

The final R-101 paranormal incident was the most startling of all. Two days after the crash, the spirit of the airship's dead captain, Royal Air Force Flight Lt. H. Carmichael Irwin, unexpectedly broke into a séance that psychic Garrett was conducting. She had been trying to contact the spirit of the recently deceased author, Sir Arthur Conan Doyle. One of those attending the séance recorded Irwin's ghostly yet vivid description of the problems he encountered on his last flight. His narrative was amazingly complete, with accurate and highly detailed technical facts of which Garrett, ostensibly, could have had no knowledge.

There is an ironic epilogue to the series of supernatural occurrences surrounding R-101—the dead airship was reincarnated. Zeppelin, the German airship company, salvaged several tons of the burnt and twisted metal remains of R-101. They melted down the valuable Duralumin alloy and recycled it for use in another great airship—the *Hindenburg*.

⬛

The ghosts of Flight 401 may or may not have been real except to those claiming to have seen them. However, the legend remains. The ghosts from this ill-fated flight, as well as aviation's other supernatural events reported over the past century, remain real enough in some circles to start a lively discussion.

Flight 401 has become a textbook example of how even seasoned professionals can be lulled into a dangerous in-flight complacency. The environment in which pilots operate is one that tolerates no such inattentiveness. The deadly distraction that occurred in the cockpit of Flight 401 that dark evening over the Everglades was only the latest version of a scenario that had played out many times in the past—and that can still occur in any cockpit at any time.

In 1900, Wilbur Wright, three years prior to his and brother Orville's historic first powered flight on the sands of Kitty Hawk, wrote: "I have learned that carelessness and overconfidence are usually far more dangerous than deliberately accepted risks." His wise observation remains as true today as when he wrote it. Only strict and constant attention to the demands of airmanship can prevent future reoccurrences of such needless flights of no return.

CHAPTER SEVENTEEN

LOST LADY OF THE DESERT

**"A FATAL COMBINATION OF
INEXPERIENCE AND BAD LUCK."**

On the afternoon of April 4, 1943, twenty-five US Army Air Forces B-24D Liberators lifted off from their base in North Africa. Their mission was a high-altitude bomb run to Naples, Italy. As the loose formation proceeded toward the target, the bombers drifted further apart, until one of them lost all contact with the rest. The bomber and its nine-man crew never returned, and they left no clue as to their fate.

The big bomber's unexplained disappearance was unusual but not unheard of. It was just one of thousands of aircraft in World War II to depart for a mission and never come back. What makes this story unique is what happened *after* the flight ended. The tragic facts surrounding the disappearance of this airplane and crew would not surface until fifteen years later, when—almost literally, out of nowhere—they reemerged onto the public scene in spectacular fashion.

A Mission Destined to Fail

The bomber was B-24D number AC41-24301, bearing a big white "64" on its nose along with the name *Lady Be Good*. The name may have originated from a 1924 Gershwin Brothers Broadway musical starring the rising young performer Fred Astaire, but its significance to this bomber is a secret lost to history. The airplane was brand new, having recently rolled out of the Consolidated Aircraft Company's San Diego factory. The US Army Air

Ill-fated crew of *Lady Be Good*. From left: Hatton, Toner, Hays, Woravka, Ripslinger, LaMotte, Shelley, Moore, and Adams. On April 4, 1943, they became lost on their very first mission and had to bail out at night over the Libyan Desert. It would take more than fifteen years for the rest of the world to learn their fate. *US Air Force*

Forces accepted the ship on December 8, 1942, and it arrived at Soluch Airfield just in time for the April 4 mission.

The airfield at Soluch was a makeshift US Army Air Forces bomber base located thirty miles southeast of Benghazi, Libya. Here, the new Liberator found its way to the 514th Squadron of the Ninth Air Force's 376th Bomb Group.

The crew designated to fly *Lady Be Good* on the April 4 mission was as new as the bomber, having recently arrived from stateside. They were: pilot 1st Lt. William J. Hatton; copilot 2nd Lt. Robert F. Toner; navigator 2nd Lt. "Dp" Hays; bombardier 2nd Lt. John S. Woravka; engineer Tech. Sgt. Harold J. Ripslinger; radio operator Tech. Sgt. Robert E. LaMotte; and gunners Staff Sgts. Guy E. Shelley Jr., Vernon L. Moore, and Samuel E. Adams. All were in their early to midtwenties, just out of training, untested, and inexperienced. It would therefore be the first wartime mission for both bomber and crew. It would also be their last.

US Army Air Forces B-24D Liberator, built by the Consolidated Aircraft Company. This is the same model as *Lady Be Good*, which was lost on April 5, 1943, in the Libyan Desert during its first, last, and only wartime mission. *US Air Force*

Lady Be Good was one of twenty-five B-24 Liberators that took off on Mission 109 the afternoon of April 4. Their objective was Naples Harbor, 750 miles to the northwest, on the far side of the Mediterranean Sea. The plan was to hit the target at dusk and then scoot home under cover of darkness. The challenging navigational aspect of this 1,500-mile overwater roundtrip increased the difficulty of the mission, but the B-24 was well suited for it. Though an ugly duckling compared to its sleek older sibling, the Boeing B-17 Flying Fortress, the thirty-ton, high-wing Liberator was equally capable. Powered by four 1,200-horsepower Pratt & Whitney turbo-supercharged radial engines, the twin-tailed B-24 could top three hundred miles per hour, reach altitudes up to thirty-five thousand feet, and fly as far as 3,000 miles nonstop. If attacked, its crews could defend themselves with a bristling armada of a dozen or more .50-caliber machine guns. Most important, bombardiers on this outstanding airplane could employ its top-secret Norden bombsight to drop with devastating precision—at least for 1943—a four-ton payload of high explosives. The Liberator's value to the US war effort is best gauged by the approximately 18,500 that were built—more than any other US combat airplane in history.

Lady Be Good and the other twenty-four bombers accomplished their mass takeoff from Soluch that day with difficulty, in the midst of a sandstorm. Several of the big bombers had to return with engines fouled from the blowing desert sand that sucked into their inner workings. The rest headed out in a scattered formation over the Mediterranean toward Italy. *Lady Be Good* was among the last of a second wave of thirteen bombers to take off. She struggled off the graded sand runway at 3:10 p.m., more than ninety minutes after the first wave of twelve bombers had departed. By this time, they had long since disappeared into the distance. Meanwhile, nine of those in the second wave turned back with mechanical problems, leaving only *Lady Be Good*, with her rookie crew, and three other bombers to find their way to the target and back alone. It was a bad start, and things would only get worse.

No one knows exactly what happened during *Lady Be Good*'s first and last mission. If the bomber actually reached Naples, the crew probably did not have sufficient

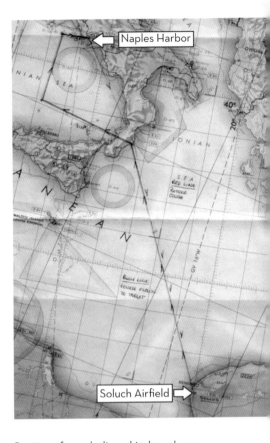

Portion of map believed to have been used in the *Lady Be Good* search operation. It shows the bomber's course from its base at Soluch, Libya, to its target at Naples, Italy, and back. *US Air Force (labels added by author)*

visibility to drop their bombs with any accuracy. With no clear target in sight, and possibly other problems plaguing them as well, they would have turned back toward home and eventually jettisoned their bombs into the sea. By this time, they had definitely separated from the other three bombers with which they started the mission. Failing to hit the target was bad enough, but the neophyte crew now had to make the formidable overwater flight back home alone, in total darkness, and under strict wartime conditions of blackout and radio silence.

Some have suggested that the plane's navigator, Lieutenant "Dep" Hays, was simply not up to the task. The twenty-three-year-old former bank clerk—whose first name really was "Dp," or sometimes, "D.P."—was perhaps too inexperienced to tackle a navigational problem as complex as the one he faced on his first mission. Had things gone as expected, he would have had little to do; his pilot would simply have followed the rest of the formation to the target and back. Now, he found himself alone and a long way from home, at night, and with virtually no visible checkpoints or other navigational aids to guide him. For this mission, the bomber carried only slightly more than enough fuel to get home, so there was not much room for error.

But did Hays fail? At around midnight that night, the men anxiously waiting for plane No. 64 back at Soluch heard the unmistakable deep throb of a Liberator's big radial engines high over the airfield. They fired off flares to alert it, but it continued to drone on until the sound faded into the southeastern sky. This was undoubtedly *Lady Be Good* since, by now, they had accounted for all the other bombers on that day's mission. Apparently, Hays had managed to guide his plane back home, after all. But why did they not land? And why did no one aboard apparently see the flares as they were passing over it?

The likely answer is that they were not looking for either the airfield or the flares. Navigator Hays probably had no idea he was anywhere near Soluch when they overflew it. As far as he knew, they were still well out over the Mediterranean. To his credit, he had maintained the proper course, but a strong tailwind had carried them much faster and further than anticipated. Consequently, they were still at relatively high altitude and probably not even looking down when they passed over the airfield. Any flares sent up therefore went unnoticed in the dusty haze below, as *Lady Be Good* droned ever deeper into the Sahara Desert.

None of this was clear to anyone at the time—either the nine men inside *Lady Be Good* or those at Soluch listening to the bomber fly over. The fate of the plane and crew was a complete mystery. In the ensuing days, the military authorities conducted a cursory search, both in the Mediterranean and the desert, but to no avail. When no traces of bomber or crew appeared, the Army listed them as "missing in action," and that officially closed the book on *Lady Be Good*.

Desert Discovery

That is, until fifteen years later. On May 16, 1958, the mystery of the lost bomber resurfaced in the most dramatic way imaginable. A British civilian oil exploration team flying across the desolate and mostly uncharted Libyan Sahara Desert—an area nearly twice the size of Texas—spotted

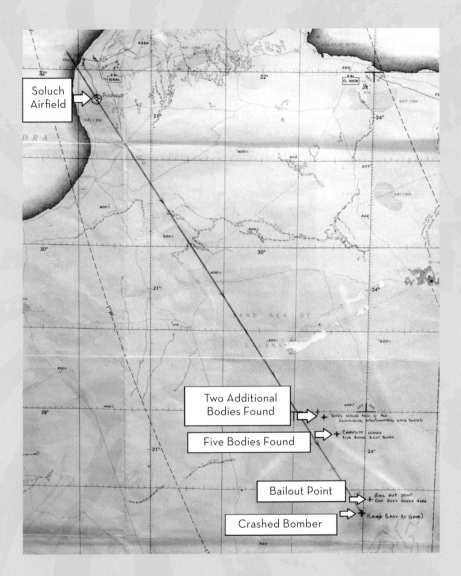

Soluch
Airfield

Two Additional
Bodies Found

Five Bodies Found

Bailout Point

Crashed Bomber

Map, also thought to have been used in the *Lady Be Good* search operation, showing the lost bomber's course after overflying Soluch and crashing in the desert four hundred miles to the southeast. Had the crew walked southwest instead of northwest after bailing out, they would have found the downed bomber, with its life-saving supplies and still-functioning radio. *US Air Force (labels added by author)*

Lady Be Good after lying unmolested and undetected in the desert for more than a decade and a half. *US Air Force*

The bomber was in remarkably good shape after its pilotless 1943 crash landing. *US Air Force*

something on the sand below that looked very much out of place. It was a derelict airplane. They noted its approximate location before continuing. Unknown to them, sitting there in the sand four hundred miles southeast of Soluch was the broken body of the long-lost *Lady Be Good*.

US and British military officials learned of the derelict, but showed no immediate inclination to investigate it. It was just another of the many unidentified wrecks that littered this desert where so much fighting had occurred only a few years earlier. This particular one was sitting hundreds of miles deep into the desert, in an area said to be so forbidding that even the tough and fearless native Bedouins refused to enter it. Consequently, military authorities did not consider this unidentified airplane important enough to warrant further investigation.

On February 27, 1959, an oil ground-survey team came upon the downed airplane previously sighted from the air. They found the derelict, which they recognized as a US B-24 bomber, lying broken on a desert plateau in an area of the Libyan Desert known as the Calanscio Sand Sea. It had obviously belly-landed and skidded nearly seven hundred yards to its present location. The painted number "64" was still clearly visible on the nose. The case of the missing *Lady Be Good* had just been reopened.

Though damaged by the crash, the bomber was in remarkably good condition. The crew might have even walked away from it. However, since no parachutes were aboard, it seemed more likely that the men had bailed out and left the bomber to crash. But instead of crashing, the pilotless Liberator somehow executed a belly landing that night that would have made any Army pilot proud. Many questions remained. Where did this misplaced mystery bomber from the past come from? When and how did it end up here? And most important, what happened to the men who had been aboard it?

The oilmen spent a considerable amount of time exploring the derelict, taking photos, and collecting souvenirs. By all appearances, they were the first humans to lay eyes on the bomber since the day it had crashed. It was amazingly well preserved; although it had been baking in the sun for nearly sixteen years, it looked as though it could have arrived there only yesterday. The arid atmosphere had maintained the big bomber as well as any climate-controlled museum could have. There was practically no corrosion, and most of the paint covering the bomber's aluminum skin was intact; two of its three tires were still fully inflated. Inside, nothing was disturbed—navigational instruments, neatly hung items of clothing, cigarette butts, food, water, chewing gum. Even the coffee remaining in a thermos still tasted like coffee. In addition, most of the Liberator's equipment appeared to function as well as the day it rolled out of the factory; when one of the oilmen pulled the trigger on a .50-caliber machine gun, it fired. The mysterious bomber in the sand was about to become an aviation legend, but the most dramatic discoveries were still to come.

Hell on Earth

When US military authorities learned the specifics of the derelict in the desert and determined its identity, they finally became interested. The unexpected find had generated an international whirlwind of media attention, and family members of the lost fliers demanded answers. Its discovery also fueled some wild speculation: some conjectured that marauding nomads had captured the "Ghost Bomber's" missing crew and sold them into slavery. If so, perhaps they were still alive.

The Army thought otherwise. They quickly dispatched a mortuary team to initiate a search for the remains of the lost crew. From July through October 1959, the team—with support from the US Air Force at Wheelus Air Base, near Tripoli, examined the area for miles around the wreckage. The extensive air and ground expedition eventually turned up a trail of discarded crew equipment, including boots and parachutes formed into crude arrows pointing northward—a ghostly message from the past. The search team's physician and resident survival expert estimated that no man could cover a total of more than twenty-five miles under such harsh conditions as existed in this desert; therefore, their bodies had to be nearby. However, after three exhaustive months of searching, the team reluctantly gave up, empty-handed, and accepted the obvious conclusion: the nine crew members lay buried somewhere in their final resting places beneath a decade and a half of blowing sand. No one would ever know where.

Then, on February 11, 1960, events spectacularly disproved this assumption. Another oil team working its way through the desert stumbled upon the skeletal remains of five humans. They were lying close together in what one member of the team described as a "pathetic little camp," littered with equipment that identified them as airmen. All had apparently died at about the same time. Though the bodies were located some eighty miles northwest of where *Lady Be Good* had come to rest, there could be no doubt: they were the missing crew members from the unlucky bomber.

Among the personal effects found was a diary belonging to the copilot, 2nd Lt. Robert Toner. This terse narrative related some of the details of the doomed crew's last mission. It also graphically described the ordeal they suffered in their final days of life:

NOSEWHEEL AND TIRE.
TRANSFERRED FROM
WHEELUS AIR BASE, LIBYA

⬆ One of the four engines from *Lady Be Good*. Its pilotless belly landing in the sand damaged it, but even after years of baking in the sun, much of the paint is still readily evident. *Steven A. Ruffin*

⬅ The nose wheel from *Lady Be Good* displayed at the National Museum of the US Air Force. The tire still held air and, even today, appears unaffected by its years in the desert sun. *Steven A. Ruffin*

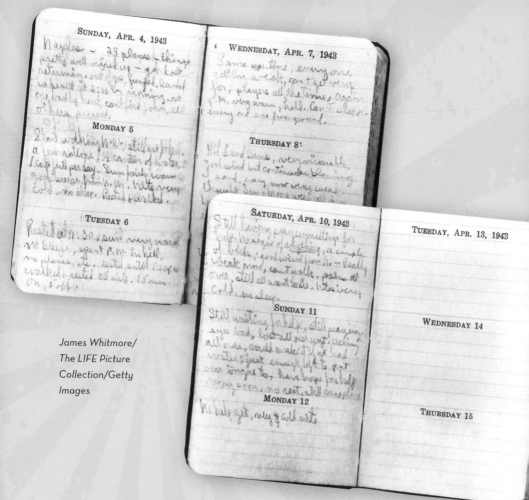

James Whitmore/
The LIFE Picture
Collection/Getty
Images

Sunday, Apr. 4, 1943
Naples–28 planes–things pretty well mixed up–got lost returning, out of gas, jumped, landed in desert at 2:00 in morning, no one badly hurt, can't find John, all others present.

Monday 5
Start walking N.W., still no John. A few rations, 1/2 canteen of water, 1 cap full per day. Sun fairly warm, good breeze from N.W. Nite very cold, no sleep. Rested & walked.

Tuesday 6
Rested at 11:30, sun very warm, no breeze, spent P.M. in hell, no planes, etc. rested until 5:00 P.M. Walked & rested all nite. 15 min on, 5 off.

Wednesday, Apr. 7, 1943
Same routine, everyone getting weak, can't get very far, prayers all the time, again P.M. very warm, hell. Can't sleep. Everyone sore from ground.

Thursday 8
Hit Sand Dunes, very miserable, good wind but continuous blowing of sand, every[one] now very weak, thought Sam & Moore were all done. La Motte eyes are gone, everyone else's eyes are bad. Still going N.W.

Friday 9
Shelly [sic], Rip, Moore seperate [sic] & try to go for help, rest of us all very weak, eyes bad, not any travel, all want to die. still very little water. nites are about 35°, good n wind, no shelter, 1 parachute left.

Saturday, Apr. 10, 1943
Still having prayer meetings for help. No signs of *anything*, a couple of birds; good wind from N.–Really weak now, can't walk, pains all over, still all want to die. Nites very cold. No sleep.

Sunday 11
Still waiting for help, still praying. eyes bad, lost all our wgt. aching all over, could make it if we had water; just enough left to put our tongue to, have hope for help very soon, no rest, still same place.

Monday 12
No help yet, very cold nite

The diary ended here. It was now clear that the crew bailed out of their fuel-starved bomber at around 2:00 a.m. on April 5. All except for missing bombardier John Woravka formed up and headed northwest on foot. This was the direction from which they had flown, and therefore, where they hoped they would find help. Little did they know how utterly futile their efforts would be; there was nothing but desert for hundreds of miles in that direction. Having only a half canteen of water between them, they trudged through the sand until crew members Hatton, Toner, Hays, LaMotte, and Adams could go no further. There they succumbed to dehydration and the harsh desert environment of sandstorms, 130-degree days, and freezing nights.

The three remaining men—Sergeants Shelley, Moore, and Ripslinger—grimly continued on, in hopes that help would be just over the next sand dune. There was nothing ahead, however, but more sand, more suffering—and ultimately, death.

Tragically, the men's still-intact Liberator had bellied in only a few miles southwest of where they had parachuted and initially assembled. Had they elected to head in that direction, they would have found the bomber—and in it, shelter, provisions, and a working radio. Of course, they had no way of knowing where—or in what kind of shape—it had ended its flight.

The dramatic discovery of the five bodies spawned a second US expedition to find the four still-missing crew members. The search continued through May 1960, but once again, civilian oilmen came to the rescue. On May 12, 1960, members of a work team discovered the remains of Guy Shelley. His body lay baking in the sand more than twenty miles further northwest from where he, Ripslinger, and Moore had left their five comrades to die. Then, five days later, a US helicopter crew member spotted Harold Rislinger's sun-dried remains lying, like all the others, on top of the sand in plain view. He had travelled several miles beyond even Shelley. Incredibly, both men had somehow managed to wade through the sand for more than a hundred miles and survive for an entire week—with virtually no food or water, in the worst environment on Earth. It was far more than anyone thought humanly possible—an amazing feat of strength and determination—but sadly, one that ended no less tragically. They were still three hundred miles away from civilization. The body of Vernon Moore, the third man who had pressed on with Shelley and Rislinger, was never found.

On August 11, 1960, oilmen made what was to be the final discovery relevant to the mystery of *Lady Be Good*. They found the skeleton of missing bombardier John Woravka imbedded in the sand only a few hundred yards from where the rest of the crew had landed and assembled. The discovery finally answered the question of why he had not joined his comrades that fateful night: he died during the parachute jump. Ironically, he may have been the luckiest of all, considering the unimaginable suffering his eight comrades endured before joining him in death.

⫷✦⫸

The tragic series of events associated with *Lady Be Good* and crew prompted some to label it a "jinx" or "ghost" plane. This idea found support in the disastrous fate of other aircraft using parts salvaged from the lost bomber. These included an Air Force C-47 using a radio receiver from *Lady*: it ditched in the Mediterranean, killing the pilot. A C-54 using parts from the "jinx" bomber experienced propeller problems and barely avoided catastrophe. And most significantly, in January 1960, a US Army U-1A Otter fitted with an armrest from *Lady Be Good* went down off the coast of Libya in the Gulf of Sidra. None of the ten people aboard the Otter were ever found, but one of the few bits of aircraft debris that eventually washed ashore was the ill-fated armrest.

The US Army and Air Force salvaged several parts from the crashed bomber and brought them back to the States for further evaluation, but what remained of the derelict continued to languish in the desert for

A portion of the stained glass window from the chapel at the former Wheelus US Air Base, Libya. It memorializes the nine crewmembers of *Lady Be Good* who perished in the Sahara desert in 1943. *Steven A. Ruffin*

decades until the Libyan government finally decided to retrieve it and haul it back to civilization. At last report, *Lady Be Good* lay in pieces at a Libyan government compound near Tobruk. Fortunately, many of its parts and artifacts originally brought back to the United States are still on display in various museums across the country. As for the bodies of her crew, all— except for that of the still-missing Vernon Moore—made their belated trip back to the United States for burial.

Seven decades have passed since the first, last, and only mission of *Lady Be Good*, but her legend lives on. She is undoubtedly the best-known B-24 Liberator ever built—equal in notoriety to her luckier Boeing B-17 Flying Fortress counterpart, *Memphis Belle*. However, while the iconic Belle and her crew, operating from a base in England, were widely feted as the war's first to complete twenty-five deadly bombing sorties intact, *Lady Be Good* and her crew failed to complete a single mission. In spite of the celebrity surrounding the strange reincarnation of the doomed *Lady*, nothing can detract from the tragedy of nine young lives snuffed out in the cruelest way imaginable, after a mission that accomplished nothing—all because of a fatal combination of inexperience and bad luck.

CHAPTER EIGHTEEN

THE GHOST BLIMP
OF DALY CITY

"NOTHING . . . HAS GIVEN A SATISFACTORY
EXPLANATION OF WHAT HAPPENED."

On the lazy Sunday morning of August 16, 1942, the citizens of Daly City, California, gazed upward at a curious sight. Drifting silently in from the sea with the incoming breeze was a big silver blimp with the large black letters "US Navy" stenciled on its sides. It was floating at low altitude with its cabin door propped open and both engines off. It was so low that two swimmers at the beach tried—without success—to grab the drifting airship and pull it down. Golfers, sunbathers, and hikers watched open-mouthed as it touched down and rose slightly. Then, it drifted into a rocky crag rising up over the beach, causing a cylindrical object to fall from the airship and crash to the ground. The object was a 325-pound depth charge designed to destroy enemy submarines; fortunately, it did not explode.

The errant blimp, now short one of its two heavy bombs and sagging in the middle, rose from the hilly peak that had snagged it. It continued to drift inland and over the town, descending slowly toward the ground—so low that it bumped along the tops of buildings and pulled down power lines along the way. Eventually, it touched down and scraped to a halt in the middle of the street at 444 Bellevue Avenue.

The partially deflated and crewless L-8, as it appeared over Daly City, California, on August 16, 1942. *US Navy*

↑ The L-8 "Ghost Blimp" soon after it came to rest on Bellevue Avenue, Daly City, California. Rescuers looking for the missing crewmembers damaged the airship's envelope, but the navy would soon return the gondola to service. *US Navy via Otto Gross*

← An opposite view of the grounded L-8. *US Navy via Otto Gross*

This was something different for the citizens of this quiet coastal community on the southern outskirts of San Francisco. It was not every Sunday morning that a navy blimp landed in the middle of their town. But the biggest surprise was yet to come.

Onlookers cautiously approached the now-stationary airship sitting silently in the street. They were justifiably apprehensive—the United States was at war. Perhaps the blimp was booby-trapped, or maybe enemy agents were inside. Soon, however, their curiosity got the best of them. Like a scene from a vintage science fiction movie, the rapidly growing crowd of Daly City citizens slowly approached the motionless gondola sitting mysteriously, like an alien spaceship, in the middle of the street. The metal and glass car extending below the huge, sagging envelope was resting on the pavement with the door to the crew compartment wide open. When they cautiously peered inside, they found to their astonishment that there was no one aboard. The bystanders searched high and low, and even ripped open the huge air bag to make sure there was no one trapped inside; however, it soon became obvious that the strange object they had before them was a derelict US Navy blimp. So, where was the crew who should have been at the controls?

The mystery of the US Navy blimp, designated L-8, is one of the most enduring and perplexing missing-persons cases to come out of World War II. The explanation for the disappearance of its two-man crew is as elusive now as the day it came to rest on Bellevue Avenue. This strange mission remains one of history's most intriguing.

US Navy Blimp L-8

At 6:03 a.m. on the morning of August 16, 1942, US Navy blimp L-8 lifted off from the Treasure Island Naval Air Facility, located in the middle of San Francisco Bay. Its mission, designated Patrol Flight 101, was to reconnoiter the harbor entrance and other Pacific waters off the California coast.

It was a routine patrol, but an important one. Only eight months had passed since the devastating December 7, 1941, Japanese sneak attack on Pearl Harbor. The danger of enemy submarines lurking off the western coast of the United States was real, and potentially deadly. Less than six months earlier, on February 23, 1942, the Imperial Japanese Navy submarine I-17 had the audacity to surface and shell a US oil refinery just north of Santa Barbara, California. The damage was insignificant, but the public hysteria resulting from it was anything but. Then, on June 21, Japanese submarine I-25 fired on Fort Stevens, a coastal defense installation in Oregon. These attacks sparked widespread fear of an impending Japanese invasion of the West Coast.

Alert levels were justifiably high. No one wanted another sunrise surprise attack at the hands of the Japanese Empire, and navy blimps were ideal for patrolling the coastal waters for marauding submarines. They carried enough fuel to remain aloft for up to twelve hours, they could fly high or low as needed, and they could hover indefinitely above anything of interest in the waters below.

L-8 was one of twenty-two "L-class" nonrigid airships built by the Goodyear Tire & Rubber Company. The navy accepted the blimp at Moffett Field, California, on March 5, 1942, and assigned it to Airship Patrol Squadron 32 (ZP-32). The blimp was then shuttled over to Treasure Island, thirty miles to the northwest, where it began flying operational missions.

L-8—like all in its class—was relatively small, as airships go. Still, it was half as long as a football field and its rubberized cloth envelope held 123,000 cubic feet of buoyant, inert helium gas. A gondola, suspended below, housed the flight deck and crew. Attached to the gondola were the two 145-horsepower Warner radial engines that propelled the blimp to speeds of up to sixty miles per hour. Its respectable payload of more than a ton included a crew of two or three men, 150 gallons of fuel, a .30-caliber machine gun with ammunition, and two Mark 17 aircraft depth charges. Thus, L-8 could not only locate enemy submarines, it could attack and destroy them.

The Goodyear-built US Navy Airship L-8 was one of twenty-two of its type. Powered by two 145-horsepower radial engines, it could carry a crew of up to three, two depth charges, and a .30-caliber machine gun. These features made it exceptionally well suited for antisubmarine patrol work. *US Navy*

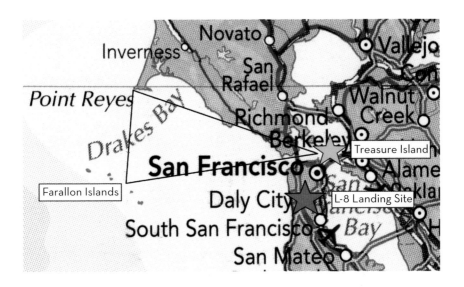

The triangle represents the planned patrol route for L-8 on August 16, 1942. Lieutenant Cody had completed the first leg, from Treasure Island to just east of the Farallon islands, when he reported a "suspicious oil slick." No further transmissions were ever received from the blimp's crew.

A Highly Qualified Crew

As the helium-filled navy blimp slowly ascended into the cool air above San Francisco Bay that Sunday morning, its pilot set a course toward the Farallon Islands, located about thirty-five miles west of Treasure Island. The patrol routine then called for a turn northward to Point Reyes, followed by a southeasterly course along the California coastline to Montara, and finally back to Treasure Island. What actually happened on this mission, however, was far from routine and more strangely tragic than anyone could possibly have imagined.

Navy Blimp L-8 normally carried a crew of three, but on the morning of August 16, 1942, only the command pilot, Lieutenant Ernest DeWitt Cody, and his passenger, Ensign Charles E. Adams, were on board. The latter, a newly assigned member of ZP-32, was aboard L-8 that morning for a familiarization flight. Both were highly competent and reliable officers.

Cody, a twenty-seven-year-old native of Mayville, Michigan, was a ten-year veteran of the navy and a 1938 graduate of the US Naval Academy at Annapolis. Having accumulated 758 flight hours as an airship pilot, nearly 400 of which were in L-type ships, he was one of the squadron's senior

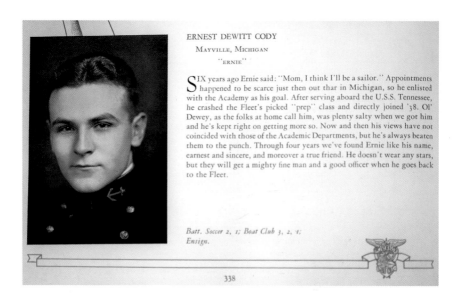

ERNEST DEWITT CODY

MAYVILLE, MICHIGAN

"ERNIE"

SIX years ago Ernie said: "Mom, I think I'll be a sailor." Appointments happened to be scarce just then out thar in Michigan, so he enlisted with the Academy as his goal. After serving aboard the U.S.S. Tennessee, he crashed the Fleet's picked "prep" class and directly joined '38. Ol' Dewey, as the folks at home call him, was plenty salty when we got him and he's kept right on getting more so. Now and then his views have not coincided with those of the Academic Departments, but he's always beaten them to the punch. Through four years we've found Ernie like his name, earnest and sincere, and moreover a true friend. He doesn't wear any stars, but they will get a mighty fine man and a good officer when he goes back to the Fleet.

Batt. Soccer 2, 1; Boat Club 3, 2, 1;
Ensign.

338

The entry for Midshipman Ernest Dewitt Cody from the US Naval Academy yearbook, the *Lucky Bag*. His peers considered him "like his name, earnest and sincere, and moreover a true friend." On August 16, 1942, he and Ensign Charles E. Adams disappeared during a routine patrol flight in US Navy Blimp L-8. *US Navy*

aviators. Only four months previously, on April 3, he had distinguished himself in L-8 when he piloted it—with the help of air crewman Chief Boatswain's Mate Desmond—to a tricky and highly secret Pacific Ocean rendezvous with the US Navy aircraft carrier *Hornet*, soon after the ship's departure from San Francisco harbor. The purpose of the blimp's mission that day was to deliver a three-hundred-pound package of parts for the sixteen US Army Air Forces B-25B bombers sitting on the carrier's deck. Unknown to anyone, except those at the highest levels, these bombers were the aircraft in which the famed Doolittle Raiders would soon make history. Their April 18, 1942, surprise bombing attack on mainland Japan, led by Lt. Col. James H. Doolittle, would strike America's first real blow of the war. Lieutenant Cody and L-8 had helped make this iconic mission possible.

Ensign Adams, on the other hand, was thirty-eight years old and an unrated pilot. He was, however, a seasoned lighter-than-air veteran, having served in navy airships for several years as an enlisted man. Prior to his recent commissioning as an officer, he had achieved the well-deserved senior enlisted rank of chief petty officer. During his action-filled fifteen years in the navy, he had repeatedly found himself in critical situations

US Navy Blimp L-8, piloted by Lt. j.g. Ernest D. Cody, delivering important cargo to the USS *Hornet* on April 3, 1942. The carrier, with sixteen US Army Air Forces North American B-25B Mitchell bombers parked on its flight deck, had just departed San Francisco for an undisclosed destination. The bombers, commanded by Lt. Col. Jimmy Doolittle, would soon take off from that very deck and deliver America's first real blow to the Empire of Japan. *US Navy*

that, in retrospect, make him a sort of Forrest Gump of the Navy Airship Service—he seemed to always be wherever things were happening. On June 24, 1931, he was present to help extinguish a fire aboard the US Navy airship *Los Angeles*, and on February 12, 1935, he was aboard the navy airship *Macon* when it crashed into the Pacific Ocean. Then, on May 6, 1937, he was a member of the ground crew at Naval Air Station Lakehurst, New Jersey, when the airship *Hindenburg* erupted into flame and crashed before his eyes. Finally, on December 7, 1941—only eight months before his fateful flight on L-8—Adams happened to be aboard the US Navy destroyer *Henley* during the Japanese attack at Pearl Harbor. There he helped down an attacking enemy airplane and assisted in dropping depth charges on a midget submarine. Whether Adams was cursed for having so many dangerous experiences or blessed to have survived them all, he was, by any measure, an experienced and capable man.

The third crew member scheduled for that morning's mission in L-8 was Aviation Machinist's Mate 3rd Class James Riley Hill, a mechanic. Lieutenant Cody scrubbed him at the last minute because the blimp was—for reasons unknown—two hundred pounds overweight. Depending on the circumstances surrounding Adams and Cody's later disappearance, this may have been a very lucky day for Hill. However, had he been aboard, his presence might have made all the difference in the outcome of the ill-fated flight.

A Suspicious Oil Slick

Nothing appeared amiss that August morning as L-8 drifted out over the Golden Gate Bridge and faded into the western sky. At 7:42 a.m.—a little over an hour and a half into the flight—Lieutenant Cody radioed back to Wing Control, "Am investigating suspicious oil slick—stand by." He was at this time about four miles east of the Farallon Islands. Such an observation could indicate, among other things, the presence of an enemy submarine lurking beneath.

The cause of the oil slick remains to this day unknown, however, because this was the last transmission received from L-8. Wing Control tried repeatedly to contact the crew for follow-up information, but received no response. Not until three hours later, at just before 11:00 a.m., did other aircraft in the area report seeing L-8. It was near the coastline north of Daly City and appeared to be in no distress. In reality, however, it was in trouble—something had gone terribly wrong. At approximately 11:15, the unmanned blimp made its dramatic appearance in Daly City.

Navy officials soon received the alarming report that one of their blimps had dropped a depth charge onto a golf course and then crash-landed in the middle of Daly City with no one aboard. One can only imagine the consternation this news must have caused. They immediately dispatched a team to secure the downed blimp, and then launched a search operation to locate the missing men.

Searchers first focused on the land over which the blimp had flown. When this failed to turn up any leads, they accepted that Adams and Cody had—for reasons unknown—gone into the water. Two life jackets were missing from the blimp's cabin, so it seemed certain that the two men were wearing them when whatever happened to them had occurred. They were probably still alive and floating in the Pacific Ocean. With luck, perhaps someone had already picked them up, and they were on their way back home with a very embarrassing story to tell. However, no bodies, alive or otherwise, ever turned up. The two men simply vanished—seemingly into thin air—leaving L-8 to find its own way back home.

An Inexplicable Occurrence

What could possibly have caused two experienced US Navy officers to abandon a perfectly good airship in midair? An investigation of the gondola revealed that in addition to the door being wide open, both engine ignition switches were still in the "on" position; and although the engines were no longer running, the fuel valves were still open and there was plenty of fuel remaining in the tanks. The helium gas valves were in their proper setting, and all components—radio included—were in good working order. The only notable discrepancy was the ship's drained battery, which any number of things could have caused. There was no evidence of foul play, and it was ascertained that the gondola never contacted saltwater at any time during its flight. All rescue equipment, including a life raft and parachutes, was still safely stowed and available for use. Even the classified codebooks aboard were undisturbed. The only things missing, in fact, were the two crew members and the life jackets they routinely wore as a safety precaution.

The condition of L-8 was such that the only reason it had descended at all was that it had automatically released some of its helium. A sudden rise to a higher altitude—possibly, when the two men exited the craft— caused the gas to expand and increase in pressure, resulting in an automatic helium release. Consequently, the partially deflated blimp slowly descended to the ground.

The crews of a fishing vessel and a Liberty ship were the only known eyewitnesses to L-8, as it circled for more than an hour above the oil slick. They reported that it descended to a very low altitude and dropped a smoke flare before eventually ascending and heading back toward

San Francisco. They saw nothing else falling from the blimp—including human bodies. In short, Navy investigators failed to find anything about the abandoned airship or its mission that seemed suspiciously amiss. Their official statement reflected this: "Nothing the Navy knows now has given a satisfactory explanation of what happened." It was one of the most perplexing occurrences imaginable and has remained so ever since.

Espionage or Accident?

Over the years, various theorists have proposed explanations to explain this strange incident. Disregarding those involving alien abductions, time warps, and black holes, one of the more believable scenarios is that a Japanese submarine might somehow have captured the two officers from L-8. This, however, also seems unlikely. There is simply no evidence to support this, and it is difficult to imagine how anyone *could* have captured them without first bringing the airship down. Furthermore, logic would dictate that Cody or Adams would have immediately radioed back to their base had they encountered the enemy.

Others have speculated that the two men perhaps had some sort of dispute, during which they fell out of the airship and into the water. Once again, there is nothing to support such a bizarre occurrence; moreover, it seems safe to assume that officers of their caliber were professional enough to save such a confrontation for a later time and place.

Another interesting theory came from the commander of Airship Patrol Squadron 32, Lieutenant Commander George F. Watson. He stated under oath that he was puzzled as to why the blimp was two hundred pounds overweight that morning. Others had speculated, perhaps unrealistically, that moisture accumulating on the blimp overnight might have caused it, but Watson doubted this and suggested that an enemy agent might have stowed away on the ship. He could have killed or disabled the two officers, dumped them overboard, and then escaped to a waiting submarine. To support this idea, he testified that only two weeks prior to the L-8 incident, an armed intruder had attempted to break into the hangars at Treasure Island. A guard had exchanged shots with the intruder during a running gun battle. Watson conceded, however, that there was virtually no place in the tiny gondola for a stowaway to hide. Moreover, since none of the classified materials aboard were missing, it seems unlikely that the two men's demise came at the hands of a spy.

Probably the most logical explanation for this bizarre incident is that the two men simply fell out of the gondola into the ocean. Admittedly, it seems somewhat preposterous, but there are many possibilities as to how

↑ The original L-8 gondola in 1942 US Navy colors, as displayed at the National Naval Aviation Museum, Naval Air Station Pensacola, Florida. *Steven A. Ruffin*

➡ A close-up of the left engine of L-8. Crewmembers occasionally had to climb out of the cabin door and onto the engine struts, while in flight, to service the engines. Did either Lieutenant Cody or Ensign Adams—or both—fall from the blimp while doing just that? *Steven A. Ruffin*

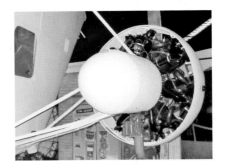

this could have happened. Perhaps while cruising with the door open for better viewing below, a gust of turbulence catapulted them both out of the cabin; or maybe they fell from outside the gondola while working on a stalled engine. If they did fall, they almost certainly died on impact with the water far below. However, it is puzzling why no bodies ever turned up, given the heavy ship traffic in the area at the time—especially since both men were almost certainly wearing life jackets that would have kept them afloat indefinitely.

Speculation aside, the facts remain unchanged: to this day, no one knows what happened to the two missing crew members of US Navy blimp L-8. Whether they encountered a spy, an enemy submarine, body-snatching aliens, or just bad luck, the result was the same: two good men were gone forever.

A final ironic twist occurred five years later that made the whole affair seem even weirder. On August 22, 1947, Lieutenant Cody's widow, Helen, wrote a letter to the US Navy Bureau of Personnel that ended up in Cody's Department of Defense personnel file. In this letter, she stated that her mother had recently seen her son-in-law, Ernest DeWitt Cody, in Phoenix, Arizona!

Helen explained that her mother, who had known Cody very well, described him as looking "peculiar, as though he were suffering from shock, or a mental illness." For that reason, as well as the fact that Helen had since remarried, she declined to approach him. Helen ended the letter by requesting that the navy look into the matter. However, it is unlikely that they had any inclination to do this.

Did Cody's mother-in-law see a ghost, or did she simply mistake someone else for Cody? And if it really was Cody, how did he survive, and why did he never return home to his wife? Could his disappearance have been the result of some secret mission on which he and Ensign Adams were engaged? As with just about every other aspect of this baffling incident, it appears that no one will ever know.

On August 17, 1943, exactly one year and one day after Cody and Adams disappeared, the secretary of the navy officially listed them as "presumed dead." As for the Ghost Blimp itself, the navy retrieved it from the Daly City street on which it landed, repaired it, and put it back into operation. It served honorably for the remainder of the war before returning, like most other veterans, to civilian life. Goodyear regained possession of it, but kept it in mothballs for the next two decades.

Finally, in 1966, the company decided to restore the gondola, and in 1969, the indomitable blimp returned to service—this time as the Goodyear blimp N10A, *America*. The reincarnated L-8 gondola once again became famous, as millions of people over the next decade watched it droning above major sporting events, flashing advertisements and providing aerial TV coverage to the networks. Finally, in 1982, the war-weary blimp retired for the last time.

However, like a cat with nine lives, the remains of the old L-8 rose once again—at least figuratively. In 2003, Goodyear donated the historic gondola to the National Naval Aviation Museum, located at Naval Air Station Pensacola, Florida. Here, it was restored to its original US Navy configuration and placed on display. It remains there today for visitors to peruse and to contemplate its dark secret from the past.

As the ghostly gondola sits there in eerie silence, who knows what stories it would tell if only it could speak. However, after seventy-plus years—and counting—the world's most famous Ghost Blimp remains silent. Whatever happened during that fateful August 16, 1942, patrol will forever remain a secret.

CHAPTER NINETEEN

FATAL RENDEZVOUS WITH A UFO

**"IT APPEARS TO BE A METALLIC OBJECT. . . .
I'M TRYING TO CLOSE IN FOR A BETTER LOOK."**

On the afternoon of January 7, 1948, an eerie series of events occurred in the skies over southern Kentucky. They culminated in the death of an American fighter pilot and an escalating sense of public anxiety nationwide. On that day, a Kentucky Air National Guard pilot crashed to his death in a field near Franklin, Kentucky. While tragic, that alone was not the reason for the widespread consternation it caused. Rather, it was due to the highly unusual mission he was performing when he died: the hot pursuit of an unidentified flying object.

A Call for Help

On that fateful day, Capt. Thomas F. Mantell Jr. was leading a flight of four North American F-51 Mustang fighters. They had taken off from Marietta Army Airfield, Georgia, and were ferrying the aircraft to Standiford Field in Louisville, Kentucky. Mantell, though only twenty-five years old, was a seasoned World War II combat pilot with more than two thousand hours of flight time. His unit was the 165th Fighter Squadron, 123rd Fighter Group of the newly activated Kentucky Air National Guard, based at Standiford Field.

At about 2:45 p.m., Mantell's flight was passing over Godman Army Air Field. Located on Fort Knox, approximately twenty-five miles southwest

A flight of three Kentucky Air National Guard F-51 Mustang fighters. The US military had only recently adopted the "F" designation—it was previously called the P-51. This formation presents a similar image to the January 7, 1948, flight that Capt. Thomas F. Mantell Jr. was leading, while in hot pursuit of an unidentified flying object. *US Air Force*

of Standiford, Godman was Mantell's last navigational checkpoint before landing. At that time, he received an unusual radio message from the Godman control tower. The controller informed Mantell that there was an object of unknown identity flying in the vicinity and asked him to investigate it.

Witnesses had first sighted the object in the sky some fifty-five miles southeast of Fort Knox. Local law enforcement officers had then alerted authorities at the army base, who ruled out any known military explanation for the object. At around 1:45 p.m., Godman tower personnel sighted the object high in the sky—by then, to their southwest. The observers in the tower, who included the base commander, collectively described the object as being several hundred feet in diameter, white with a red border, and resembling an ice cream cone or a parachute. It appeared to be stationary or moving very slowly. All agreed that they had never seen anything like it before.

The men in the tower had been watching the strange object for nearly an hour when Mantell and his flight of four Mustang fighters roared in from the south. When the tower operator requested their assistance, Mantell first checked his fuel gauge and then agreed to investigate. He immediately turned back to the southwest and began climbing toward the unknown object lurking somewhere in front of him. Two of the three other members of his flight accompanied him, while the remaining pilot continued on to Standiford, low on fuel.

The three fighters continued to climb southwesterly in pursuit of the mysterious object. Mantell had no idea what they were chasing, but at least he, too, could now see it. At fifteen thousand feet, he radioed: "The object is directly ahead of and above me now, moving at about half my speed. It appears to be a metallic object . . . and it is of tremendous size. I'm still climbing. I'm trying to close in for a better look."

Mantell continued to climb toward the object, but at some point his two wingmen leveled off and lost sight of their leader, still climbing ahead of them. They heard him say in a somewhat garbled transmission that he intended to go up to twenty-five thousand feet for ten minutes and then come back down. Exactly what happened next is a matter of conjecture—because no one ever heard from Mantell again.

A few minutes later, a witness on the ground near Franklin, Kentucky, a small town eighty-five miles southwest of Godman Field, heard Mantell's airplane in the sky, still so high that it was barely visible. He observed as the fighter circled three times and then fell into a power dive. The engine screamed, as the sleek fighter accelerated in the dive to a fantastic speed, probably sending both its engine tachometer and air speed indicator off the dial. As the man watched, he heard an explosion and then saw the fighter break apart in midair, before crashing to the ground in pieces. Although the wreckage covered an area a half mile in diameter, Mantell's body was still strapped into what was left of the cockpit. His shattered wristwatch marked his death precisely at 3:18 p.m. He had just become the Kentucky Air National Guard's first flying fatality—and aviation history's first victim of an unidentified flying object. The town of Franklin, where Mantell crashed, was also the town in which he had been born on June 30, 1922.

The Flying Saucer Phenomenon

The term "unidentified flying object," or "UFO," did not become a part of the public vernacular until 1952. However, human sightings of unknown objects in the sky date back almost to the beginning of time. More recently, Allied aircrew members flying in both the European and Pacific theaters of operations during World War II routinely reported unexplainable objects and lights in the sky. There were so many of these sightings that they gave the objects a name: "foo fighters." What they were, no one knows even today.

Only a few months before Mantell's encounter, two highly publicized otherworldly events had occurred, and these had a profound effect on the public's attitude toward these mysterious objects. First, on June 24, 1947, a civilian pilot in Washington State named Kenneth Arnold reported seeing nine "saucer-shaped" objects traveling at humanly impossible speeds while he was flying near Mount Rainier. He was widely regarded as a reliable witness, and his descriptions of these objects resulted in a term that quickly became a household word: "flying saucer." Then, just two weeks later, the most notorious of all out-of-this-world incidents occurred near Roswell, New Mexico. On July 8, 1947, an officer at Roswell Army Air Field announced that they had recovered a crashed "flying disk." Furthermore, there were rumors that they had found an alien body in the wreckage. The military quickly retracted the announcement and said that the object was really just a weather balloon—but the damage was done. Flying saucers—and aliens from other worlds—were now on everyone's radar.

Because of these recent sightings, people the world over became obsessed with UFOs and extraterrestrial beings. When news of the eerie events surrounding Mantell's death made headlines, it was just more evidence that aliens were about to take over Earth. Mantell's case, however, was much more sinister than previous sightings: now, a flying saucer had apparently attacked and killed an American fighter pilot. What were these strange craft and what were the intentions of the beings inside them? Was an alien invasion imminent? A public mass hysteria was in the making, in large part because the authorities refused to provide credible answers.

The sensational worldwide news coverage of the Mantell incident did little to help the situation. The next day's edition of the *New York Times* proclaimed in its headlines, FLIER DIES CHASING "FLYING SAUCER" and PLANE EXPLODES OVER KENTUCKY AS THAT AND NEAR STATES REPORT STRANGE OBJECT. Dramatic, perhaps, but also true. For the first time, a military aviator had died trying to intercept an unidentified object in the sky. His Mustang fighter—one of the best and strongest airplanes ever built—had exploded or disintegrated in the air for no known reason, and the pilot had not even attempted to bail out. It was strange.

Moreover, if the facts were ominous, the rumors were downright frightening. Some falsely alleged that Mantell had radioed fantastic statements about what he saw: "My God, I can see people in this thing!" Others suggested that the alien spacecraft had shot his plane out of the sky, or that the occupants had abducted him from his airplane, or that Mantell's body had been shot full of strange holes. None of this was true, but it stoked the growing fires of public hysteria.

What really happened to Mantell is a matter of conjecture, but there is no doubt that he died under very unusual circumstances. No one ever positively identified the mysterious object he was chasing, but it was definitely more than a figment of everyone's imagination: many reliable witnesses, including Mantell himself, saw it. The absence of any definitive answers makes this infamous incident a compelling mystery. However, a logical explanation exists that even the most ardent "ufologist" can accept.

Postmortem

Capt. Thomas Mantell was by all accounts an experienced, careful, and skilled pilot who normally did not take unnecessary risks. He was also a courageous man, as evidenced by his many wartime citations and by the unhesitating manner in which he went in pursuit of the unknown object. If he had any limitation in his résumé at all, it is that most of his flight hours had been logged flying transports at low altitudes—and not as a fighter pilot. Thus, his experience in high-altitude, high-performance fighters was surprisingly little: only sixty-seven hours.

Since Mantell intended his flight that day to be at low level, none of the three Mustangs was carrying an adequate supply of oxygen. Therefore, military regulations strictly limited the pilots on this mission to a maximum altitude of 14,000 feet. Above that, the air is simply too thin to safely pilot an aircraft without supplemental oxygen. Mantell undoubtedly knew this, but obviously felt that the situation warranted the risk to pursue a potential enemy. His two wingmen, who may have had more high-altitude experience than Mantell, chose the more cautious approach. They broke off the chase when they had gone as high as they felt they could safely go.

Mantell's unrestrained charge upward may have been—both literally and figuratively—his downfall. As his airplane ascended to higher altitudes, perhaps eventually as high as thirty thousand feet, he almost certainly passed out from lack of oxygen. It is difficult to understand why he believed he could remain at twenty-five thousand feet for ten minutes without supplemental oxygen, as he had indicated in his last radio transmission. In reality, he could only have remained conscious for three to five minutes, at most. These actions may have simply reflected his inexperience with high-altitude flight in a non-pressurized aircraft like the Mustang.

Air Force investigators postulated that after Mantell passed out, his aircraft, trimmed for climb, likely continued upward on its own until it finally fell out of control. It ended up in an uncontrolled power dive that probably exceeded the speed of sound—a deadly and all-too-common occurrence for World War II-era high-performance aircraft. Eventually, the sturdy fighter, with a still-unconscious pilot at its controls, broke apart under the tremendous forces. This sudden structural failure—or perhaps a sonic boom resulting from the high-speed dive—was in all likelihood the "explosion" that the ground witness reported. Mantell died instantly when he hit the ground—that is, if not already dead from oxygen starvation or the excessive forces he experienced on the way down.

This logical explanation seems to put to rest the cause of Mantell's death. He did not die at the hands of an alien spaceship. He simply failed to abide by an important safety regulation—and paid for it with his life.

The Mysterious Object

Just what it was that Mantell and his two wingmen were chasing is not so easy to answer. The official explanation was that he was erroneously chasing the planet Venus that winter afternoon. Military authorities went to great pains to explain that the planet was, at the time, visible in the southwestern sky and that it set at about the same time the object reportedly disappeared from sight. Still, it was a stretch of anyone's imagination. It seemed ridiculous—even insulting—to propose that the faint appearance of a planet in broad daylight could have fooled hundreds of people on the ground, the experienced and reliable observers in the Godman tower, and a pilot of Mantell's ability. Because of the seemingly preposterous nature of this explanation, many accused military investigators of covering up the real story—that Mantell had actually died at the hands of an alien spacecraft.

What *was* the "real" story? No one knows for sure what Mantell was chasing, but even some dedicated UFO proponents question that the object in the sky that day was an alien spaceship, or anything else of extraterrestrial design. It simply did not fit the pattern of most of the sightings they consider legitimate. Rather, the most logical explanation is that the unidentified flying object causing all the commotion that day was something decidedly earthly.

Specifically, it may have been a massive high-altitude US Navy research balloon developed for a program known as Project Skyhook. Very few people at the time knew about this extremely specialized unmanned balloon. The navy had launched the first of these on September 25, 1947, only three months before Mantell's death. The colossal helium-filled craft could carry a payload of scientific and photographic equipment to heights exceeding one hundred thousand feet.

Because of the secrecy surrounding the research these balloons were conducting, none of the observers in the Mantell incident—either on the

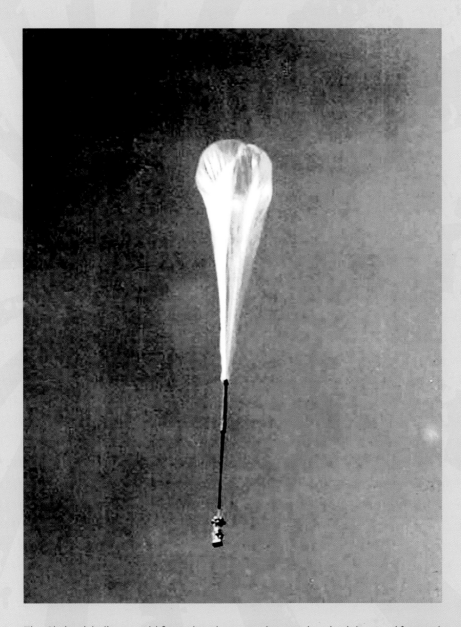

This Skyhook balloon could fly at altitudes exceeding one hundred thousand feet and expand to an enormous size. With its ice cream cone shape and polyethylene plastic surface shimmering in the sunlight, it may have been what Captain Mantell and others saw in the skies over Kentucky on the afternoon of January 7, 1948. *US Navy*

ground or in the air—had ever seen one or even heard about them. It is now a matter of public record, however, that these balloons were consistent in size and appearance with most of the descriptions of the object observed in the sky over Kentucky that day. Made from reflective polyethylene plastic, Skyhook balloons could expand at very high altitudes to an amazing size—several hundred feet in diameter and as high as a skyscraper; their maximum gas volume could expand to at least *twice* that of one of the largest airships ever built, the *Hindenburg*. In short, at high altitude one of these gigantic balloons would have been clearly visible to observers on the ground for, perhaps, as far away as a hundred miles in any direction. Additionally, it would have appeared as a white, shimmering parachute or ice cream cone hanging in the sky—just as the Godman Field control tower personnel described it.

Unfortunately, the navy kept the Skyhook launches so secret that it is still difficult to establish whether any of these balloons were actually floating over Kentucky that day. There is evidence to suggest that a Skyhook was launched on the previous day from a base in Minnesota. However, there are no records proving that it or any other balloon flew over Kentucky on January 7, 1948. Consequently, no one can say for sure what the mysterious object in the sky that day really was.

≠✴≠

Later that year two additional incidents involving credible witnesses added yet more fuel to the flames of worldwide flying saucer paranoia. On July 24, 1948, two Eastern Airlines pilots flying a Douglas DC-3 over Alabama nearly collided with a silent, wingless, torpedo-shaped craft they could not identify. Three months later, on October 1, a North Dakota Air National Guard pilot—who, like Mantell, was flying an F-51 Mustang fighter—had a protracted encounter with a UFO. In this case, now widely known as the "Gorman Dogfight," Lieutenant George F. Gorman actually flew a series of combat maneuvers against an unidentified object he confronted in the sky.

In the years since 1948, there have been hundreds more UFO sightings throughout the United States and the rest of the world. Along with these have been a number of claims of alien contact of one type or another, including alien sightings and abductions, alien attacks on people and animals, and UFO crashes. Some of these sightings and claims were little more than overly imaginative minds misinterpreting natural phenomena or futuristic-looking secret military aircraft. Others have been out-and-out hoaxes perpetrated by misguided individuals looking for fame, fortune, or amusement. However, a few of these incidents seem to be credible and are still unexplained.

Of all the many UFO sightings that have occurred over the centuries, the Mantell incident was one of the most provocative ever recorded. After all, he died a mysterious death while in pursuit of an unidentified object in the sky. He was the first ever known to die in this manner—but he would not be the last. At least three other fliers met a similar fate while encountering UFOs. On November 23, 1953, US Air Force pilot Lt. Felix E. Moncla Jr. and his radar operator, Lt. Robert L. Wilson, disappeared in their Northrop F-89C Scorpion jet over Lake Superior while attempting to intercept a UFO. Twenty-five years later, on October 21, 1978, a young Australian civilian pilot named Frederick Valentich disappeared in his Cessna 182 over Bass Strait, after radioing that he was being harassed by a large, lighted metallic object hovering in the sky over him. Many people have proposed logical explanations for each of these incidents, but they remain unsolved.

A roadside marker honoring Capt. Thomas F. Mantell Jr. It is located just south of Franklin, Kentucky, at the intersection of I-65 and US Highway 31W. He crashed and died near here on January 7, 1948, while pursuing an unidentified flying object. Coincidentally, Mantell was also born in Franklin. *Steven A. Ruffin*

CHAPTER TWENTY

THE CURIOUS CASE OF FLIGHT 19

"...AS IF THEY HAD FLOWN TO MARS."

A t 2:10 p.m., on December 5, 1945, a formation of five US Navy torpedo bombers took off from Naval Air Station Fort Lauderdale, Florida. The mission for Flight 19, so named because it was the nineteenth flight on the roster that day, was routine. It was a bombing and navigational training run over a three-hundred-mile triangular course. Aboard the planes, in addition to the five pilots, were nine enlisted crew members.

The lumbering single-engine Grumman TBM Avengers lifted off and headed east in formation. As they slowly disappeared into the haze over the Atlantic Ocean, no one could have imagined that the five planes or the fourteen men aboard would never return. This infamous flight was destined to become one of history's most intriguing and memorable aviation legends.

Navigation Problem No. 1

The task for the flight's experienced instructor pilot, US Navy Lt. Charles Taylor, was straightforward. He was to accompany his four advanced student pilots—one navy officer and three marines—on a standard training mission. Almost the entire flight would be over the waters of the Atlantic Ocean. The three-legged course they had planned ran 123 miles east, 73 miles north, and then 120 miles southwest back on the final leg to the Naval

Flight of five US Navy Grumman TBM Avengers, assigned to Naval Air Station Fort Lauderdale, Florida. Flight 19 must have looked much like this as it departed Fort Lauderdale for the last time on December 5, 1945. The final destination of the aircraft and crew is as much a mystery today as it was then. *US Navy via NAS Fort Lauderdale Museum*

Air Station. Four of the Avengers carried a crew of three men each—the pilot and two enlisted members—while the fifth carried only two.

Each of the student pilots was near the end of his advanced training and already wore the "Wings of Gold," designating him as a full-fledged naval aviator. As a group, they averaged more than 360 flight hours apiece. Consequently, for them, this mission—officially called Navigation Problem No. 1—was not particularly challenging. As they headed out over the Atlantic Ocean, they were probably already thinking about the cold drinks they would be sipping at the officers' club in less than three hours. Unfortunately, those drinks would never be poured.

The subsequent disappearance of the five TBMs and their crews should have been sufficient to satisfy the greedy gods of the sea, but it was not. A Martin PBM-5 Mariner patrol aircraft, sent out later that evening to search for the overdue Flight 19, also vanished with its thirteen-man crew. Despite an extensive five-day search operation, no definitive trace of any of the missing men or aircraft ever turned up. It was, as one US Navy investigator later put it, "as if they had flown to Mars."

US Navy Martin PBM-5, similar to the one that disappeared with thirteen men aboard while searching for lost Flight 19. Did it succumb to the malevolent powers of the Bermuda Triangle, as so often suggested? Or did it simply experience a fuel leak and explode in midair? *US Navy*

The Bermuda Triangle

Exactly what happened to the Flight 19 Avengers and the Martin Mariner flying boat remains a mystery. Innumerable books, articles, and documentaries have appeared over the years, describing these strange and tragic disappearances and attempting to explain them. Unfortunately much of this is fraught with inaccuracy, hyperbole, and wild speculation. Yet, the fact remains that, to this day, no one knows exactly what happened to the twenty-seven men and six aircraft that vanished that December afternoon in 1945.

Vanishing airplanes and ships are not particularly uncommon. Disappearances of craft on, above, or beneath the ocean have taken place with appalling regularity ever since man first ventured out onto the unforgiving seas. Unpredictable weather systems, strong currents, and the sheer vastness of Earth's great oceans have always provided more than enough cause for maritime disasters. These conditions apply to all large bodies of water, but there are those who believe that some are more treacherous than others—and one of the most infamous of these purportedly cursed ocean regions, known as the Bermuda Triangle, lies beneath the airspace in which Flight 19 and the Mariner disappeared. Different authors have defined this four-hundred-thousand-square-mile area of nautical intrigue in various ways. Most, however, describe it roughly as the area of the Atlantic Ocean within a triangle formed by Bermuda, Puerto Rico, and Miami, Florida.

The name given this region dates back to an article appearing in the February 1964 issue of *Argosy* magazine, entitled "The Deadly Bermuda Triangle." Its author, Vincent F. Gaddis, coined the term—and it stuck. However, the area's many recorded idiosyncrasies date back long before. Since Christopher Columbus himself, seafarers sailing through these regions have described anomalies, such as rogue waves, strange aquatic life, lights in the sky, powerful currents, and magnetic compass deviations.

These disarmingly enchanting Caribbean waters, which supposedly possess such mysterious forces, have also established a reputation for danger. The so-called "graveyard of the Atlantic," infamous for its extreme meteorological conditions and powerful currents, has devoured hundreds of ships and aircraft. Some of these have vanished without a trace and for reasons still unknown. Various authors have suggested an innate supernatural evil associated with the Bermuda Triangle—a sinister force that greedily snatches up ships, aircraft, and unsuspecting human travelers at will. Others contend that this important high-traffic area experiences no higher losses, proportionally, than any of the earth's other heavily traveled ocean areas.

Unquestionably, however, some of the most publicized and puzzling ship and aircraft disappearances ever recorded have occurred in this area. Bizarre as many of these tragedies were, the strangest vanishing act of all was that of Flight 19. This incident, more than any other, solidified the legend of the Bermuda Triangle.

An Explosion in the Sky

The disappearances of the Flight 19 Avengers and the Martin Mariner sent out to look for them are in many ways as baffling now as they were on the day they occurred. Some of the many theories proposed to explain their loss seem credible, while others are considerably less so. Different authors have hypothesized about huge, deadly methane gas bubbles escaping from the sea and interfering with the men and aircraft; or electromagnetic anomalies that disabled the planes' navigational equipment; or even that the unlucky aircraft fell into a time warp or a black hole.

Some have even suggested that aliens abducted the planes and men—as portrayed in the 1977 Steven Spielberg movie *Close Encounters of the Third Kind*. In the exciting opening segment of the film, viewers experience the inexplicable discovery of what appears to be the Flight 19 Avengers sitting completely undamaged in the middle of a remote desert— more than thirty years after their disappearance. Later in the movie, the men—ostensibly from the lost flight—reappear as guests of the aliens who have come to Earth. This science fiction classic is undoubtedly more fiction than science, but it illustrates the widespread mystical aura that has hovered for all these decades over the Flight 19 incident.

No matter what happened to these aircraft, those experienced in search operations agree on one point: rarely does anything ever simply "disappear," even in the ocean. When a ship or aircraft goes down, it nearly always leaves behind traces, usually in the form of floating debris and an oil slick.

The Mariner search plane may have left just such a calling card. At 7:50 p.m.—only twenty-three minutes after the Mariner took off from its base at Banana River, Florida—the crew of the tanker SS *Gaines Mills*, cruising off the coast of Florida nearby, witnessed what appeared to be an airplane explode in flame and crash into the sea. They later went through a pool of oil floating on the water, but found no bodies or anything else to confirm that it was—or was not—from the Mariner.

Many popular accounts suggested that the big flying boat was, like Flight 19, a victim of the malevolent forces of the Bermuda Triangle; this, however, is highly debatable, since the oil pool was near the location where the airplane disappeared from ground radar. Thus, at least circumstantially, there is a rational explanation as to the fate of the Mariner and crew. However, this did not explain the loss of Flight 19. Even after the ensuing five-day search, an entire flight of five US Navy aircraft and fourteen men were missing without any trace—and everyone wanted to know where they had gone.

A Case of Directional Disorientation

As is so often the case, the most likely explanation for an unusual occurrence is not necessarily the most exciting. What *probably* happened to the five lost US Navy torpedo bombers is not mysterious at all. Logic dictates that instead of aliens, black holes, time warps, and supernatural vortices from other dimensions, the blame should go to something more believable—like human error.

The most plausible explanation for the tragedy of Flight 19 is that the pilots simply became lost, ran out of fuel, crashed into the sea, and sank before searchers could locate them. The evidence is compelling. At the heart of the issue was the instructor pilot, Lieutenant Taylor. Although he was the leader of the flight, and a veteran with more than 2,500 flight hours, he had recently transferred to Fort Lauderdale from Naval Air Station Miami. Because of this, he was relatively unfamiliar with the assigned mission area.

To complicate things, Taylor had—for reasons still not clear—tried to excuse himself from flying that day. Some suggest he had a premonition, while others assert he simply had a hangover from the night before or otherwise did not feel up to par. Whatever the case, no replacement pilot was available, so he had no choice but to fly. This delayed the scheduled 1:45 p.m. takeoff time by almost half an hour. The mission was already off to a bad start.

The first indication that Flight 19 was having problems occurred at 3:50 p.m., less than two hours after the five torpedo bombers departed Fort Lauderdale. At this time, Lt. Robert Cox, another US Navy instructor pilot assigned there, was flying south of Fort Lauderdale. He picked up part of a radio conversation between Lieutenant Taylor and one of his student pilots, Marine Capt. Edward Powers. Cox heard Powers report, "I don't know where we are. We must have got lost after that last turn." When Cox heard this, he radioed Taylor and asked what the problem was. Taylor responded, "Both my compasses are out and I'm trying to find Fort Lauderdale, Florida. I'm over land but it's broken. I'm sure I'm in the Keys but I don't know how far down and I don't know how to get to Fort Lauderdale."

US Navy Lt. Charles Taylor, before promotion to full lieutenant. How did a pilot of his considerable experience get his entire flight of five Grumman TBM Avengers so hopelessly lost on a routine training mission? *US Navy via NAS Fort Lauderdale Museum*

Why *both* of Taylor's compasses were apparently malfunctioning is a mystery in itself. Typically, the Avenger carried, like most other aircraft at that time, two types of compasses: one magnetic, the other gyroscopic. Since these operate on completely different principles, it is highly unlikely that both would go haywire at the same time. Was Taylor simply confused, or was some unknown force affecting his navigational gear?

Since Taylor had stated that he was in "the Keys," which lie off the southern coast of Florida, Cox advised him to "put the sun on your port wing . . . and fly up the coast until you get to Miami." This was sound advice, provided the formation actually was over the Keys. Minutes later,

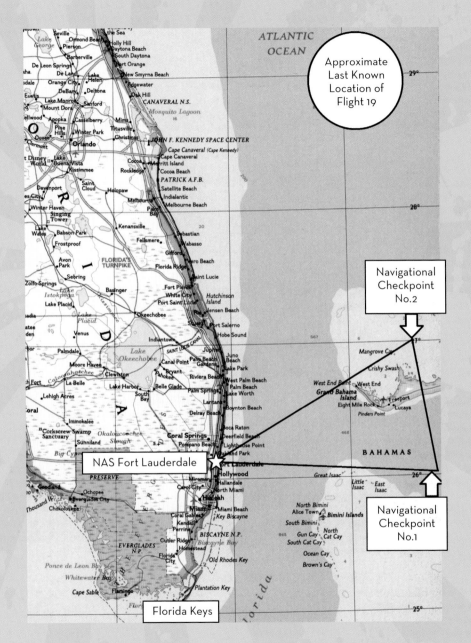

The triangle marks the intended course of Flight 19 on December 5, 1945. However, Lieutenant Taylor incorrectly believed, for reasons unknown, that he had strayed down into the Florida Keys. The white circle marks the approximate location of the flight's last radio fix. This also may be where they crashed into the sea.

Taylor transmitted, "We have just passed over a small island. We have no other land in sight." This could only mean that he had somehow missed the entire peninsula of Florida—which was unlikely—or else that he was somewhere entirely different from where he thought he was. Unfortunately for the men of Flight 19, they almost certainly were not over the Florida Keys. They were probably not even near the Keys; nor for that matter, should they have been. This would have put them well over a hundred miles southwest of their planned route, which seems highly unlikely. Instead, they were probably more or less on course, over a group of islands near the Bahamas that could easily be mistaken for the Florida Keys.

As the minutes ticked away, those on the ground became increasingly concerned. The navy alerted area coastal radar stations, ships, and the Coast Guard. At 5:03 p.m., Lieutenant Taylor, still flying north and still convinced he had been south of Florida over the Keys, instructed his flight to turn east. He apparently had decided that they must somehow be *west* of Florida, in the Gulf of Mexico. However, since he was in reality already more than a hundred miles *east* of Florida and north of the Bahamas, heading in that direction only took him and his doomed flight further out to sea.

Ironically, Taylor, the experienced veteran and leader of the flight, may have been the only pilot in the formation so completely confused. When he gave the order to turn east, two of his student pilots expressed their disagreement. One said, "Dammit, if we could just fly west we would get home; head west...!" Not until thirteen minutes later, at 5:16 p.m., did Taylor finally heed his students' advice and turn his flight—correctly—back toward the west, and mainland Florida. They would continue, he advised, "until we hit the beach or run out of gas."

By then, however, it was too late. Hitting the beach was no longer an option. Flight 19 was now not only well out to sea, totally lost, and getting low on fuel—they were suddenly also facing rapidly deteriorating flying conditions. The lost flight of Avengers was heading into a storm, with gusty winds and rain, decreased visibility, and rough seas, and it was getting dark. The final curtain was about to fall.

Gone Forever

By 6:00 p.m., ground radio stations finally managed to obtain a fix, which definitively placed Flight 19 north of the Bahamas, halfway up the eastern coast of Florida. Instead of flying west for the past hour as Taylor indicated they were going to do, the five Avengers had apparently—for reasons unknown—been flying north. The ground radio stations failed to pass this information on to Lieutenant Taylor—although by now, it would not have helped anyway. At approximately 6:20 p.m., Taylor radioed his pilots: "All planes close up tight . . . we'll have to ditch unless landfall . . . when the first plane drops below ten gallons, we all go down together." This was the last transmission from Flight 19 ever heard. By 8:00 p.m., the formation was no longer airborne based on projected fuel exhaustion. They had either ditched or crashed into the sea.

Many researchers have puzzled over how five torpedo bombers and fourteen men managed to disappear so completely without a trace. Part of the explanation could be in the conditions they encountered near the end of their flight. Their visibility had become very poor on what was by now a dark and stormy night at sea. It is reasonable to assume that when they ran out of fuel and went into the rough sea that evening, they all went straight to Davy Jones's locker before anyone could escape. Even if they managed to make a relatively controlled ditching into the stormy sea, there was little chance of survival. The Grumman Aircraft Company did not build its seven-ton "Iron Birds," as Avengers were affectionately called, to float on water—especially after crashing into the rolling waves at a hundred miles per hour. In all likelihood, when the formation went into the drink, all five aircraft—and the men in them—went straight to the bottom. If they were far enough out to sea when they ditched, the nearly limitless depth of the ocean and the northeasterly flowing current of the powerful Gulf Stream would have erased any traces of the planes and rendered future discovery all but impossible.

The official navy board of inquiry into the matter ended in 1946, after a thorough investigation and a four-hundred-page report. It concluded that Lieutenant Taylor's misidentification of the Bahamas as the Florida Keys "plagued his future decisions and confused his reasoning . . . . He was directing his flight to fly east . . . even though he was undoubtedly east of Florida." Later that year, however, in response to a legal challenge from Taylor's mother—who took serious exception to her lost son bearing the responsibility for the tragedy, the Board of Correction of Naval Records officially removed the blame from Lieutenant Taylor and attributed the loss of Flight 19 to "causes or reasons unknown." That cryptic official conclusion is the final verdict as it stands today.

Recent Developments

In 1986, it appeared that proof of the fate of Flight 19 might be at hand. In the aftermath of the tragic loss of the Space Shuttle *Challenger*, divers combing the ocean floor thirty-five miles off the coast of Cape Canaveral for fragments of the doomed spacecraft unexpectedly came upon an airplane sitting on the sandy floor at a depth of 390 feet. Further examination confirmed that the airplane was a TBM Avenger. Had the final resting place of at least one of the missing Flight 19 aircraft at last been located? It seemed likely, given that this airplane was almost exactly where a researcher named Jon Myhre had previously calculated that Flight 19 probably ditched. Hopes of finally learning the secret of the infamous lost flight were deep-sixed, however, when divers were unable to positively identify this airplane or find others near it.

Five years later, in 1991, an underwater salvage crew made an even more compelling find. This team discovered a cluster of five Avengers lying six hundred feet below the ocean's surface off the eastern coast of Florida. At last, they had solved the mystery of Flight 19 . . . or had they? Closer examination revealed discrepancies that ruled out any possibility that they were the aircraft of Flight 19. Neither the model type nor the serial numbers matched those of the lost flight, but it seemed utterly impossible that *another* formation of five TBMs had simultaneously ditched in this same area. Experts explained this by concluding that these five aircraft had not crashed into the sea together but individually over a period of years near a low-level practice-bombing target.

In 2010, researcher Gian J. Quasar proposed a novel alternative explanation for the loss of Flight 19: the formation may not have crashed into the ocean at all. He argues rather convincingly that, based on all available evidence, Flight 19 made landfall and crashed into southern Georgia's Okefenokee Swamp. Unfortunately, this theory is impossible to test. The area in question is a national wildlife refuge, making any search for sunken torpedo bombers strictly forbidden.

⇥✦⇤

After more than seven decades of theorizing, conjecture, and calculation—with at least two false sightings thrown in for good measure—no one knows what happened to Flight 19. The final resting place of the men and their aircraft remains a matter of ongoing speculation, and chances grow slimmer that anyone will ever find them in the nearly infinite expanse of the mighty Atlantic Ocean or the murky depths of a Georgia swamp. With still no secrets revealed, the mystery of this most curious flight to nowhere remains unsolved.

BUT NOT LAST

"GOOD NIGHT. MALAYSIAN THREE-SEVEN-ZERO."

Questions ... and More Questions

At forty-one minutes and forty-three seconds past midnight on March 8, 2014, a Malaysian Airlines Boeing 777 took off from Kuala Lumpur International Airport, Malaysia. The flight, designated MH370, was bound for Beijing, China, nearly three thousand miles to the northeast. Aboard were 227 passengers and a crew of 12. Within minutes, Lumpur radar cleared the airliner to climb to thirty-five thousand feet and, at 1:19:24 a.m., handed it off to Ho Chi Minh Air Traffic Control. The flight crew acknowledged this with a routine signoff, "Good night. Malaysian three-seven-zero." Two minutes later, the big airliner disappeared from the radar screen, and was never seen again.

Satellite analysis later indicated that the jet continued to fly for at least another six hours in total radio silence and—with neither of its two transponders apparently sending out signals—effectively invisible to radar. Instead of landing on time at Beijing Capital International Airport, the incomprehensible journey of MH370 is believed to have ended somewhere over the southern part of the Indian Ocean—thousands of miles off course and in the opposite direction from its intended destination. Here, in all likelihood, it ran out of fuel and crashed into the sea. No one knows why it lost contact or why it deviated from its course and proceeded to meander across a major portion of the Eastern Hemisphere. Nor does anyone know

Malaysian Airlines Boeing 777-2H6ER, registration number 9M-MRO, at Amsterdam Airport Schiphol, May 5, 2013. On March 8, 2014, this airliner disappeared after taking off from Kuala Lumpur International Airport, Malaysia. Lost with it were 227 passengers and a crew of 12. *Bernhard Ebner*

what terrible things must have transpired inside the cabin and cockpit of MH370 during those final hours.

The ensuing search and recovery operation became the largest multinational air-sea search ever conducted. It eventually involved eighty-two aircraft, eighty-four surface vessels, and various support services from at least twenty-six countries. The vaguely defined search area was also the largest in history—nearly three million square miles—and the operation continued in full force until April 28. After more than seven weeks of general confusion, numerous false sightings, dead-end leads, baseless speculation, and ratings-driven 24/7 coverage by the cable TV news networks, it was apparent that any chance of finding debris still floating on the surface was nil. Consequently, aerial and surface search operations were suspended.

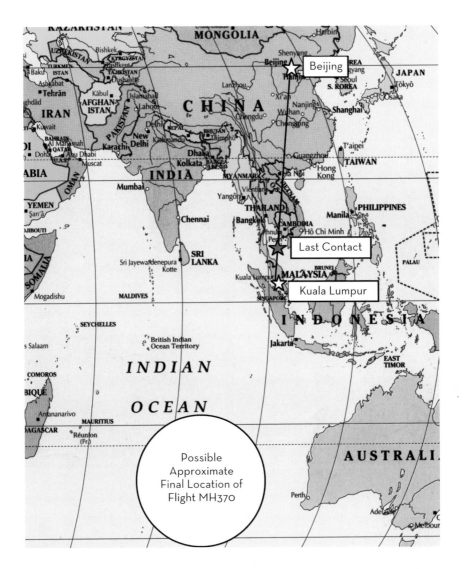

Malaysian Airlines Flight MH370 took off from Kuala Lumpur bound for Beijing, China, some three thousand miles to the northeast. Instead, it veered west and then south to points unknown. The white circle marks the area where it may have ended its flight.

Even after this unprecedented effort, no one had so much as a clue as to the whereabouts of the lost jetliner or the reason it went missing in the first place. Much conjecture ensued and dozens of possibilities were suggested, but none had even a shred of evidence to support it. Most of the more plausible theories seemed to center around one of two broad scenarios.

The first is that there was a catastrophic onboard event—a fire, explosion, sudden high-altitude decompression, or other problem causing an electrical failure. This probably would have knocked out all of the jet's communications and avionics equipment and incapacitated everyone aboard. Eventually, according to this theory, the airliner ran out of fuel and crashed into the sea.

The second scenario hinges on criminal activity—that one or more of the passengers or crew perpetrated a terrorist attack, hijacking, or other wrongdoing. This led to the destruction of the aircraft or a forced landing in some undisclosed place. Since no one apparently made any ransom demands, the latter possibility is doubtful, at best. The jetliner almost certainly crashed.

The list of less probable scenarios is almost endless. For example, one writer suggested in a widely cited April 18, 2014, OpEdNews.com article, that the US might have shot the airliner down—either intentionally or unintentionally—and then covered it up by failing to disclose known traces of the wreckage. However, the best source of unsubstantiated explanations came from TV news commentators, who found themselves with too much airtime and no real news to report. Some augmented their neverending coverage by quizzing guest experts on such matters as whether the big Boeing might have fallen into a black hole or been the victim of alien abduction. Such ridiculous speculation was so widespread that people actually started to believe it. A May 2014 CNN poll indicated that nine percent of Americans—one out of every eleven—believed that "space aliens or beings from another dimension" were somehow involved in the disappearance of MH370.

However, despite the comprehensive search and abundance of theories, the facts of this mysterious incident have remained as conspicuously absent as the airliner itself. It seems at this writing that unless someone comes forward with useful information, the only hope of ever finding answers to the many questions about Malaysian Airlines Flight 370 rests on future searches of the ocean's floor. Meanwhile, friends and families of the 239 victims can only grieve, wonder where and why their loved ones were taken, and imagine the terrible ways in which they might have met their end.

Eventually, the world may learn the secret of Flight MH370. Until then, it will remain—with the likes of Amelia Earhart, Nungesser and Coli, and Flight 19—one of aviation's great mysteries.

✈

Though unique in circumstances, the disappearance of MH370 is but a recent example of a scenario that has played out thousands of times and in many ways over the past 230-plus years of manned flight. Yet, flying has never been more reliable. Improved aircraft and engine design, coupled with major technological advances in navigation and weather prediction, have made it the safest of all forms of transportation—even walking. Arnold Barnett, MIT professor of statistics, calculated that the risk of being on a fatal commercial aircraft flight in the United States was one in forty-five million. Given those odds, a person could—statistically speaking—fly every day for an average of 123,000 years before being involved in a fatal crash.

In spite of odds so overwhelmingly in favor of air travelers, it is also a statistical fact that the next flight a person takes *could* be his last. This is merely a reflection of the uncertainty of life in general. In the end, a flier's chances of arriving at his destination boil down to something far less scientifically definable than statistical analysis. Renowned aviation author Ernest K. Gann called it "fate." In his autobiographical novel *Fate Is the Hunter*, his conclusion about two fatal aircraft accidents he had just described could probably apply to all such occurrences: "In both incidents the official verdict was 'pilot error,' but since their passengers who were innocent of the controls also failed to survive, it seemed that fate was the hunter. As it had been and would be."

Aviation technology will continue to advance, and aircraft will fly through the skies faster, higher, and farther. With these advancements, aviation safety and reliability will also improve. However, since human beings will always be a part of the process, the possibility of error or intentional wrongdoing will continue to exist. For that reason, flights of no return will unfortunately always be a small but tragic part of aviation.

BIBLIOGRAPHICAL REFERENCES

Prologue

Crouch, Tom D. *The Bishop's Boys: A Life of Wilbur and Orville Wright*. New York: W. W. Norton & Company, 1989.

Hennessy, Juliette A. *The United States Army Air Arm, April 1861 to April 1917*. Washington, DC: Office of Air Force History, 1985.

Jackson, Donald Dale. *The Aeronauts*. Alexandria, PA: Time-Life Books, Inc., 1980.

Kelly, Fred C. *The Wright Brothers: A Biography Authorized by Orville Wright*. New York: Harcourt, Brace and Company, 1943.

Lilienthal, Otto. *Birdflight as the Basis of Aviation: A Contribution Towards a System of Aviation*. Hummelstown, PA: Markowski International Publishers, 2000.

"Monsieurs Rozier and Romain, the World's First Deaths in an Air Crash – 15 June 1785." the British Newspaper Archive, posted June 14, 2013. *blog. britishnewspaperarchive.co.uk/monsieurs-rozier-and-romain-the-worlds-first-deaths-in-an-air-crash-15-june-1785*.

Moolman, Valerie.*The Road to Kitty Hawk*. Alexandria, VA: Time-Life Books, Inc., 1980.

Prendergast, Curtis.*The First Aviators*. Alexandria, VA: Time-Life Books, Inc., 1980.

Rolt, L. T. C. *The Aeronauts: A History of Ballooning, 1783-1903*. London: Longmans, 1966.

Villard, Henry Serrano. *Contact! The Story of the Early Birds: Man's First Decade of Flight from Kitty Hawk to World War I*. New York: Thomas Y. Crowell Company, 1968.

Chapter One

Behar, Michael. "The Search for Steve Fossett: One Tough Job for the US Civil Air Patrol." *Air & Space*, March 2008.

Bingham, John. "Steve Fossett: Conspiracy Theories Challenged by Discovery of Human Remains." *Telegraph*, October 3, 2008.

Fédération Aéronautique Internationale (FAI), International Air Sports Federation. *www.fai.org/records*. Accessed 2013.

Fossett, Steve, with Will Hasley. *Chasing the Wind: The Autobiography of Steve Fossett*. London: Virgin Books, Ltd., 2006.

Garrison, Peter. "Why Steve Fossett Crashed." *Los Angeles Times*, July 27, 2009.

Irvine, Chris. "Adventurer Steve Fossett May Have 'Faked His Own Death.'" *Telegraph*, July 27, 2008.

National Transportation Safety Board. Factual Report, Aviation, NTSB Identification SEA07FA277, Washington, DC, September 3, 2007.

National Transportation Safety Board. Probable Cause, NTSB Identification SEA07FA277, Washington, DC, July 9, 2009.

Vlahos, James "Steve." *The New York Times Magazine*, New York edition, December 23, 2008. MM48.

Chapter Two

Bak, Richard. *The Big Jump: Lindbergh and the Great Atlantic Air Race*. Hoboken, NJ: John Wiley & Sons, Inc., 2011.

Cussler, Clive. *The Sea Hunters II: More True Adventures with Famous Shipwrecks*, Part 11, "L'Oiseau Blanc." New York: G.P. Putnam's Sons, 2002.

Hansen, Gunnar. "The Unfinished Flight of the White Bird." *Yankee Magazine*, June 1980.

"Looking for l'Oiseau Blanc." *whitebird.over-blog.net/*. Accessed 2013.

Moffett, Sebastian. "Charles Lindbergh Won the Prize, but Did His Rival Get There First?" *Wall Street Journal*, September 6, 2011. *online.wsj.com/news/articles/SB1000142405311190448090457649806149 1234304*.

"Nungesser and Coli Disappear Aboard l'Oiseau Blanc – May 1927." French Ministry of Transport, General Inspector of Civil Aviation and Meteorology Report, June 1984. *tighar.org/Projects/PMG/FrenchReport. htm*, 2013.

TIGHAR, The International Group for the Recovery of Historic Aircraft. "Project Midnight Ghost: The Search for History's Most Important Missing Airplane." *tighar.org/Projects/PMG/PMG.html*. Accessed 2013.

Chapter Three

Archbold, Rick. *Hindenburg: An Illustrated History*. New York: Chartwell Books, 2005.

Bain, A. "The Hindenberg Disaster: A Compelling Theory of Probable Cause and Effect." *Proceedings: National Hydrogen Association*, 8th Annual Hydrogen Meeting, Alexandria, VA, March 11–13, 1997. 125-128.

Botting, Douglas. *Dr. Eckener's Dream Machine: The Great Zeppelin and the Dawn of Air Travel*. New York: Henry Holt & Co., 2001.

"Commerce Department Accident Report on the Hindenburg Disaster," *Air Commerce Bulletin*, US Dept. of Commerce, Vol. 9, No. 2, August 15, 1937.

"Destruction of Airship Hindenburg," Federal Bureau of Investigation, File Number 70-396, Washington, DC, June 17, 1937.

Dick, Harold G. and Douglas H. Robinson. *The Golden Age of the Great Passenger Airships Graf Zeppelin & Hindenburg*. Washington, DC: Smithsonian Books, 1992.

Duggan, John. *LZ 129 "Hindenburg": The Complete Story*. Ickenham, UK: Zeppelin Study Group, 2002.

Grossman, Dan. "Airships: The Hindenburg and Other Zeppelins." *www.airships.net/zeppelins*. Accessed 2013.

Hoehling, A. A. *Who Destroyed the Hindenburg?* Boston: Little, Brown and Company, 1962.

Hoehling, A. A. and Martin Mann, "The Biggest Birds That Ever Flew," *Popular Science*, May 1962, pp. 85–95.

"'LZ-129,' the Latest Airship." *Popular Mechanics Magazine*, June 1935, 846–847, 138A.

Majoor, Mireille. *Inside the Hindenburg*. Boston: Little, Brown and Company, 2000.

Mooney, Michael. *The Hindenburg*. New York: Dodd, Mead & Company, 1972.

Robinson, Douglas Hill. *Giants in the Sky: A History of the Rigid Airship*. Seattle: University of Washington Press, 1973.

Toland, John. *The Great Dirigibles: Their Triumphs & Disasters*. Mineola, NY: Dover Publications, Inc., 1972.

Chapter Four

Briand, Paul. *Daughter of the Sky*. New York: Duell, Sloan, Pearce, 1960.

Brink, Randall. *Lost Star: The Search for Amelia Earhart*. New York: W.W. Norton & Co. Inc., 1993.

Butler, Susan. *East to the Dawn: The Life of Amelia Earhart*. Reading, MA: Addison-Wesley, 1997.

Devine, Thomas E. *Eyewitness: The Amelia Earhart Incident*. Frederick, CO: Renaissance House, 1987.

Earhart, Amelia. *20 Hrs., 40 Min.: Our Flight in the Friendship*. New York: Harcourt, Brace and Company, 1928.

——. *Last Flight*. New York: Crown Publishing Group, 1996.

Goerner, Fred. *The Search for Amelia Earhart*. Garden City, NY: Doubleday & Company, Inc., 1966.

Jourdan, David W. *The Deep Sea Quest for Amelia Earhart*. Ocellus, 2010.

Klaas, Joe and Joseph Gervais. *Amelia Earhart Lives: A Trip through Intrigue to Find America's First Lady of Mystery*. New York: McGraw-Hill, 1970.

Long, Elgen M. *Amelia Earhart: The Mystery Solved*. New York: Simon & Schuster, 1999.

Loomis, Vincent V. *Amelia Earhart, the Final Story*. New York: Random House, 1985.

Lovell, Mary S. *The Sound of Wings*. New York: St. Martin's Press, 1989.

Rich, Doris L. *Amelia Earhart: A Biography*. Washington DC: Smithsonian Institution Press, 1989.

Strippel, Dick. *Amelia Earhart - The Myth and the Reality*. New York: Exposition Press, 1972.

TIGHAR, The International Group for the Recovery of Historic Aircraft. "The Earhart Project." *tighar.org/Projects/Earhart/AEdescr.html*. Accessed 2013.

Chapter Five

"The Airmen of Note." United States Air Force Band. *www.usafband.af.mil/ensembles/BandEnsembleBio.asp?EnsembleID=58*. Accessed 2013.

Atkinson, Fred W. Jr., "A World War II Soldier's Insight Into the 'Mysterious Disappearance' of Glenn Miller," *www.mishmash.com/glennmiller*. Accessed 2013.

British Broadcasting Company. "The Mysterious Disappearance of Glenn Miller." July 20, 2004. *www.bbc.co.uk/dna/place-lancashire/plain/A2654822*.

Butcher, Geoffrey. *Next to a Letter from Home: Major Glenn Miller's Wartime Band*. North Pomfret, VT: Trafalgar Square Publishing Co., 1997.

Downs, Hunton. *The Glenn Miller Conspiracy: The Never-Before-Told Story of His Life—and Death*. Beverly Hills, CA: Global Book Publishers, 2009.

Lennon, Peter, "Glenn Miller 'Died Under Hail of British Bombs.'" *Guardian, December 15, 2001. www.guardian.co.uk/uk/2001/dec/15/humanities.research*.

Missing Air Crew Report, relating to the disappearance of Glenn Miller's airplane, War Department, Headquarters US Army Air Forces, Washington, DC, December 22, 1944.

"Noorduyn UC-64 Norseman," National Museum of the US Air Force Fact Sheet, *www.nationalmuseum.af.mil/factsheets/factsheet.asp?id=515*, 2013.

Official Site of Glenn Miller. *www.glennmiller.com*, 2013.

Simon, George T., *Glenn Miller & His Orchestra*. New York: T.Y. Crowell Co., 1974.

Wolfe, Clarence B., and Susan Goodrich Giffin. *I Kept My Word: The Personal Promise between a World War II Army Private and His Captain about What Really Happened to Glenn Miller*. Bloomington, IN: AuthorHouse, 2006.

Chapter Six

Andersen, Christopher. *The Day John Died*. New York: Avon Books, 2000.

Landau, Elaine. *John F. Kennedy Jr.* Brookfield, CT: Twenty-First Century Books, 2000.

Levine, Alan, Kevin Johnson, and Deborah Sharp, "Pilot Kennedy was 'Conscientious Guy,'"*USA Today*, July 21, 1999.

National Transportation Safety Board. NTSB Identification NYC99MA178, Washington, DC, July 6, 2000.

Terenzio, RoseMarie. *Fairy Tale Interrupted: A Memoir of Life, Love, and Loss.* New York: Gallery Books, 2012.

Chapter Seven

"Astronaut Stories: The World's first Spaceplane," *AirSpaceMag.com*, February 28, 2011.

Bredeson, Carmen. *The Challenger Disaster: Tragic Space Flight.* Berkeley Hts., NJ: Enslow Publishers, 1999.

Cook, Richard C. *Challenger Revealed: An Insider's Account of How the Reagan Administration Caused the Greatest Tragedy of the Space Age.* New York: Thunder's Mouth Press, 2006.

Dunar, Andrew J., and Stephen P. Waring. *Power to Explore: History of Marshall Space Flight Center 1960-1990*, Chapter IX, "The Challenger Accident." Washington, DC: National Aeronautics and Space Administration, NASA History Office. Also available online at: *history.msfc.nasa.gov/book/chptnine.pdf,* 2013.

Feynman, Richard P., and Ralph Leighton. *What Do You Care What Other People Think? Further Adventures of a Curious Character.* New York: W.W. Norton & Company, 2001.

McDonald, Allan J. with James R. Hansen. *Truth, Lies, and O-Rings: Inside the Space Shuttle* Challenger *Disaster.* Gainesville, FL: University Press of Florida, 2009.

National Aeronautics and Space Administration. *www. nasa.gov.* Accessed 2013.

——. "Report of the Presidential Commission on the Space Shuttle Challenger Accident," NASA History Office, Washington, DC, June 6, 1986. *history.nasa. gov/rogersrep/genindex.htm.* Accessed 2013.

——. "The Space Shuttle Decision: NASA's Search for a Reusable Space Vehicle." NASA History Office, Washington, DC, 1999.

——. "Report from Joseph P. Kerwin, Biomedical Specialist from the Johnson Space Center in Houston, Texas, Relating to the Deaths of the Astronauts in the Challenger Accident, July 28, 1986." NASA History Office. *history.nasa.gov/kerwin. html.* Accessed 2013.

Vaughan, Diane. *The Challenger Launch Decision: Risky Technology, Culture, and Deviance at NASA.* Chicago: University of Chicago Press, 1996.

Chapter Eight

Bickers, Richard Townshend. *Von Richthofen: The Legend Evaluated.* Annapolis, MD: Naval Institute Press, 1996.

Bodenschatz, Karl, and Jan Hayzlett, trans. *Hunting with Richthofen. The Bodenschatz Diaries: Sixteen Months of Battle with JG Freiherr von Richthofen No. 1.* London: Grub Street, 1996.

Burrows, William E. *Richthofen: A True History of the Red Baron.* New York: Harcourt, Brace & World, Inc., 1969.

Carisella, P. J., and James W. Ryan. *Who Killed the Red Baron?* Greenwich, CT: Fawcett Publications, Inc., 1969.

"Death of the Red Baron." *Unsolved History,* Discovery Communications, Inc., 2002.

Fischer, Suzanne Hayes. *Mother of Eagles: The War Diary of Baroness von Richthofen.* Atglen, PA: Schiffer Publishing, Ltd., 2001.

Franks, Norman, and Alan Bennett. *The Red Baron's Last Flight: A Mystery Investigated.* London: Grub Street, 1997.

Gibbons, Floyd. *The Red Knight of Germany: The Story of Baron von Richthofen.* Garden City, NY: Garden City Publishing Co., Inc., 1927.

Hyatt, T. L., and D. R. Orme, "Baron Manfred von Richthofen—DNIF (Duties Not Including Flying)," *Human Factors and Aerospace Safety*, Vol. 4, No. 1 (2004): 67–81.

Kilduff, Peter. *Richthofen: Beyond the Legend of the Red Baron.* New York: John Wiley & Sons, Inc., 1993.

McGuire, Frank. *The Many Deaths of the Red Baron: The Richthofen Controversy 1918–2000.* Calgary, AB: Bunker to Bunker Publishing, 2001.

Schurmacher, Emile C. *Richthofen: The Red Baron.* New York: Paperback Library, 1970.

Titler, Dale. *The Day the Red Baron Died: A Full Account of the Death of Baron Manfred von Richthofen.* New York: Ballantine Books, 1970.

Ulanoff, Stanley M., ed., and Peter Kilduff, trans. *The Red Baron: The Autobiography of Manfred von Richthofen.* New York: Barnes & Noble Books, 1995.

Von Richthofen, Captain Manfred Freiherr (translated by J. Ellis Barker). *The Red Battle Flyer.* New York: Robert M. McBride & Co., 1918.

"Who Killed the Red Baron?" *NOVA*, Corporation for Public Broadcasting, 2003.

Chapter Nine

Adams-Ray, Edward. *The Andrée Diaries, Being the Diaries and Records of S.A. Andrée, Nils Strindberg and Knut Frænkel . . . .* London: John Lane, The Bodley Head Ltd., 1931.

"Andrée Expeditionen," Grenna Museum, The Andrée Expedition Polar Centre, *www.grennamuseum.se/,* 2013.

Martinsson, Tyrone. *Nils Strindberg, en biografi om fotografen på Andrées Polarexpedition.* Lund, Sweden: Historical Media, 2006.

——. "Recovering the Visual History of the Andrée Expedition: A Case Study in Photographic Research," *Research Issues in Art Design and Media*, ISSN 1474-2365, Issue 6, Summer 2004. *www.biad.bcu. ac.uk/research/rti/riadm/issue6/abstract.htm,* 2013.

Putnam, George Palmer. *Andrée: The Record of a Tragic Adventure.* New York: Brewer & Warren, Inc., 1930.

Sollinger, Günther, "S.A. Andrée: the Beginning of Polar Aviation 1895-1897," *The Geographical Journal*, 172(4), December 2006, p. 350.

Stefansson, Vilhjalmur. *Unsolved Mysteries of the Arctic*. New York: Macmillan Co., 1972.

Sundman, Per Olaf. *The Flight of the Eagle*. New York: Pantheon, 1970.

Wilkinson, Alec. *The Ice Balloon: S.A. Andrée and the Heroic Age of Arctic Exploration*. New York: Alfred A. Knopf, 2011.

Chapter Ten

Begich, Tom, and Dr. Nick Begich Jr., "Alaska's Bermuda Triangle or Lack of Government Accountability?" *www.freedomwriter.com/issue17/ak1.htm*, July 12, 2001.

"Boggs, Thomas Hale Sr.," Biographical Directory of the United States Congress, 1774 to Present, *bioguide. congress.gov/scripts/biodisplay.pl?index=B000594*, 2013.

Gibson, Dirk C. "Hale Boggs on J. Edgar Hoover: Rhetorical Choice and Political Denunciation." *Southern Speech Communication Journal 47*, Fall 1981, pp. 54–66.

Fensterwald, Bernard. *Coincidence or Conspiracy?* New York: Kensington Publishing Corp., 1977.

"Hale Boggs," Check-Six.com. *www.check-six.com/lib/ Famous_Missing/Boggs.htm*, 2013.

"History's Mysteries: Alaska's Bermuda Triangle," The History Channel, 2005.

Jonz, Don, "Ice Without Fear," *Flying*, October 1972, pp. 66–68, 123.

——. "Light Planes and Low Temperatures," *National Pilots Association Service Bulletin*, Vol. XII, No. 1, January 1972; and Vol. XII, No. 2, February 1972.

National Transportation Safety Board Aircraft Accident Report, "Pan Alaska Airways, Ltd. Cessna 310C, N1812H, Missing between Anchorage and Juneau, Alaska, October 16, 1972," Report Number NTSB-AAR-73-1, File No. 3-0604, Washington, DC, January 31, 1973.

Chapter Eleven

Allen, Martin. *The Hitler-Hess Deception*. London: HarperCollins Publishers, 2003.

Allen, Peter. *The Windsor Secret: New Revelations of the Nazi Connection*. New York: Stein and Day, 1984.

Costello, John. *Ten Days to Destiny: The Secret Story of the Hess Peace Initiative and British Efforts to Strike a Deal with Hitler*. New York: William Morrow, 1991.

Galland, Adolf. *The First and the Last*. New York: Bantam Books, Inc., 1979.

Harris, John. *Rudolf Hess: The British Illusion of Peace*. Northampton, UK: Jema Publications, 2010.

Harris, John, and M. J. Trow. *Hess: The British Conspiracy*. London: Andre Deutsch, Ltd. 2011.

Harris, John, and Richard Wilbourn. *Rudolf Hess: A New Technical Analysis of the Hess Flight, May 1941*. Staplehurst, UK: Spellmount, 2014.

Hess, Wolf Rüdiger. *My Father, Rudolf Hess*. London: W. H. Allen, 1986.

Kilzer, Louis C. *Churchill's Deception: The Dark Secret That Destroyed Nazi Germany*. New York: Simon & Schuster, 1994.

Masters, Anthony. *The Man Who Was M: The Life of Charles Henry Maxwell Knight*. London: Grafton Books, 1986.

Nesbit, Roy Conyers, and Georges Van Acker. *The Flight of Rudolf Hess: Myths and Reality*. Stoud, UK: Sutton Publishing, Ltd., 2002.

Padfield, Peter. *Hess: Flight for the Fuhrer*. London: Weidenfeld & Nicolson, 1991.

Picknett, Lynn, Clive Prince, and Steven Prior with additional historical research by Robert Brydon. *Double Standards: The Rudolf Hess Cover-Up*. London: Little, Brown, and Co., 2001.

Schwärzwaller, Wulf. *Rudolf Hess, the Deputy*. London: Quartet Books, 1988.

Smith, Alfred. *Rudolf Hess and Germany's Reluctant War, 1939–41*. Sussex, UK: The Book Guild Ltd., 2001.

Stafford, David, ed. *Flight From Reality: Rudolf Hess and His Mission to Scotland, 1941*. London: Pimlico, 2002.

Thomas, W. Hugh. *The Murder of Rudolf Hess*. New York: Harper & Row, 1979.

Chapter Twelve

"A Byte out of History: The D. B. Cooper Mystery." Federal Bureau of Investigation Website, November 24, 2006. *www.fbi.gov/news/ stories/2006/november/dbcooper_112406*. Accessed 2013.

"D. B. Cooper," FBI Records: The Vault. Federal Bureau of Investigation. *vault.fbi.gov/D-B-Cooper%20*. Accessed 2013.

"D. B. Cooper Redux: Help Us Solve This Enduring Mystery." Federal Bureau of Investigation, December 31, 2007. *www.fbi.gov/news/stories/2007/december/ dbcooper_123107*. Accessed 2013.

Forman, Pat and Ron. *The Legend of D. B. Cooper: Death by Natural Causes*. Borders Personal Publishing, 2008.

Gates, David, with Mark Kirchmeier, "D. B. Cooper, Where Are You?" *Newsweek*, December 26, 1983.

Gilmore, Susan. "D. B. Cooper Puzzle: The Legend Turns 30," *Seattle Times*, Nov. 22, 2001.

Gorney, Cynthia. "Vanishing Act: The Hunt for D. B. Cooper," *Washington Post*, February 18, 1980.

Gray, Geoffrey. *Skyjack: The Hunt for D. B. Cooper*. New York: Crown Publishing Group, 2012.

——. "Unmasking D. B. Cooper." *New York Magazine*,

October 21, 2007. nymag.com/news/features/39593.

Gunther, Max. *D.B. Cooper: What Really Happened.* Chicago: Contemporary Books, 1985.

Himmelsbach, Ralph P., and Thomas K. Worcester. *NORJAK: The Investigation of D. B. Cooper.* West Linn, OR: Norjak Project, 1986.

Martz, Ron. "D. B. Cooper Is Alive: The Legend Won't Let Him Die." *Chicago Tribune,* December 5, 1985.

Olson, Kay Melchisedech. *D. B. Cooper Hijacking: Vanishing Act.* Mankato, MN: Compass Point Books, 2010.

Pasternak, Douglas, "Skyjacker at Large: A Florida Widow Thinks She Has Found Him," *U.S. News and World Report,* June 24, 2000.

Porteous, Skipp, and Robert Blevins. *Into the Blast: The True Story of D. B. Cooper.* Seattle: Adventure Books of Seattle, 2010.

Rhodes, Bernie, and Russell Calame. *D. B. Cooper: The Real McCoy.* Salt Lake City: University of Utah Press, 1991.

Seven, Richard. "D. B. Cooper—Perfect Crime or Perfect Folly?" *Seattle Times,* Nov. 17, 1996.

——. "Man Still Trying to Track Legendary Hijacker D. B. Cooper," *Seattle Times,* Nov. 20, 1996.

Skolnik, Sam, "30 Years Ago, D. B. Cooper's Night Leap Began a Legend," *Seattle Post-Intelligencer,* Nov. 22, 2001.

"Sluggo's Northwest 305 Northwest Hijacking Research Site." n467us.com/index.htm

The Skyjacker That Got Away. Edge West, Inc. with National Geographic Television for National Geographic Channel, 2009.

Tosaw, Richard T. *D. B. Cooper: Dead or Alive? The True Story of the Legendary Skyjacker.* Tosaw Publishing Company, 1984.

Vartabedian, Ralph, "A New Lead in the D. B. Cooper Mystery." *Los Angeles Times,* August 1, 2011.

Chapter Thirteen

"A New Kind of War: The Story of the FAA and NORAD Response to the September 11, 2001 Attacks," *Rutgers Law Review,* www.rutgerslawreview.com/2011/a-new-type-of-war, 2013.

"Debunking the 9/11 Myths: Special Report – The Planes." *Popular Mechanics,* March 2005. www.popularmechanics.com/technology/military/news/1227842. Accessed 2013.

Elias, Barbara, ed. "Complete Air-Ground Transcripts of Hijacked 9/11 Flight Recordings Declassified." National Security Archive Electronic Briefing Book No. 196, August 11, 2006. www.gwu.edu/~nsarchiv/NSAEBB/NSAEBB196/index.htm.

Full [9/11] Audio Transcript, *Rutgers Law Review,* www.rutgerslawreview.com/2011/full-audio-transcript. Accessed 2013.

National Commission on Terrorist Attacks Upon the United States, "The 9/11 Commission Report," www.9-11commission.gov/. Accessed 2013.

Chapter Fourteen

Churchill, Winston S. *The Hinge of Fate.* New York: Houghton-Mifflin, 1950.

Colvin, Ian. *Flight 777: The Mystery of Leslie Howard.* London: Evans Brothers, 1957.

Eforgan, Estel. *Leslie Howard: The Lost Actor.* London: Vallentine Mitchell Publishers, 2010.

Goss, Chris. *Bloody Biscay: The Story of the Luftwaffe's Only Long Range Maritime Fighter Unit, V Gruppe/Kampfgeschwader 40, and Its Adversaries 1942–1944.* London: Crécy Publishing, 2001.

Howard, Leslie Ruth. *A Quite Remarkable Father: A Biography of Leslie Howard.* New York: Harcourt Brace and Co., 1959.

Howard, Ronald. *In Search of My Father: A Portrait of Leslie Howard.* London: St. Martin's Press, 1984.

Nesbit, Roy Conyers. *Failed to Return: Mysteries of the Air 1939–1945.* Wellingborough, Northamptonshire, UK: Patrick Stephens Limited, 1988.

Rosevink, Ben and Lt. Col. Herbert Hintze, "Flight 777," *FlyPast,* Issue 120, July 1991.

Chapter Fifteen

"Accident Description." Aviation Safety Network, Flight Safety Foundation, aviation-safety.net/database/record.php?id=19721013-0. Accessed 2013.

Andes Accident Official Website. www.viven.com.uy/571/eng/default.asp. Accessed 2013.

Parrado, Nando, and Vince Rause. *Miracle in the Andes: 72 Days on the Mountain and My Long Trek Home.* New York: Three Rivers Press, 2006.

Read, Piers Paul. *Alive: The Story of the Andes Survivors.* New York: Lippincott, 1974.

Chapter Sixteen

Caidin, Martin. *Ghosts of the Air: True Stories of Aerial Hauntings.* Lakeville, MN: Galde Press, Inc., 1994.

Currie, Jack. *Echoes in the Air: A Chronicle of Aeronautical Ghost Stories.* Manchester, UK: Crécy Publishing Ltd., 1998.

"Eastern Air Lines Flight 401." sites.google.com/site/eastern401. Accessed 2013.

"Eastern Flight 401: The Story of the Crash." Miami Herald Media Company, December 2007. www.miamiherald.com/multimedia/news/flight401.

Elder, Rob and Sarah. *Crash.* New York: Atheneum Press, 1977.

Fuller, Elizabeth, *My Search for the Ghost of Flight 401.* New York: Berkley Books, 1978.

Fuller, John G. *The Airmen Who Would Not Die.* New York: Putnam, 1979.

———. *The Ghost of Flight 401.* New York: Berkley Books, 1983.

Job, Macarthur. "Hey—What's Happening Here?" *Air Disaster, Volume 1,* 98–111. Fyshwick ACT, Australia:

Aerospace Publications Pty, Ltd., 1994.

Kilroy, Chris. "Special Report: Eastern Air Lines Flight 401." *www.airdisaster.com/special/special-ea401.shtml*. Accessed 2013.

McKee, Alexander. *Great Mysteries of Aviation*. New York: Stein and Day, 1981.

Monan, W. P. "Distraction—A Human Factor in Air Carrier Hazard Events," *NASA Aviation Safety Reporting System: Ninth Quarterly Report*, 2–23. Moffett Field, CA: National Aeronautics and Space Administration, 1978.

National Transportation Safety Board. Aircraft Accident Report Number NTSB-AAR-73-14, Washington, DC, June 14, 1972. *www.airdisaster.com/reports/ntsb/AAR73-14.pdf*. Accessed 2013.

Titler, Dale M. *Wings of Mystery: True Stories of Aviation History*. New York: Tower Publications, Inc., 1962.

Chapter Seventeen

Ali Mohamed, Dr. Fadel. "The Return of the *Lady Be Good*." *After the Battle*, Issue 89, 28–31.

Fuller, Captain Myron C., Jr., and Wesley A. Neep. "Report of Investigation, US Army Quartermaster Mortuary System, Europe, Case: B-24 Bomber Lost 4/5 April 1943 and the 1959 Libyan Desert Search for the Nine Missing Crewmembers." November 17, 1959.

——. "Report of Investigation, US Army Quartermaster Mortuary System, Europe, Case: Final Search for Sour Unrecovered Airmen of B-24 Bomber *Lady Be Good* Lost April 1943 in the Libyan Desert." June 20, 1960.

Hanna, William, "The Ordeal of the *Lady Be Good*." *American History Illustrated*, Vol. 16(7), November 1981, pp. 8-15.

Holder, William G. "Epitaph to the *Lady*—30 Years After." *Air University Review*, Vol. 9(3), March–April 1973, 41–50. *www.airpower.au.af.mil/airchronicles/aureview/1973/mar-apr/holder.html*. Accessed 2013.

"*The Lady Be Good*." *After the Battle*, Issue 25, 26–49.

"Lady Be Good." National Museum of the US Air Force Factsheet. *www.nationalmuseum.af.mil/factsheets/factsheett.asp?id=2475*. Accessed 2013.

"Lady Be Good." US Army Quartermaster Foundation, Fort Lee, Virginia, *www.qmfound.com/lady_be_good_b-24_bomber_recovery.htm*. Accessed 2013.

"Lady Be Good.net: A repository for online information about World War II's Ghost Bomber." *www.ladybegood.net*. Accessed 2013.

Martinez, Mario. *Lady's Men: The Saga of Lady Be Good and Her Crew*. Annapolis, MD: Naval Institute Press, 1995.

McClendon, Dennis E. *The Lady Be Good: Mystery Bomber of World War II*. New York: Day, 1962. (Reissued by Aero Publishers, Inc., Fallbruck, CA with a new epilogue in 1982.)

"North African Desert Gives Up Its Secret: 17-Year-Old Mystery of the 'Lady Be Good' and Her Crew Is Finally Solved." *LIFE* magazine, March 7, 1960 (Vol. 48, No. 9), 20–27.

"The Truth about the Ship That Vanished in the Desert." *www.ladybegood.com*. Accessed 2013.

Walker, James W. "Lady Be Good." 376th Heavy Bomb Group website, *376hbgva.com/aircraft/ladybegood.html*. Accessed 2013.

——. *The Liberanos: World War II History of the 376th Bomb Group*. 219–281. Waco, TX: 376th Vets Association, 1994.

Chapter Eighteen

"Airship Accident, All West Coast." US Navy Publication, March 1944. Lighter-Than-Air Library, Naval Air Warfare Center, Aircraft Division, Warminster, PA.

"Airship Accidents of World War II." US Navy Publication, September 1945. Lighter-Than-Air Library, Naval Air Warfare Center, Aircraft Division, Warminster, PA.

Cook, Jeffrey, "The Flying Dutchman: the Mystery of the L-8." *The Noon Balloon*, Official publication of the Naval Airship Association, Inc. Issue 74, Summer 2007, 14–17.

Gross, Otto K., "L-8: The Ghost Blimp." *links. ghostblimp.com* and *ghostblimp.blogspot.com*. Accessed 2013.

Hansen, Zenon C.R. *The Goodyear Airships*. Blooming-ton, IL: Airship International Press, 1979. Updated in 2005 by James R. Shock and David R. Smith.

"History of Blimp Squadron 32." Official declassified US Navy document. *www.warwingsart.com/LTA/ZP-32%20Squadron%20Diary.pdf*. Accessed September 12, 2014.

"Record of Proceedings of a Board of Investigation Convened at the US Naval Air Station Moffett Field, California, by Order of Commander, Western Sea Frontier, San Francisco, California, to Inquire into the Accident to the US Navy Non-rigid Airship L-8 on August 16, 1942." Official US Navy document dated August 18, 1942.

Shock, James R. *US Navy Airships 1915-1962: A History by Individual Airship*. Edgewater, FL: Atlantis Productions, 1992.

Vaeth, J. Gordon. *Blimps & U-Boats: US Navy Airships in the Battle of the Atlantic*. Annapolis, MD: Naval Institute Press, 1992.

Chapter Nineteen

Beaty, David. *Strange Encounters: Mysteries of the Air*. New York: Atheneum, 1984.

Blundell, Nigel, and Roger Boar. *The World's Greatest UFO Mysteries*. London: Bounty Books, 1991.

Brookesmith, Peter. *UFO: The Complete Sightings*. New York: Barnes & Noble Books, 1995.

Clark, Jerome. *The UFO Book: Encyclopedia of the Extraterrestrial.* Canton, MI: Visible Ink Press, 1998.

Emenegger, Robert. *UFO's Past, Present & Future.* New York: Ballantine Books, 1974.

Jacobs, David M. *The UFO Controversy in America.* Bloomington, IN: Indiana University Press, 1975.

Keyhoe, Donald E. *The Flying Saucers Are Real.* New York: Fawcett Publications, 1950.

Lorenzen, Coral E. *Flying Saucers: The Startling Evidence of the Invasion from Outer Space.* New York: New American Library Signet Books, 1966.

"Mantell Accident Report and Mantell Case File No. 136." *Project Blue Book* files, 1948. National Archives: Washington, DC, Microfilm Roll T-1206-2.

Peebles, Curtis. *Watch the Skies! A Chronicle of the Flying Saucer Myth.* Washington, DC: Smithsonian Institution, 1994.

Randle, Kevin D. "An Analysis of the Thomas Mantell UFO Case." *www.nicap.org/docs/mantell/analysis_mantell_randle.pdf.* Accessed 2013.

Randle, Kevin D. *Project Blue Book—Exposed.* New York: Marlowe and Co., 1997.

———. *The UFO Casebook.* New York: Warner Books, 1989.

Ruppelt, Edward. J. *The Report on Unidentified Flying Objects.* Garden City, NY: Doubleday and Co., 1956.

Steiger, Brad, ed. *Project Blue Book.* New York: Ballantine Books, 1987.

Story, Ronald D. *The Encyclopedia of UFOs.* Garden City, NY: Doubleday and Co., 1980.

Stringfield, Leonard H. *Situation Red, the UFO Siege!* Garden City, NY: Doubleday and Co., 1977.

Wilkins, Harold T. *Flying Saucers on the Attack.* New York: Ace Books, 1954.

Chapter Twenty

Berlitz, Charles. *The Bermuda Triangle: The Incredible Saga of Unexplained Disappearances.* New York: Doubleday, 1974.

Berlitz, Charles. *Without a Trace: New Information From the Triangle.* New York: Doubleday, 1977.

Bermuda Triangle Exposed. Discovery Channel, 2010.

Gaddis, Vincent H., "The Deadly Bermuda Triangle," *Argosy,* February 1964.

———. *Invisible Horizons: True Mysteries of the Sea.* Philadelphia: Chilton Books, 1965.

Kusche, Lawrence D. *The Bermuda Triangle Mystery – Solved.* New York: Harper & Row, 1975.

———. *The Disappearance of Flight 19.* New York: Harper & Row, 1980.

McDonell, Michael. "Lost Patrol. "*Naval Aviation News,* June 1973, 8–16.

MacGregor and Bruce Gernon. *The Fog: A Never Before Published Theory of the Bermuda Triangle*

Phenomenon. Woodbury, MN: Llewellyn Worldwide, Ltd., 2005.

Myhre, Jon H. *Discovery of Flight 19: A 30-Year Search for the Lost Patrol in the Bermuda Triangle.* Orange, CA: The Paragon Agency, 2012.

Quasar, Gian J. *They Flew Into Oblivion: The Disappearance of Flight 19—A True Story of Mystery, Irony, and Infrared.* Lulu Enterprises, Inc., 2010.

Spencer, John Wallace. *Limbo of the Lost.* New York: Bantam Books, 1975.

"US Navy Board of Investigation to Inquire into the Loss of the 5 TBM Avengers in Flight 19 and PBM Aircraft." Microfilm reel, NRS 1983-37, Operational Archives Branch, Naval History & Heritage Command, Washington, DC. Selected excerpts available at: *www.ibiblio.org/hyperwar/USN/rep/Flight19/index.html.* Accessed September 12, 2014.

Winer, Richard. *The Devil's Triangle.* New York: Bantam Books, 1974.

Epilogue

"10 Theories about Missing Flight MH370." *New York Post, March 19, 2014 (originally appearing in News.com.au). nypost.com*

Brumfield, Ben, and Holly Yan. "MH370 Report: Mixed Messages Ate Up Time Before Official Search Initiated," CNN.com, May 2, 2014.

Chuckman, John. "The Second Mystery around Malaysia Airlines Flight MH370."OpEdNews.com, April 18, 2014.

"Flight MH370 Conspiracy Theories: What Happened to the Missing Plane?" *The Week, www.theweek.co.uk,* May 9, 2014.

Gann, Ernest K. *Fate Is the Hunter,* London: Hodder & Stoughton Ltd., 1961.

"Missing Plane MH370 Conspiracy Theory Goes Viral: Was Passenger Jet Shot Down by American Military Forces?" *Huffington Post UK,* April 23, 2014. *www.huffingtonpost.co.uk*

Mouawad, Jad, and Christopher Drew. "Airline Industry at Its Safest Since the Dawn of the Jet Age." *New York Times,* February 11, 2013.

"MH 370 Preliminary Report." Office of the Chief Inspector of Air Accidents, Ministry of Transport, Malaysia, Serial 03/2014, April 9, 2014.

Neuman, Scott. "Search For Flight MH370 Reportedly Largest in History." *The Two-Way,* March 17, 2014. *www.npr.org/blogs/thetwo-way.*

Sanchez, Ray. "Nearly 80% of Americans Think No One Survived Flight 370, CNN Poll Finds." CNN.com, May 7, 2014. *edition.cnn.com.*

"The Search for Flight MH370," BBC News Asia, April 11, 2014. *www.bbc.com/news/world-asia-26514556.*

Yan, Holly, and Elizabeth Joseph. "Flight 370 Search Chief: Hunt for Plane Is the Most Difficult in History." *CNN World,* May 12, 2014. *www.cnn.com.*

INDEX

Page numbers in italics indicate a photograph or illustration